T0162615

*f***P**

PEDDLING PERIL

HOW THE SECRET
NUCLEAR TRADE
ARMS AMERICA'S ENEMIES

David Albright

FREE PRESS

NEW YORK   LONDON   TORONTO   SYDNEY

Free Press
A Division of Simon & Schuster, Inc.
1230 Avenue of the Americas
New York, NY 10020

Copyright © 2010 by The Institute for Science and International Security

First Free Press hardcover edition March 2010

FREE PRESS and colophon are trademarks of Simon & Schuster, Inc.

For information about special discounts for bulk purchases, please contact
Simon & Schuster Special Sales at 1-866-506-1949 or business@simonandschuster.com.

The Simon & Schuster Speakers Bureau can bring authors to your live event.
For more information or to book an event contact the Simon & Schuster Speakers Bureau
at 1-866-248-3049 or visit our website at www.simonspeakers.com.

Designed by Level C

Manufactured in the United States of America

10   9   8   7   6   5   4   3

Library of Congress Cataloging-in-Publication Data

Albright, David
    Peddling peril : how the secret nuclear trade arms America's enemies / David Albright.
—1st Free Press hardcover ed.
       p. cm.
1. Nuclear weapons—Pakistan—History.   2. Khan, A.Q. (Abdul Qadeer), 1936–
3. Technology transfer—Islamic countries.   4. Technology transfer—North Korea.
5. Nuclear nonproliferation.   6. Security, International.   7. Nuclear terrorism.
8. National security—United States.   I. Title.
    U264.5.P18A425 2010
    355.02'17—dc22   2009031899

ISBN: 978-1-4767-4576-3

Dedicated to all those who strive for a world
free of nuclear weapons and terror

Contents

Introduction

In the early hours of September 6, 2007, Israel launched an audacious raid near the small town of Al Kibar, in a desert region of eastern Syria where the Euphrates River cuts across mostly barren land. The target was identified as a soon-to-be-completed nuclear reactor, hidden inside an ordinary, nondescript building. The attack was authorized before the reactor was operational in order to prevent the potential release of dangerous radioactive material if it were bombed later.

Israeli jets destroyed the reactor but the act initially went unreported. In 1981, when Israel destroyed Iraq's Osirak reactor near Baghdad, Israel trumpeted its actions. Now Israel was silent, as was the United States. Even Syria was tight-lipped, making only a brief announcement that its air defenses had forced Israeli planes to flee its air space. U.S. officials confirmed the attack but provided no further details about the target, and no official condemnation was issued.[1] While in Israel several months later, President George W. Bush commended his Israeli hosts for the strike, but still declined to comment publicly about the nature of the raid.[2]

For its part, the Israeli government imposed heavy censorship on Israeli reporters trying to dig up information.[3] Admission of Israeli's involvement in the strike could lead to international condemnation and might push Syria into military retaliation. In an interview with the BBC three weeks after the raid, Syrian President Bashar al-Assad would only say that Israeli jets had attacked an unused "building under construction related to the military . . . there's no people in it, there's no army, there's nothing in it."[4]

In mid-September Glenn Kessler of *The Washington Post* had reported the troubling news that Israel had provided the United States with evidence of North Korea's cooperation with Syria on building a nuclear facility.[5] Several experts charged Kessler with perpetuating rumors, insisting that the site was nonnuclear, and was likely a missile, chemical weapons, or radar installation. A North Korean foreign ministry official quickly dismissed the accusation as "sheer misinformation."[6] The level of mistrust following the Bush administration's disastrous hyping of Iraq's weapons of mass destruction (WMD), and the media's often uncritical reporting of those claims, was so high that Kessler was accused of reporting unsubstantiated intelligence information from Bush administration hard-liners. These same hard-liners, the argument went, aimed at destroying ongoing U.S. negotiations with North Korea to limit its nuclear weapons programs, which were reaching fruition.

Kessler noted that the Israeli raid was the subject of "some of the tightest censorship in years," making confirmation difficult. George Friedman, chief executive officer of Stratfor, a leading private intelligence organization, said that Israel and the United States had "worked hard to create a mystery wrapped in a riddle."[7] Following weeks of searching for possible nuclear sites, the organization I work for, ISIS (the Institute for Science and International Security), located the probable site of Israel's attack. Using commercial satellite imagery of the site before the attack, we were able to determine that the building destroyed was consistent in appearance with a North Korean reactor.[8] For the next six months, our analysis remained the only independent assessment of the attacked site. To see this analysis and other satellite images, photographs, documents, and drawings discussed in *Peddling Peril*, please visit www.isis-online.org/peddlingperil.

Finally, in April 2008, striking proof emerged that the target was in fact a nuclear reactor, and the evidence showed that North Korea had almost surely collaborated with the Syrians in building it. The Central Intelligence Agency (CIA) released a dramatic video complete with a matter-of-fact voice-over that explained that the carefully camouflaged nuclear reactor was clearly built with North Korean technology. The most powerful pieces of evidence were photographs obtained by Israel in late 2006 showing the interior and exterior of the reactor building at different stages of construction. The most recent photo, taken in 2006, shows what looks like the top of a North Korean–style reactor, a gas-graphite model based on a North Korean design. It's not an exact copy, but one closely modeled on the five megawatt electric reactor at Yongbyon nuclear center. Sometime in 2002 or 2003, the facade and roof of the building were altered to deceive spy satellites.

U.S. intelligence officials asserted that the reactor was within weeks or months of operation when it was bombed. When operating close to full power, this reactor would be able to produce enough plutonium for a nuclear weapon every one to two years. Start-up could have quickly followed the completion of the water cooling system, which was finished in the summer of 2007. Since none of the photos of the inside of the reactor building were taken in 2007, the extent of progress at the time of the Israeli strike cannot be authoritatively determined.

The full extent of North Korean assistance is still unclear, but it apparently included design and engineering expertise, the supply of reactor components, and help in procuring other reactor components and equipment illicitly, likely from Europe, China, and Japan. It probably involved direct transfer of nuclear equipment from North Korea to Syria. North Korea also used its own trading companies, some with offshore offices, to buy items in a foreign country illicitly for sale to Syria, in essence serving as a smuggling service for Syria's secret nuclear program.

The relationship between North Korea and Syria has been an open secret in intelligence circles for years. The North Koreans have provided Syria with a steady stream of missile components and military technologies, particularly for liquid-fueled rockets, and have recently assisted with the development of modern solid fuel rockets.[9] One of North Korea's most important sources of income is the export of missiles and conventional arms to Egypt, Iran, and Pakistan, along with Syria.

How had Syria gotten so far in its reactor project, right in Israel's backyard, without being detected by the world's foremost intelligence agencies and the International Atomic Energy Agency (IAEA), whose mission is to detect secret nuclear facilities? And how was North Korea's assistance, which involved numerous international purchases and shipments, likewise missed for so many years? Despite long-standing suspicions, until this reactor was revealed no one could prove North Korea was engaging in nuclear proliferation. Israel's raid temporarily ended the threat, but how long will it be before Syria tries again? Israeli's bombing of Iraq's Osirak reactor in 1981 merely intensified Saddam Hussein's work on nuclear weapons and led Iraq to institute even greater secrecy measures. The final outcome of the Syrian raid has yet to be determined but it demonstrates how persistent illicit trade in nuclear technology is, and how motivated the many players on the world stage—governments, private companies who reap enormous profit, and terrorist groups—truly are. The revelation on September 25, 2009, that Iran was illegally hiding another nuclear facility, this time deep in a mountain near the holy city of Qom, underscores the threat of Iran obtaining nuclear weapons. Two of the most underappreciated (and terrifying) facets of global nuclear proliferation are how much it has depended on nuclear smuggling to thrive, and how inadequate our ability is to detect or prevent the construction of secret nuclear facilities.

———

SINCE THE START of the nuclear age, experts have worried about the proliferation of nuclear weapons. After the United States acquired nuclear technology essentially from scratch with the Manhattan Project, the Soviet Union stole atomic secrets from that project and tested its own bomb in 1949. Britain, the next nuclear power, acquired technology with help from the United States, while France followed suit by acquiring help wherever it could.

The prevailing view up to the 1960s was that only the most developed (i.e., first world) states had the ability to build nuclear weapons. Then China detonated a nuclear explosive in 1964. The relatively new state of Israel followed, building its first bomb in 1967. Unlike the first five nuclear weapon states, Israel kept its success a secret, fearing harsh reactions from its main enemy Egypt, and from its increasingly important ally, the United States, which did not want to see nuclear weapons in the volatile Middle East.

During the 1960s, nuclear proliferation fears reached new heights. President John F. Kennedy said that more than twenty nations might have nuclear weapons by the early 1970s. Tom Lehrer, a satiric folk singer, captured the mood of the time in "Who's Next," a song that wondered, in the midst of the American civil rights struggle, whether we would "stay serene and calm when Alabama gets the bomb."

Those pessimistic forecasts did not materialize; proliferation happened more slowly than expected. Of the more than thirty countries that have sought nuclear weapons, only ten are known to have succeeded.[10] Of these ten, South Africa remains the only country that has subsequently dismantled its weapons program. While nine countries with nuclear weapons is an alarming statistic, particularly since more are trying, it is far less than predicted.

Why were these early projections so wrong? Part of the reason is the underlying assumption that any country with the necessary technical infrastructure would build nuclear weapons, regardless of their security needs. Instead, many countries feared that nuclear weapons could worsen their security or bankrupt their treasuries. In 1949, Canada, a country that had participated in the Manhattan Project and after the war developed the capability to make nuclear weapons, decided not to move forward. Sweden also abandoned its quest for the bomb by the early 1960s after building a nuclear weapons production infrastructure. Many other states also did the same.

Another reason was that countries with stronger security incentives to build nuclear weapons faced more problems than expected in developing the sufficient technical infrastructure to do so. They needed facilities to produce and separate plutonium or enrich uranium up to the level needed in nuclear weapons, commonly called highly enriched uranium. While successfully building these facilities is a daunting technical feat, building up a nuclear weapons capability is a much trickier, costlier process than popular belief suggests. China overcame this limitation because the Soviet Union provided it with an entire set of facilities to produce nuclear explosive materials, plutonium and highly enriched uranium. The Soviet Union later changed its mind on the deal, albeit too late to stop China, but it did not make that mistake again. Israel was also an exception, secretly buying both a reactor and a plutonium separation plant from France.

A final reason was the 1968 Nuclear Non-Proliferation Treaty (NPT), which aims to stop any more countries from getting nuclear weapons. This treaty was possible only because the United States and the Soviet Union decided that preventing nuclear proliferation was in both their strategic interests. The NPT was difficult to negotiate and contained many loopholes. It was a delicate balancing act between commitments to foreswear nuclear weapons in exchange for access to peaceful nuclear energy and promises that the nuclear weapons states would disarm. It was a compromise many states resisted as inadequate.

The NPT formally recognized the five states that had tested nuclear weapons by 1968—Britain, China, France, the Soviet Union, and the United States—as acknowledged nuclear weapon states with special rights. However, the treaty required all signatories not to proliferate. China and France did not sign the treaty until 1992, and China helped Pakistan develop nuclear weapons and is suspected of helping North Korea. It also secretly provided a nuclear reactor to Algeria, which stopped its nuclear weapons effort in the early 1990s after U.S. intelligence's discovery of the project led to intense international condemnation.

The NPT contained a fundamental loophole that both signatories and nonsignatories exploited. The treaty legitimized the sale of civil nuclear facilities, some of which could make nuclear explosive materials, if the recipient state or private company promised to place these facilities under IAEA inspections and not to misuse them to make nuclear weapons. India, which refused to sign the NPT, conducted an underground nuclear explosion in 1974 using plutonium produced in a reactor that had been provided by Canada, ostensibly for peaceful purposes. Unable to build nuclear facilities on its own, India had sought nuclear weapons under the cover of civil nuclear energy development. India called its test a "peaceful nuclear explosion," but few were fooled by this misnomer.

The Indian test led the United States to reevaluate the wisdom of moving forward with several commercial deals, mostly involving European allies, that would sell civil nuclear facilities to a range of countries suspected of seeking nuclear weapons, including Taiwan, South Korea, South Africa, Pakistan, Argentina, and Brazil. The United States exerted enormous diplomatic pressure on its allies Britain, France, and Germany not to sell these facilities themselves. Of particular worry was the selling of plutonium separation plants, or "reprocessing" plants. The separated plutonium could be recycled into a nuclear power reactor as fuel, but it could also be used in nuclear weapons.

While the United States accelerated its effort to prevent the sale of whole facilities that could make nuclear explosive materials, other countries found new loopholes to exploit. South Africa was the first to realize nuclear facilities could be bought piecemeal. It pursued this strategy in the late 1960s and early 1970s, regularly shopping in Europe for sensitive equipment, components, and materials for its uranium enrichment and other nuclear weapon production facilities. Some commercial purchases were important subcomponents of these facilities; some were "dual-use" items that could be used either in a nuclear facility or in other, nonnuclear industries. The ambiguity surrounding such dual-use goods made controlling their export that much more difficult. Under the NPT, European supplier states could sell these sensitive and dual-use subcomponents without any commitment by the buyer to use them only for civil purposes or to place a resulting facility under IAEA inspections.

Pakistan's Abdul Qadeer Khan took advantage of this loophole on an unprecedented scale. A.Q. Khan stole the secrets of how to construct European gas centrifuges which then allowed Pakistan to buy the individual pieces for a gas centrifuge plant in Europe, Japan, and the United States. With China providing nuclear weapon designs and its initial weapon-grade uranium, Pakistan succeeded in obtaining nuclear weapons by 1984. Khan would then go much further, selling secrets and nuclear weapons capabilities to Iran, Libya, and North Korea.

The reality of the last thirty years is that states that have sought to join the "nuclear club" have done so almost exclusively through illicit trade. Surprisingly, governments and business have too frequently overlooked or downplayed this pathway to the bomb. Revelations about nuclear smuggling have complicated international diplomacy, embarrassed major corporations, and jeopardized profit margins.

Peddling Peril details a state's journey to the bomb by start-

ing with the story of A.Q. Khan. After Khan committed industrial espionage in the Netherlands, the Dutch government
missed a critical opportunity to arrest him before he fled back
to Pakistan. Within a few short years, Khan secretly assembled
the necessary parts for a gas centrifuge plant via an ingenious
network, a tangled web of companies and contacts that formed
a global network to outfit Pakistan's nuclear weapons program.

The middle chapters chart the Khan network's shift to proliferation. That network was able to do what only states had done
before—sell complete nuclear facilities, and the know-how for
making nuclear weapons. Khan's network set out in the 1980s to
sell fellow Muslim countries and targets of opportunity the bomb,
but early efforts to deal with Iran, Libya, Iraq, South Africa, and
perhaps Egypt were largely unsuccessful. By the 1990s, though,
the network landed a major sale to Libya valued at over $100 mil-
lion that came close to arming Muammar Qaddafi with nuclear
weapons. To make this sale, Khan mobilized his entire overseas
network, stretching from Switzerland to South Africa, through
Turkey and Dubai to Malaysia. The Khan network sold North
Korea vital gas centrifuges and teamed up with that dictatorship
to proliferate nuclear technology together. It also provided Iran
with essential centrifuge components which still plague the international community today. The network's singular failure was
Syria, which balked at its offer to sell centrifuges in 2001.[11]

Khan likely lost out in this sale to North Korea, which after
decades of illegally obtaining items for its own nuclear weapons
program, saw the money-making potential in nuclear trafficking.
Peddling Peril covers North Korea's assistance to Syria, but who
are its other customers? And will Iran follow in North Korea's

footsteps and become a major international supplier to pariah states who desire nuclear weapons?

Sultan Bashiruddin Mahmood, one of Khan's longtime rivals in Pakistan's nuclear weapons program, also had ambitions to spread nuclear weapons technology throughout the Muslim world. A devout fundamentalist and resentful of his own government, he held talks with senior al Qaeda personnel including Osama bin Laden, to help that terrorist organization get nuclear weapons. Only the fall of the Taliban in 2001 stalled this effort. Mahmood's subsequent detention was the first warning bell of a dangerous threat that Pakistan's own nuclear assets could cause enormous damage through theft by terrorists or a takeover of the country by fundamentalist forces.

Peddling Peril recounts efforts to stop these traffickers. Iran's two-decade march toward nuclear weapons, along with Khan's vital assistance, were first exposed by the IAEA, the United Nations nuclear watchdog organization located in Vienna. Khan's network was finally busted after a ten-year, joint CIA/MI6 intelligence operation. Key to this operation's success was the CIA's recruitment in 2003 of the Swiss businessman Friedrich Tinner, along with his sons Marco and Urs. "The Three Tinners" were key network members the CIA cornered and pressured to turn against Khan. This intelligence operation was so successful that it helped convince Libya to dismantle its clandestine nuclear weapons program.

Busting Khan's network went little further than an initial rounding up of its members. Few members served much jail time; ironically, the Tinners spent more time in jail than almost anyone else in the network. After five years, a myriad of national prosecutions in Britain, Germany, Japan, Malaysia, South Africa,

South Korea, Switzerland, and Turkey did not serve the cause of justice or create the deterrence needed to stop others from pursuing nuclear smuggling. While the successes against the Khan network represent outstanding accomplishments, they depended largely on luck and strategies such as military intervention and cargo seizures that constitute the last line of defense. Sorely missing are successful strategies to detect and stop illicit trade before it occurs. Bolstering these first lines of defense is critical to preventing illicit nuclear trade.

I explore a model for such a strategy by looking in depth at the German company Leybold, which transformed itself from a major exporter to dangerous nuclear programs in the 1970s and 1980s into a leader in preventing nuclear proliferation worldwide. It now serves as a valuable lookout for illicit trade by Pakistan, Iran, and other countries seeking nuclear weapons.

Peddling Peril's portrayal of the hidden world of nuclear trafficking, which begins with A.Q. Khan, forces us to ask a simple question: why has illicit nuclear trade, something so critical to nuclear proliferation, flourished for so long? Looking at Khan's beginnings might provide us with the answer.

Out of the Cold

December 1975 was a busy time at the tiny single terminal at Amsterdam's Schiphol airport. Amid the holiday travelers was a young man traveling with his wife and two small daughters. To any casual observer, this handsome, personable man appeared no different from any of the other harried vacationers and tourists.

In fact, Dr. Abdul Qadeer Khan was fleeing to Pakistan, having pulled off history's most dangerous act of nuclear espionage.

Khan was "coming out of the cold"[1] just as Dutch authorities were growing suspicious of his activities in the fall of 1975. A pioneer in nuclear smuggling who laid the foundation for pariah governments to acquire nuclear weapons, the Pakistani scientist was an unlikely spy. Born in 1936 into an educated Muslim family of military men, magistrates, and teachers, Khan's middle-class childhood (he loved ice hockey, fishing, and kite flying) ended with the political and religious turmoil created by Indian independence. With the partition of the South Asian subcontinent in 1947, the large Muslim minority in his home state of Bhopal found itself part of Hindu-dominated India.

His older brothers and sisters left for the safe haven of Pakistan. Abdul Qadeer stayed behind to finish high school. At sixteen, he headed to Karachi to join his siblings, making the hard journey alone, first by train, then barefoot across a four-mile stretch of desert that burned blisters on his feet.

Reunited with his family, he pursued his dream of becoming a teacher like his father, earning a bachelor's degree in mathematics and physics. After a brief turn as an inspector of weights and measures, Khan left in 1961 to study at the Technical University of Berlin, then to the Netherlands to study engineering at the Delft Technological University. The engaging, charismatic Khan developed close relationships with his professors and classmates wherever he studied, making international connections that would serve him well during his rise to notoriety.

It was also in the Netherlands that Khan met and married a Dutch woman named Hendrina Reterink in March 1964. Khan was a devoted family man who enjoyed making dinner for his wife and, later, his two young daughters, cooking pilaf, kebabs, meat curry, and *parathas*, a flatbread fried in butter. His neighbors and colleagues were fond of Khan, an avid street volleyball player. One friend recalled that he was "a great source of pleasure in all social gatherings."

In 1965, while he was studying in Holland, war broke out between India and Pakistan over Kashmir, a dispute that ended in a stalemate. Deeply disturbed by a documentary he saw that blamed Pakistan for the conflict, Khan embarked on a solitary letter-writing campaign to Dutch newspapers to set the record straight. His letter-writing skills would ultimately prove to be a catalyst that changed both Khan's and Pakistan's future.

In 1971, a pivotal year for Khan, he obtained a doctorate in metallurgy from the University of Leuven in Belgium, and war broke out again between India and Pakistan. When Pakistan was created in 1947, its eastern and western halves were separated by thousands of miles of Indian territory. Growing pressures in East Pakistan, which later became Bangladesh, for greater autonomy from West Pakistan triggered a bloody crackdown by the army. Millions of East Pakistani refugees streamed into India to escape the violence and the destruction caused the previous year by the Bhola cyclone, the deadliest tropical cyclone on record. Televised images of the utter devastation, along with George Harrison's Concert for Bangladesh in August 1971, led to an outpouring of support for Bangladesh. For Khan, though, the portrayal of his countrymen as murderers embittered him toward the West.

Further humiliation arrived when Pakistan's army was routed in December 1971. The Indo-Pakistani war lasted two weeks, culminating with the mass surrender of Pakistan's army and the loss of East Pakistan in the face of rapidly advancing Indian troops. Khan and his fellow countrymen had believed that they were a martial race—"one Pakistani can handle ten Indians." This myth had survived the 1965 stalemate, but the loss in 1971 created an identity crisis for both Pakistan and Khan.

In May 1972, Khan and his family moved to Zwanenburg, a quiet Amsterdam suburb, and he began a new job at a technical consulting firm, Physical Dynamic Research Laboratory [Fysisch Dynamisch Onderzoek-Technische Adviseurs] (FDO). FDO was part of Werkspoor Amsterdam, an important private contractor to the secretive Ultra-Centrifuge Nederland (UCN). UCN controlled all Dutch gas centrifuge work and was a partner with British and German companies in the URENCO uranium enrichment consortium. Founded in 1971, URENCO combined the resources of countries with the ambition to build commercial gas centrifuge facilities but without the sufficient funding to do so alone. These gas centrifuges produce low enriched uranium for nuclear reactors, but could also be used to make highly enriched uranium (HEU) for nuclear weapons. HEU was the fissile material used in the "Little Boy" bomb dropped on Hiroshima.

Compared to other methods, a gas centrifuge plant is one of the cheapest ways to produce HEU for nuclear weapons. The core of a centrifuge is an ingeniously designed rapidly rotating tube, or "rotor," in which uranium gas spins. The spinning separates the lighter, rare isotope uranium-235 from the more plentiful and less useful uranium-238. In nature, uranium contains less than one percent uranium-235. When centrifuges increase the fraction of uranium-235 in the uranium to a level of 3 or 4 percent, the enriched material can be used in nuclear reactors. When the fraction of uranium-235 exceeds 20 percent, it is called HEU and is usable in nuclear explosives. Bomb makers typically want HEU enriched to at least 80 to 90 percent uranium-235, because at that level the bomb will need far less of it. A crude nuclear weapon requires several hundred kilograms of 20 percent enriched material, but needs only 15 to 20 kilograms of HEU enriched to 90 percent uranium-235, commonly called weapon-grade uranium. If the weapon must be small enough to fit under an aircraft or on top of a ballistic missile, the amount of HEU used matters.

Khan was hired as a metallurgist at FDO by A. Langstraat, a fellow engineering student at Delft Technological University who liked Khan and had since become head of FDO's Metallurgy Department.[2] He also came highly recommended by his professors, but there was a problem: Khan's hiring was a violation of URENCO's rules, set in part by the United States which at the time had a virtual monopoly on the supply of enriched uranium. If a nonnational were to work in a top secret gas centrifuge consortium, with the range of classified centrifuge information routinely found at FDO, his application would need to be submitted to the "Joint Committee," run by the three governments involved in the URENCO partnership. (Nonnationals of the three countries were not allowed access without special permission.) According to a classified 1979 Dutch report, it was "highly unlikely" that the Ministry of Economic Affairs (the Dutch ministry responsible for the enrichment work) would have approved Khan's employment.[3]

Yet the report makes clear that FDO was willing to take advantage of URENCO's nascent security rules. To avoid Khan's application being sent to the Joint Committee, FDO explained that Khan's area of work would be limited to metallurgical research, and that FDO experts had "estimated" that Khan would only have access to information classified lower than the level that would require Joint Committee approval.[4] Khan's supporters in FDO also told UCN security officers that Khan had already lived in Europe for eleven years and wished to settle down permanently in the West, preferably in the Netherlands. An investigation at the time by BVD, the Dutch domestic security service, turned up nothing suspicious on Khan despite the inherent risk of hiring a Pakistani at a time when his country most wanted sensitive nuclear information. FDO, UCN, and Dutch government officials never followed through to ensure that Khan actually applied for citizenship, but whether the story about settling in the Netherlands originated with Khan or his advocates, Khan was deeply attached to Pakistan and had never taken steps to sever those ties.

Mr. L.L. Strappers, a senior security officer at the Ministry of Economic Affairs, granted Khan a security clearance for *only* low-level Dutch centrifuge information. He was not authorized to see centrifuge information from the Netherlands' partners, Britain and Germany. However, once Khan started working at FDO, his friendliness and helpfulness allowed him to quickly strike up relationships with his new colleagues. When returning from annual vacations in Pakistan, he always brought little presents for his co-workers. In addition, Khan became known as a key "materials expert" for the entire UCN centrifuge project,[5] and his colleagues ignored his lack of security clearance to see sensitive information. Later, when Khan violated basic security rules, they ignored that too.[6] Collectively, FDO and UCN had no established procedures to block Khan from seeing a wide variety of classified centrifuge information from all three countries.

Khan's expertise led to visits to the Almelo enrichment plant near the Dutch-German border and many other sensitive UCN facilities. URENCO relied on an excellent network of high-tech European contractors to make centrifuge parts and supply vital equipment and as part of Khan's job he visited several URENCO suppliers, contacts that would later be invaluable when Khan shopped for his own centrifuge program. Because Khan was fluent in Dutch and German, he was also assigned by FDO in 1974 to help translate the overwhelming number of German documents FDO accumulated. His work took him to the restricted facility known as the "brain box," a temporary building located next to the factory at Almelo. There he had access to scores of highly classified centrifuge designs and manufacturing documents and was treated as a fully accredited member of the team.

Through his work at FDO, Khan obtained detailed designs of

the Dutch SNOR and CNOR centrifuges, and the German G2 centrifuge. He also gained information about the more advanced Dutch M4 centrifuge, and most likely the German G4 centrifuge. Khan was so confident of how much he'd learned that he confided to a colleague he commuted to work with that he knew all the secrets of the centrifuge project and was himself capable of making a centrifuge.[7]

In less than a decade, Khan would make good on his boast. He christened Pakistan's first and second generation centrifuges—duplicate versions of the Dutch and German centrifuges whose designs he had access to—P1 and P2.

───────■■■───────

THERE IS NO doubt that Khan had the means and the opportunity to become a spy. But why did he do it? The official Dutch investigation in 1979 concluded he was unlikely to have been a plant by the Pakistani government. URENCO officials speculated he was recruited by Pakistani officials early in his employment at FDO and told to stay in the Netherlands for a couple of years to collect information and experience.[8]

Khan—who likes to talk—tells his story this way.

When India detonated its first nuclear device (code-named "Smiling Buddha"), in 1974, the memories of the Indo-Pakistani war were still fresh. In his mind, his country had been dismembered and its people humiliated. Now nuclear weapons were in the hands of a mortal enemy. A bolder approach than writing letters to Dutch newspapers was required. In an emotional letter to Pakistan's Prime Minister Zulfikar Ali Bhutto in September 1974, delivered via Pakistan's ambassador in Belgium, Khan argued that no less than the survival of his country was at stake.

"Why was a long struggle made for the creation of Pakistan and why were hundreds of thousands of mothers, sisters and brothers martyred at the hands of the Hindus? . . . We must chalk out a line of action and start work on it immediately, as it is the demand of our security and welfare."[9] He volunteered his help in meeting this national emergency.

"He seems to be talking sense," Bhutto scribbled in the margin of Dr. Khan's letter. Bhutto referred the letter with his comments to the head of the Pakistan Atomic Energy Commission (PAEC), Munir Ahmad Khan. Munir Khan had been trying, without success, to obtain a reprocessing plant from France to separate plutonium.[10] Munir asked his point man in Europe, S.A. Butt, a science and technology minister in the Pakistani embassy in Brussels, to verify Khan's claims. "I checked on A.Q. Khan," Butt said, "and reported that he was really engaged in pioneering work on centrifuge technology and can be helpful in Pakistan's nuclear program."[11]

Bhutto had reason to be excited, having started his country on the path to nuclear weapons. Pakistani nuclear scientists were faced with difficulties in purchasing overseas facilities to make plutonium. The unknown, European-educated Khan offered Bhutto another way. Pakistan could produce an atomic weapon based not only on plutonium but on highly enriched uranium as well. Khan's offer held out the prospect of help from someone with up-to-date scientific knowledge, access to critical new technology, and a list of European companies happy to supply the equipment. Still, it was a monumental gamble requiring years of hard work, hundreds of millions of dollars, and an enormous amount of faith placed in a young, unproven scientist. It was a gamble Bhutto was willing to take.

Bhutto asked Khan to meet him in Karachi.[12] When he returned to Pakistan during his Christmas break in 1974, Khan laid out his plan to Bhutto, who asked him to meet with Munir Khan. Khan met Munir Khan and his officers and advised them on how to proceed in obtaining a centrifuge plant.[13] According to later accounts by both Khan and the Pakistani government, he offered minimal direct assistance during the meeting, implying that he stole no sensitive centrifuge information while he was in the Netherlands and that he developed the P1 and P2 based only on general information.[14]

How much of Khan's story is myth? URENCO's conjecture of what transpired reveals that Khan may have been recruited in a less heroic manner. Butt was actively seeking assistance for Pakistan's fledgling nuclear weapons effort and may well have heard about this young talented Pakistani engineer and approached him directly. Why did he choose Khan? There is some evidence that Khan was gathering information before meeting Bhutto in 1974. The secret Dutch government report on Khan states that a UCN employee told Dutch investigators that during his visits to several suppliers in Germany and Switzerland in 1974, he discovered that Khan had also made inquiries at these firms, which were supplying Dutch centrifuge components to URENCO.[15] At the time, he wondered whether FDO was engaged in a centrifuge project itself, independent of URENCO. He did not even consider the possibility that one of FDO's employees was providing secrets to a foreign government.

After meeting A.Q. Khan in January 1975, Munir Khan recommended that Bhutto establish a secret gas centrifuge program.[16] The centrifuge project was code-named the Directorate of Industrial Liaison (DIL). At the same time, Munir started a

program to find the resources to make "hex"—uranium hexafluoride, the feed gas for a gas centrifuge that is difficult both to
produce and handle. He also created a team dedicated to building
an atomic bomb out of HEU. (Producing the HEU would prove
Munir's greatest challenge.)

Armed with URENCO's technology, Khan realized that he
could buy a centrifuge plant and the means to make centrifuges
piece by piece on the international market, and many suppliers
would gladly help him do it for a fat profit. "With years of experience working on similar projects in Europe," he wrote later on,
"my contacts there with the various manufacturing firms were an
invaluable asset to me."[17] Khan deserves credit for acknowledg-
ing Pakistan didn't have the technological infrastructure to build
the components needed for a centrifuge plant. Doing so would
have "cost an enormous amount of time," he wrote, and he was
"sure that the [centrifuge] project would have been aborted at the
very early stages because of this."[18] He was correct—centrifuges
require highly precise manufacturing and advanced metallurgy
generally unavailable to developing countries. Pakistan's industries were unable to produce the specialized metals needed for
centrifuges, and they lacked the equipment and technicians able
to produce the high-quality components of a centrifuge.

Rounding out Munir Khan's team was Sultan Bashiruddin
Mahmood, an exuberant thirty-three-year-old fundamentalist
who was placed in charge of the gas centrifuge project.[19] Munir
Khan placed Butt, already at the Pakistani embassy in Belgium,
in charge of procurement for the new project.[20] Thus, PAEC
launched its secret operation in Europe to purloin gas centrifuge
information and procure parts for centrifuges from European
companies.

Work started almost immediately, with Khan leading the way from his post at FDO. "A.Q. Khan did some daring things, risking his job and imprisonment," said Butt.[21] He reportedly flooded Butt, through an unknown intermediary, with steady streams of secret information on designing and building centrifuges, as well as lists of suppliers.[22]

Khan brought to his home in Zwanenburg from FDO entire packets of drawings of classified centrifuge components. He also "spontaneously" offered his wife's services to FDO as a translator from Dutch to English for classified centrifuge documents.[23] Astonishingly, the company agreed despite her not having any security clearance at all. He began receiving visitors from both the Pakistani embassies in Belgium and France at his home.[24] When Mahmood visited Europe in 1975 to shop for equipment and materials for the centrifuge program, Khan traveled to Belgium to meet both him and Butt.[25]

PAEC decided to build its P1 model based on the designs from a Dutch centrifuge, this type being considerably easier to construct than the German model centrifuges for which Khan had designs. Butt and Khan started to seek out URENCO's suppliers and began to order components. In August 1975, Butt telephoned Emerson Electric Industrial Controls Ltd., a U.S.-owned company, seeking information about frequency converters, an important component that powers a centrifuge and keeps it spinning at a precisely specified speed. He told the company he worked at Belgo-Nucleaire, a famous Belgian nuclear company, and asked about buying a specialized converter. Emerson became suspicious because this type of converter had been developed by the Dutch company Comprimo specifically for URENCO, and Belgo-Nucleaire had no known use for it. When Emerson informed Comprimo, its officials could not find any explanation for the order and UCN was notified.[26] Then in the fall of 1975, the French company Metalimphy received an order from the Pakistani embassy in Brussels for some equipment that company officials could see was drawn from a specific UCN report.[27] UCN determined that Khan appeared to be connected to this order.

Khan's questionable behavior that fall during NUCLEX (an industry wide nuclear exhibition) in Basel, Switzerland, was finally enough to raise flags. He was overheard by officials at UCN asking suspicious questions of various UCN suppliers. Khan also reconnected with Henk Slebos, an old Dutch friend from his student days at Delft Technological University. Slebos would become a lifetime friend and a key ally in finding many sensitive items for Khan's centrifuge plant.

Security officials at UCN notified the Ministry of Economics. "It seems to me I have found a spy," said a ministry official to Ruud Lubbers, the minister of economics.[28] Lubbers, who had become minister in 1973, decided not to order Khan's arrest right away. This being 1975 he "did not think about proliferation at that very moment, to be honest."[29] Lubbers viewed Khan as a commercial threat to URENCO, worrying that its secrets would fall into the hands of its American and Japanese competitors. He likely also worried about adverse reactions from his British and German partners and the Dutch public, which at the time was increasingly antinuclear.

Lubbers ordered BVD to follow Khan, who had been reassigned to a less information sensitive job at FDO. His superiors tried to convince Khan that his new job was a high priority, but it is probable he didn't believe them. Now aware his actions were being closely scrutinized by authorities, he acted much more cautiously. BVD agents were unable to find any clear evidence of espionage.

However, the wheels were already in motion for at least one order for centrifuge parts. Sometime toward the end of 1975, possibly at the NUCLEX conference, Khan asked R.W.Y. van Blijenburgh of Van Dorne's Transmissie (VDT), which provided superstrong maraging steel parts to UCN, whether his company could produce certain types of steel tubes for one of Khan's "connections."[30] Khan already knew van Blijenburgh because of his regular contact with FDO. Based on the technical details Khan provided, van Blijenburgh made a sketch, which was submitted to VDT's drawing office to prepare an official drawing.[31] The official drawing, dated November 21, 1975, was derived from classified UCN information for experimental versions of two Dutch centrifuges.[32] The tubes Khan requested were the raw materials of a particularly tricky part of a centrifuge known as a bellows, a Russian invention that prevents longer and more powerful centrifuges from breaking as they gain speed during start-up.

Austrian engineer Gernot Zippe had brought this type of bellows to URENCO. He had been captured by Soviet forces at the end of World War II and forced to work on the Russian centrifuge program until 1953. After being allowed to return to the West in 1956, he shared his new knowledge with faltering European centrifuge efforts, allowing them to make huge strides forward. Zippe's bellows and longer centrifuges were critical to producing enriched uranium at a price competitive with the more established U.S. programs. This invention would make it more affordable to enrich uranium for nuclear reactors and nuclear weapons, ironically increasing the likelihood of the very kind of nuclear proliferation Khan sought to exploit.

Pakistan would likely have encountered significant difficulty in attempting to make these parts without assistance. The tubes had to be cut into sections, then skilled machinists would carefully thin a portion of the cylinder which was placed in a machine that would create an inward facing bulge in the thinned section. Even the most capable machinists faced high rates of manufacturing error. In response to Khan's request, VDT produced a written proposal to make the tubes.

Nobody responded to the proposal. Khan left the Netherlands on December 15, 1975, with his family "on holiday" and returned to Pakistan. Lubbers believed that Khan "understood the signal" of being denied access to the centrifuge project and "came in out of the cold."[33] A month later, in January 1976, Khan's wife, Henny, returned to the Netherlands to meet Frits Veerman, one of Khan's close co-workers at FDO. Khan asked Veerman in a letter to go to Khan's office on a Saturday, collect all of Khan's materials from his filing cabinet and hand them over to Henny.[34] In that same letter, Khan asked Veerman to give Henny the home address of a mutual colleague who was an expert in the mass production of centrifuge components. He also asked Veerman to contact his brother, Abdul Lateef Khan, who was also living in the Netherlands, about making arrangements to visit Pakistan. Veerman refused these requests but later learned that Khan had nonetheless contacted their colleague.[35]

The Dutch government acted as though Khan's departure ended the case. It did not launch an investigation to determine what Khan could have stolen. Worse, it did not inform its partners Britain and Germany about Khan's breach of security, despite its treaty obligations to do so. This not only allowed Khan to steal secrets, it also enabled him to benefit from that theft of centrifuge information for years to come. Khan was now free to procure materials and know-how for his centrifuge program from all over the world. One of the very few early opportunities to stop him was lost.

After Khan's arrest in 2004, Lubbers tried to shift blame to the CIA. "Certainly, at the time he [Khan] was already known to U.S. intelligence services who were following his movements," he claimed.[36] He told the Japanese television network NHK in 2005 in a rambling interview that "Washington requested—the Dutch people—services to inform them fully, but not to take any action so that they could follow Mr. Khan and try to find out what network was developing."[37]

In the 1980s and 1990s, the CIA would certainly be guilty of letting Khan operate in order to gather more information, but it seems unlikely they were aware of Khan in 1975. A former CIA official who served as their station chief in the Netherlands in 1975 categorically denies Lubbers' statements.[38] He did not even know Khan's name at that time, and was not briefed about Khan's activities by the BVD (Dutch intelligence). He added that the CIA could not have followed Khan, even if it had wanted to, because he lacked the resources to set up such an operation. Only the BVD had the resources to set up round-the-clock surveillance on Khan, and "the Dutch BVD did not like the CIA operating inside Holland" without permission. He said that the CIA and BVD cooperated closely on many operations, running "compatible operations" on China, terrorism, and the Eastern Bloc, but never on Khan. "If someone had come up with Khan as a target in my day," he said, "I would have loved it."[39]

Stunned senior U.S. government officials didn't learn about Khan's centrifuge project until 1978, only weeks after Washington finally convinced France to cancel the sale of a plutonium separation plant to Pakistan. By then, Khan was well on his way to building the bomb, and U.S. efforts could only slow him down.

As for Khan, he had one last letter to write.

Not long after his departure, he sent word to his colleagues that he had become ill. In a letter dated January 26, 1976, Khan submitted his resignation, citing his desire to live in Pakistan. Despite suspicions about his spying, FDO sent him a testimonial regretting his departure. They wished him the best of luck, both in his future career and "perhaps for the benefit of your country."[40]

Pakistan Gets the Bomb

A fundamental weakness in the Pakistani centrifuge project was its lack of enough trained people and centrifuge "know-how." Although A.Q. Khan had acquired a vast amount of secret centrifuge technology and components in the Netherlands, building a centrifuge plant in Pakistan required more outside help. Khan would prove adept at finding that help, but a more important step needed to be taken first: wresting control of the project from Munir Khan.

A.Q. Khan has stated that he intended to return to the Netherlands in early January 1976, but Bhutto asked him to stay and save the centrifuge program.[1] However, without access to the Dutch centrifuge program and realizing he was under suspicion of espionage, Khan most likely had little choice but to stay in Pakistan and seek a prominent position in the centrifuge program.

In early 1976, PAEC had already identified a workable centrifuge design and placed several orders in Germany and Switzerland for parts. These were notable benchmarks given that the program's main pipeline for information had been cut off a few months prior. Yet in a letter to Prime Minister Bhutto,

A.Q. Khan complained about the project's progress, blaming Sultan Bashiruddin Mahmood and Munir Ahmad Khan.[2] It was a self-serving claim aimed to deflect any accusations about time lost due to Khan's removal from FDO but also geared at seizing control of the program.

A.Q. Khan was reportedly upset that Munir Khan had not given him a senior enough position in the Pakistan Atomic Energy Commission. A.Q. Khan's aim was to sow discord. In April 1976, A.Q. Khan wrote Bhutto that the project would not be able to provide the material for a nuclear weapon by 1980, as promised.[3] In a subsequent meeting with Bhutto, Khan is reported to have cited Munir Khan as a key problem.

Bhutto sided with A.Q. Khan. On July 17, 1976, Khan took over the project, renamed the Engineering Research Laboratories (ERL). While Munir remained in control of many parts of the Pakistani nuclear weapons program, including the development of the nuclear weapon itself and the effort to produce plutonium for nuclear weapons, ERL did not come under Munir Khan's PAEC and had its own budget. Signaling trouble later, it also had a weak oversight board of senior Pakistani officials with little knowledge of centrifuges and little penchant to control Khan. He was free to pursue his quest for nuclear weapons with a huge budget and minimal governmental oversight.

As the Khans fought over who would control the resource-rich centrifuge effort with dueling philosophies (Munir ran an honest, slower-moving program; A.Q. Khan led an accelerated, corrupt one), A.Q. Khan launched an aggressive effort to find highly trained personnel, luring European-educated Pakistani scientists with high salaries while also obtaining their assurance not to reveal the program to outsiders.[4] He also continued contacting his old colleagues at FDO in 1976 and 1977 asking for information, materials, and on occasion, centrifuge components. In exchange for traveling to Pakistan, they would receive a handsome fee. And there was plenty of money to go around. During 1977 and 1978, European suppliers transferred considerable amounts of funds to the personal savings account of Henny and her mother at the Rabo-Bank in Bergen op Zoom. Monies totaling NLG 400,000 (or about $200,000) were subsequently transferred to Khan in Pakistan from the Swiss vacuum firm VAT and Leybold-Heraeus in Hanau, Germany. Dutch investigators speculated that these payments were personal commissions for providing these companies with Pakistani orders.[5]

Khan's efforts became so brazen that FDO management became alarmed, and sent a confidential letter on July 29, 1977, to its employees warning them of immediate dismissal and possible criminal prosecution if they complied with such requests. Several of Khan's ex-FDO colleagues refused to help him with sensitive issues that were plaguing his project. Even his closest ex-associates, such as Frits Veerman, had no interest in assisting him to build centrifuges if it meant divulging company secrets. Yet as long as he kept his project secret, FDO and UCN were willing to ignore a wide range of warning signs that Khan was building a secret gas centrifuge plant. Despite their initial efforts, FDO management did not follow through and inform the Dutch branch of URENCO or the Dutch government about Khan's contacts with its employees and the warning letter it wrote in response.[6]

Along with his efforts to recruit FDO personnel as advisors, Khan went after FDO as a source of less sensitive equipment. In September 1976, FDO's sales manager A.C.M. Kuys visited

Pakistan to explore selling a range of dual-use equipment. Kuys was aware that Khan could have been a spy when he was at FDO, but that did not deter him from pursuing business with him.[7] On one of his trips to Pakistan, Kuys even suggested to Khan that the Dutch were suspicious that he had been a spy.[8] Khan acted surprised at the news.

Kuys stayed at A.Q. Khan's house, where Khan presented himself as a senior official of the Pakistani Ministry of Finance who was unaffiliated with Pakistan's nuclear programs.[9] While he was at FDO, Khan had not overly impressed his colleagues with his project management skills; he seemed to have difficulty implementing initiatives.[10] Kuys saw a transformed Khan in Pakistan, a man with a newfound sense of importance constantly issuing orders without a trace of the self-effacing personality Khan had at FDO.[11]

Munir Khan also met with Kuys and told him that Pakistan had no interest in gas centrifuges. Pakistan would not have the technological capability, Munir said, to build an industrial scale centrifuge plant for twenty years.[12] Munir added that Pakistan had been able to obtain an Italian gas centrifuge design, but was interested only in setting up experiments with ten to twenty centrifuges with little prospect of enlarging this effort beyond that level.

Unbeknownst to Kuys, Munir's point man in Europe, S.A. Butt, continued to seek centrifuge equipment and materials. On July 1, 1976, he sent a letter from Brussels on Pakistani Embassy letterhead that followed up on a telephone conversation with Mr. M. Niessen, the head of VDT.[13] Butt asked for "1,000 meters" of extremely durable steel tubes to be made according to a sketch included with the letter.[14] Butt did not tell Niessen what the tubes were for but the sketch was almost identical to the one A.Q. Khan had supplied to van Blijenburgh at VDT in late 1975. To manufacture the tubes, VDT used the drawing that it had sent to Khan in late 1975, in apparent recognition that the order from Khan had finally arrived. VDT officials, dismissing Pakistan's capabilities to make use of such high-specification tubes and appreciating the tidy profit, jokingly referred to the order of tubes as the "Pakistani pipeline."[15]

The initial order was enough for about 2,000 tubes, each one-half meter long. The order was subsequently expanded to 6,000 tubes.[16] Most were shipped directly to Pakistan, while the rest were delivered to Dutch, French, and English clients, as instructed by Butt in an attempt to disguise the true recipients.[17] The tubes would be cut into sections of 60 to 100 millimeters before being machined into a finished bellows. With this order, Khan could make over 30,000 bellows. Each P1 centrifuge requires three bellows, so the order was enough to make bellows for 10,000 centrifuges. If all of these centrifuges worked, they could produce about 100 kilograms of weapon-grade uranium each year, enough for four or five nuclear weapons per year.

In 1978, the procurement section of the Pakistani embassy in Germany sent VDT a letter explicitly complaining that many of the VDT tubes were not manufactured adequately to permit Pakistan to make the bellows. VDT responded in April that the tubes were fine but in a coup for the Pakistanis, VDT officials instructed the Pakistani technicians how to overcome their problems in finishing the bellows based on VDT's own past experience.

Kuys accepted Munir Khan's fabrications and FDO agreed to sell a variety of dual-use equipment to the Special Works Organization (SWO) in Rawalpindi, a secret procurement front company for the centrifuge project.* FDO also allowed three Pakistanis to receive training in the use of the equipment. The first of many front Pakistani companies ordering sensitive items for Khan, SWO's orders included equipment that FDO and UCN determined were "exclusively designed and intended" for gas centrifuge projects. Since Kuys would only sell UCN approved items, he always showed senior UCN officials SWO's orders. Many requests for items, particularly those unique to a centrifuge plant, were rejected, but again a lack of coordinated effort meant UCN didn't report to its URENCO partners about SWO's suspicious requests or take steps to stop future orders.

Although Khan stole a wide variety of centrifuge designs, he missed information for some critical components. In the early Dutch centrifuges, one of the "scoops," which extract uranium gas from the rotating cylinder, vibrated excessively. The Dutch designed parts to fix this problem, but they did not include sketches for these parts with the others. As a result, Khan's first P1 centrifuges frequently broke or "crashed." A former senior URENCO official who saw the Pakistani centrifuge designs firsthand noted Khan's earliest centrifuges even had pieces designed to hold one of the new Dutch components, but the Pakistani designers did not know actual parts were supposed to go there. This problem, and likely others, explain early media reports that the Pakistani centrifuge program was struggling. Eventually, Khan's team came up with a solution similar to the Dutch one either through invention or espionage, but his program would have never succeeded if he had relied only on his old FDO contacts.

A centrifuge plant requires thousands of components and ma-

---

*In this book, a front company is a shell or a trading company that buys items on behalf of a nuclear program, often a secret one. The company's procurements can be legal or illegal.

terials, and only a small fraction was available from FDO. Khan quickly realized he could shop around the world for the necessary items. In the 1970s, he secretly dispatched dozens of buyers to Europe, Japan, and North America. Khan's buyers easily gained valuable information and other critical items for the centrifuge plant then taking shape in secret near the town of Kahuta, outside Islamabad. They were able to contact unsuspecting or indifferent URENCO suppliers, buy centrifuge components and equipment, and obtain critical training in manufacturing centrifuge components. Some of the firms had earlier sold items to URENCO and were eager to sell the same items to Khan's front companies.[18] "Firms and people chased us with figures and details of equipment," Khan wrote. "They literally begged us to buy their equipment. It was a competition to woo us. They were willing to do anything for money, if the money was good."[19]

Khan's efforts soon produced a constant flow of equipment to Pakistan: drive mechanisms to make things turn, centrifuge components, ultrathin pipes that revolve at extremely high speed, specialized materials, and all ancillary equipment needed in the centrifuge project.[20] Most of their purchases were legal, since governments had not expected Pakistan to buy a centrifuge plant piecemeal. Pakistani officials were also placed in embassies using thinly veiled disguises to buy critical equipment. When the embassy received an especially sensitive item, it used "diplomatic pouch" couriers to transport the item while evading scrutiny by customs. Khan himself went abroad seeking contacts and items when necessary, traveling with such confidence that he returned to the Netherlands in August 1976.[21]

In a development that proved critical later when Khan became a nuclear exporter, he established a loyal network of businessmen and middlemen on three continents who became experts at ferreting out shady suppliers or, if necessary, deceiving suppliers about the true end use of a purchase. They would ultimately form a core group that sold centrifuges to other countries. It was this transnational network that would emerge as one of the greatest and most damaging legacies of Khan's theft of centrifuge know-how from the Netherlands.

One of Khan's first recruits was an old friend, Abdus Salam. Salam was a British Muslim businessman who helped set up trading companies and acted as a third-party hub from which Khan could recruit specialists for his program.[22] In one attempt to lure his old FDO colleague Frits Veerman to visit Pakistan, in June 1977 Khan sent Veerman a letter of introduction addressed to Salam.[23] In the letter, Khan wrote that if Veerman visited London, Salam should buy him an airline ticket to Pakistan: "I am sure you will help Mr. Veerman as you help my other friends."[24] Khan also wrote a series of letters in the late 1970s to a skilled friend in Montreal asking for help to get information. He asked him to visit Pakistan and work on the centrifuge project, which was codenamed in the letters in various ways, including as a "butter factory."[25]

Salam started setting up companies in Britain in 1977. He was soon joined by Peter Griffin, an engineer from South Wales who claims he met Khan after Salam, in a search for suppliers, dialed the wrong number.[26] An early order arranged by Salam and Griffin's company, Weargate, in Swansea, Wales, was for frequency converters from a British subsidiary of the U.S. company Emerson Electric. After buying the converters with funds supplied by Khan, Weargate forwarded them to Special Works Organization. A subsequent order was detected by British authorities and stopped. Weargate's relationship with Pakistan was exposed, but new trading companies were easily established.

Another of Khan's initial recruits was his university friend Henk Slebos, with whom he reconnected at the NUCLEX conference in Switzerland in October 1975. Slebos was then at the Dutch company Explosive Metal Working Holland (EHWH) and had been involved in contracts with the Dutch URENCO company. While Khan was still at FDO Slebos had visited him to discuss the explosive welding of metal pipes that connected together the centrifuges, or cascades.[27]

In July 1976, Slebos was dismissed from EHWH and formed his own engineering company near Alkmaar. Soon, Slebos was regularly traveling to Pakistan, collecting goods for Khan's centrifuge project and often running into other members of Khan's growing network, each pursuing their own sales.[28] In late 1976 or early 1977, Slebos approached Nico Zondag, his former boss at EHWH, asking him to create bellows in up to four thousand maraging steel tubes. Zondag thought Slebos's sketches looked identical to ones that originated in the URENCO project.[29] Slebos admitted the tubes were for centrifuges, most likely the tubes VDT produced for Butt, and went one step further by inviting Zondag to Pakistan.[30] "You can make more money in Pakistan than in this crappy company over here," Slebos told Zondag.[31]

Zondag rebuffed Slebos's overtures and informed UCN management. In a meeting with P. Six Dijkstra, UCN's security officer, L.L. Strappers, the senior security officer at the Ministry of Economic Affairs, and a BVD employee, Zondag gave a detailed briefing, even including Slebos's planned departure date to Pakistan.[32] The response was noncommittal. "BVD studied whether a further investigation regarding Slebos would make sense. In view of the type and weight of the available information, it was not considered useful."[33] Zondag's candid assessment was simpler: "They just did not take me seriously." In the meantime, the same order Zondag turned down was eventually given to the French company Calorstat.[34] Two UCN employees who visited Calorstat in February 1979 on unrelated business discovered the order and learned it had originated in the Netherlands, most likely from Slebos.

With Slebos on board, he was now free to recruit his own partners. Slebos picked Gunes Cire, a key business partner in Turkey who would be a reliable Khan supplier for over two decades. Cire and Slebos had attended Delft Technological University together. Cire was working for a German electronics company at the time, but left to form his own company. By 1981, he was specializing in key components for frequency converters for Khan's centrifuges. Cire and Slebos would eventually become partners in each other's companies. Slebos reportedly owned a 15 percent stake in Cire's Istanbul-based ETI company, and Cire was a member of the board of directors of Slebos's engineering office.[35]

Another key Khan recruit was Ernest Piffl, a German company official at Team Industries, who supplied frequency converters. Piffl said the order came from Pakistanis in Paris, likely Butt who by then was based in the Pakistani embassy in Paris.[36] Piffl said that Butt told him that the converters were for a textile plant. In truth, Piffl had a record of friendly contact with officials responsible for Pakistan's nuclear program dating back to 1973.[37] That friendly contact would remain until his prosecution in the 1990s for illegal exports to Pakistan.

Also affiliated with Khan was Gotthard Lerch. He was a

senior salesman at Leybold-Heraeus, a world leader in vacuum technology and its applications to the nuclear field. Leybold-Heraeus supplied URENCO with vacuum equipment, including specialized valves and vacuum pumps. Khan first visited a Dutch sales office of Leybold-Heraeus while at FDO and could have consulted directly with the company about metallurgical problems facing UCN's centrifuge program. It is assumed this led to contact with the Leybold-Heraeus branch in Hanau, near Frankfurt, where Lerch was based.

By 1978, Khan had an effective team in place. He had also unwittingly attracted the attention of Trevor Edwards, a pioneer in the British centrifuge program and an early URENCO recruit. In 1976, Edwards learned that Pakistan had ordered a specialized machine identical to those URENCO ordered from the German company Leifeld. These flow-forming machines were specially adapted to make maraging steel tubes for bellows in a Dutch centrifuge. A year later, Edwards was surprised to discover that a French company, which made maraging steel preforms for the Dutch CNOR centrifuge, had shipped off a room full of the preforms to Switzerland. The final confirmation of his suspicions about Pakistani activities came when Pakistan asked a British machine tool company to make fifty demonstration bellows out of thin-walled tubes. This was part of an order to buy the equipment necessary to make large numbers of bellows, and it included a drawing in English that contained classified URENCO data from the Netherlands. A subsequent raid of the house of Abdus Salam in Britain uncovered a full set of centrifuge drawings.[38]

Suspicion quickly fell on Khan. Edwards was head of the research and development program at the Almelo plant from 1971 to 1975 and remembered seeing A.Q. Khan there. He recalled being troubled by this as Khan was not a British, Dutch, or German national, as required by URENCO. At the time, Khan's presence reminded him of an earlier controversy at MAN New Technologies in Munich, the main supplier of centrifuges to German URENCO. MAN had Austrian and Yugoslavian machinists in their classified areas, and German URENCO ordered them removed. Dutch URENCO issued no such orders about Khan.

Edwards and his British colleagues had pieced together a disturbing picture. Pakistan was using secret URENCO designs to procure highly sensitive centrifuge components and the means to manufacture them. The Pakistanis were buying the parts to build a modified CNOR centrifuge. The modified model had four tubes connected by three bellows, one less tube and bellows than the original model, but it had a SNOR rotor tube and an improved CNOR bottom bearing. It also had an inward pointing bellows, which was more advanced and harder to make than an outward pointing bellows. In essence, Khan was copying what he stole, but building a composite, simpler design that he believed was more suited for Pakistan.

In 1978, Britain warned the United States about its growing suspicions. Previously unaware of Khan's centrifuge project, Washington now brought its huge intelligence gathering capabilities to bear, including the National Security Agency (NSA), home of the world's foremost capability to intercept communications. Pakistani orders, many of which involved telexes and unsecured phone conversations, were easy to intercept once the NSA operatives started looking. Spy satellites zeroed in on Kahuta, which was growing into an enormous facility. The British, who had better on-the-ground intelligence capabilities, penetrated Kahuta with spies.[39] Later, U.S. agents also infiltrated the program and trickled in bits and pieces about Khan's progress. By fall 1978, information was flooding in from multiple sources.[40]

In the United States, this intelligence was assigned a special "compartment" to which only a handful of government officials had access. U.S. nuclear weapons labs produced a diagram of a centrifuge based on what Khan was purchasing and gradually filled in the parts as new information emerged. Like a slowly developing picture, what emerged was devastating. Pakistan's centrifuge program was based on imports of individual components, not a whole plant, from a variety of private companies in a number of countries, not just one government-owned company in one country. In short, it was fool-proofed against the same approach the United States had taken with France to end its sale of a reprocessing plant to Pakistan. Making matters worse, most of Khan's purchases were perfectly legal, even several that he orchestrated in the United States. Export controls on nuclear facilities and equipment were in their infancy in the 1970s. The United States and other major nuclear suppliers were focusing on whole nuclear plants, such as reprocessing plants and nuclear reactors, or major components of those facilities, not components of gas centrifuge plants. Such minutely focused regulations were not considered because, in part, of the first-world belief that third-world countries like Pakistan wouldn't be able to construct a full-scale nuclear facility.

A multipronged approach was devised to thwart Khan's program. The biggest challenge by far was to convince other countries to plug the massive gaps in their regulations about what technology could and could not be sold. Few governments understood what to control since centrifuge technology was top secret. The first task was to develop a list of proscribed items. Jerry Malling, an engineer working for the Oak Ridge National Laboratory in Tennessee, was approached by his boss in the cafeteria one day in mid-1978 and asked to put together the new list. Leading a team of eight U.S. experts, Malling prepared an export guide including pictures and diagrams of key centrifuge parts as well as "dual use" items essential to operate the machines. While the British initially opposed declassifying the guide since it looked like a "how-to" book for making centrifuges, they relented when Malling documented that the information was, surprisingly, public knowledge.[41]

Armed with Malling's guide and a color-coded chart of a centrifuge showing which companies were helping Khan, American and British teams fanned out to visit the main suppliers—Germany, France, Italy, Belgium, Spain, Switzerland, Holland, and Japan. These teams shared intelligence on Pakistan's nuclear program, asked governments to stop dangerous exports, and identified the companies and people working with Khan. When British officials discovered that an employee of a company that had exported inverters to Khan was planning a vacation in Australia after stopping in Pakistan, they confiscated his passport at the airplane gate.[42]

With export control teams circling the globe, the U.S. State Department launched a new innovation, working with the American intelligence community to issue timely warnings to other governments about dangerous sales to Pakistan. Regular meetings were held to examine fresh information, usually communications intercepts, which served as the basis for these démarches (unofficially called "non-papers"). To heighten the impact of their diplomatic offensive, U.S. and British officials selectively leaked information to the media, hoping to turn public opinion against recalcitrant suppliers and to further educate governments and companies about Khan.[43]

The Netherlands undertook a full investigation of the Khan affair only after initial press reports about his activities appeared. When Britain demanded a full report, the Dutch government launched a full-scale investigation.[44] During one of the classified hearings in the Netherlands, a confiscated Pakistani centrifuge general assembly drawing was shown to the head of Dutch URENCO. He denied knowing what it was. Trevor Edwards, who was at the hearings, immediately recognized the drawings as a modified CNOR centrifuge, or what would become known as the Pakistani P1 centrifuge. He would see much later a similar design in Iran and Libya.

Overall, progress was uneven. Upon learning Switzerland ignored evidence that Pakistan was building nuclear weapons, the United States cut off desperately needed assistance for its nuclear power program, a move the Swiss ambassador in Washington called "blackmail."[45] Germany was likewise slow to hamper their export-driven economy. It was not until the early 1990s, with revelations about the role of German companies in Iraq's and Libya's WMD programs, that significant reforms were initiated. France and Japan used political pressure to stop suspicious exports as they had no laws explicitly prohibiting such sales.

Asking national governments to tighten regulations was necessary, but devising common international controls was essential. The Zangger committee, also known as the Nuclear Exporters Committee, was a group of fifteen nuclear supplier states that met in Vienna. Chaired by Professor Claude Zangger of Switzerland, the committee was charged with developing a universal set of controls on items whose export would trigger safeguards under the Non-Proliferation Treaty, thus called the "trigger list." Both the United States and Britain lobbied the committee for tough, stringent additions to the trigger list. According to one participant in the meetings, some officials complained that too many items would be controlled, limiting their countries' exports. This weighting toward profit over nonproliferation would repeatedly plague deliberations about expanding controls. Ultimately, the Zangger committee only agreed to control a small list of key centrifuge components, materials, and equipment.[46] Increasingly important "dual-use" items were made voluntary, creating an important loophole that Pakistan and many other countries exploited until after the 1991 Persian Gulf War, when dual-use controls were finally mandated.

In reaction to the greater scrutiny and tightening controls, Khan's network moved offshore and created front companies in the Gulf states that could more effectively disguise their efforts from authorities. If asked, they told suppliers that the end user was a company in the United Arab Emirates (UAE) or Kuwait. In reality, the front company was little more than an office. Sometimes, several front companies shared the same address. Once the items were delivered, agents found it easy to send the items to Pakistan without the supplier knowing.

Two of the first to set up trading companies in the Gulf states were Abdus Salam and his business associate Peter Griffin. They created Golden Castle Trading and Construction Company in Kuwait. Salam would also be linked in Kuwait to Tower International and to Khalid Jassim General Trading Establishment and Bin Belailah Enterprises in Dubai, UAE. Known as the "Hong

Kong of the Middle East," with well-known firms such as IBM and Samsung doing business there, Dubai's cosmopolitan trading zone became a hub of illicit nuclear trade. Many of Dubai's small and unknown businesses have taken advantage of the UAE's porous laws to smuggle technology for building weapons of mass destruction.[47] The UAE requires the participation of local partners to establish a registered, legitimate company. Often the name of the front company was that of the local partner, providing an additional complication in detecting shell organizations. Khan's companies hired UAE citizens who were unknown in the West.

Such was the case with both General Trading Establishment and Bin Belailah Enterprises (BBE). According to a 1981 document from Germany's own CIA, the Bundesnachrichtendienst (BND), these two companies employed Abdul Qayuum Khan (likely one of A.Q. Khan's brothers) and S. Mohammed Farooq, a Sri Lankan national. Farooq would emerge as the head of Bin Belailah and become a key player in Khan's network. By 1982, Seyed Abu Tahir Bin Bukhary, Farooq's young nephew, was working at Bin Belailah. Tahir's age earned him the nickname "Junior." He carried out many mundane duties, including filling orders, processing shipping instructions, and getting tea for participants in meetings. Tahir gradually worked his way up and in the 1990s took over Khan's Dubai operations, eventually becoming Khan's chief administrator, financial officer, and money launderer.[48]

Tahir's position in Khan's operation speaks to Dubai's prominence as an ideal base of operations. *Nuclear Caravans*, a top secret U.S. intelligence report completed in the mid-1980s and based almost entirely on intercepted telephone calls, faxes, telexes, and other communications, documented Khan's use of Dubai as a key transit point for nuclear equipment shipped from Europe to Pakistan.[49] The UAE would not institute export controls until 2007, and then only under intense U.S. pressure. These controls have yet to be effectively enforced. As a result, it remains a crucial nexus for nuclear smuggling for both Iran and Pakistan.

———————■———————

DESPITE ITS ADVANCEMENTS, Pakistan could not build the one weapon it wanted in the early 1980s: a small, reliable armament that could be delivered to India by attack aircraft or missile. The best it could hope for was a bomb weighing a few thousand pounds, akin to what the United States detonated over Japan. Once again, Pakistan would rely on the technological advances of another country for help, but this time it would use diplomacy instead of espionage.

Longtime allies united by a mutual enmity for India, Pakistan and China commenced "peaceful" nuclear cooperation in December 1976. Tom Graham, a young U.S. government official who tried to launch a diplomatic initiative to warn both countries against cooperating, ran into stiff opposition from the State Department. At a General Advisory Committee on Arms Control and Disarmament at the State Department, a Carter administration official stated skeptically, "I think they [China] are not in favor of a Pakistani nuclear explosive program and I don't think they are doing anything to help it."[50] There were, however, mounting stacks of circumstantial evidence of their collusion. Prime Minister Bhutto's death cell memoirs, published after he was hung in 1979, hinted at collaboration with China that "will perhaps be my greatest achievement and contribution to the survival of our people and our nation."[51] Moreover, Chinese academics have gone on record arguing that Mao Zedong promised Pakistan a nuclear weapon but never followed through.[52] Unfortunately, the Carter administration's new imperative after the Soviet invasion of Afghanistan in 1979 was to work closely with China and Pakistan, not to raise potentially divisive problems.[53]

For Pakistan and A.Q. Khan, cooperating with China quickly proved to be a boon. The Chinese provided Pakistan with blueprints for building a nuclear weapon, most likely the Chic-4, first tested as a missile warhead in 1966 and detonated above ground with an explosive force of twelve kilotons, equivalent to 12,000 tons of TNT.[54] They also provided 50 kilograms of weapon-grade uranium.

The heart of that bomb is a sphere of weapon-grade uranium surrounded by conventional explosives molded to the outside in shaped charges, or high explosive lenses. The explosives are covered by metal plates which when meshed together form an even larger sphere. When the conventional explosives are detonated, they compress the nuclear core which, when it reaches a critical density, triggers a specialized device to inject neutrons into the nuclear material, resulting in a nuclear explosion.

Pakistan now had the blueprint of a proven weapon. In 1981, A.Q. Khan sent his procurement agents detailed drawings of weapon components with orders to buy them from European companies.[55] One of the European agents was Slebos.[56] Another one was Khan's old university friend, Heinz Mebus, who ran an engineering bureau in Erlangen, Germany. He was Piffl's father-in-law, and he had become a middleman for Khan's centrifuge effort in the 1970s. With his boss Albrecht Migule, he supplied a complete plant to make uranium hexafluoride at Dera Ghazi Khan in the late 1970s.[57] This time, Mebus reportedly supplied Pakistan with the components for the detonating systems of nuclear weapons and metal plates for manufacturing the housing of nuclear warheads.[58] Another main intermediary was Turkish, believed to be Cire, who bought parts elsewhere.[59] U.S. intelligence learned of several efforts by Khan's agents to buy metal hemispheres and dished plates, high quality detonators with power supplies for firing them, high-speed cameras and flash x-ray equipment used in testing nuclear weapon components, and neutron generators.[60]

China's deal with Pakistan was so dramatic there was little consensus among U.S. government officials over what ultimate agenda it served. Was it the result of a rogue operation concocted by China's nuclear bureaucracy, or yet another symptom of a *laissez-faire* export policy out of control? Beijing's sales of low enriched uranium to South Africa—then practicing apartheid—and heavy water to India, its regional adversary, made economic sense but ran contrary to Chinese foreign policy. Some U.S. officials believed that China's leaders had directly approved the deal. A Special National Intelligence Estimate completed by the CIA in 1982 warned that Moscow was likely to "intensify pressure on Pakistan" because of its help in sustaining the Afghan resistance.[61] China appears to have already reached the same conclusion and provided Pakistan with nuclear assistance to bolster its security. As a bonus, China's nuclear scientists would have access to the advanced centrifuge technology Khan stole from Europe, technology that might contribute to its own nuclear weapons program. According to a former senior U.S. official, Chinese representatives were at Kahuta "all the time" during the early 1980s, both helping Pakistan and receiving information and assistance on building European centrifuges.[62]

In return, between 1981 and 1984, Pakistanis attended a series of lectures in Beijing from prominent Chinese experts in nuclear weapons and took detailed, dated, handwritten notes in English. Based on several cryptic notations apparently deriding Munir Khan's rival nuclear weapons program, some of the note takers may have worked directly for Khan.[63] These notations state that without Chinese assistance "M" or "Munir" would need a much longer time period to build a miniaturized nuclear weapon. By the early 1980s, Munir Khan's PAEC had developed a nuclear weapon design, but this weapon was significantly bigger than the one described in the notes, which had a mass of about 500 kilograms and a diameter about 0.8–0.9 meters.

The notes, which would prove crucial in Khan's later dealings with Libya, describe nuclear weapon theory, the detailed design and purpose of individual components, and step-by-step instructions on assembling an implosion-type nuclear weapon that uses a solid core of almost 25 kilograms of weapon-grade uranium. This design includes the first steps China took to reduce the size of its nuclear weapons. Drawings obtained from China or produced by Pakistani experts from the notes represent the components of this weapon design with their exact specifications. The level of technical precision and detail in the notes and drawings would have allowed Pakistan to manufacture the components with a high confidence that they would work.

These notes go far beyond anything available through open source material or on the Internet. One U.S. nuclear weapons expert said this information would be considered classified in the United States. He noted that the drawings alone would be immensely valuable, illustrating how to get around fundamental problems in building an implosion weapon. Included in these notes were a written discussion and design drawings of a relatively sophisticated neutron initiator placed at the center of the nuclear device. This initiator uses fusion materials and does not require polonium-210. This isotope, with a relatively short radioactive half-life, must be produced typically in reactors and can severely complicate the construction and deployment of a nuclear arsenal. The provision of this type of long-lasting initiator would have been a tremendous gain for Pakistan's fledgling nuclear weapons program.

While the Chinese were willing to supply various components, even they had limits as to which components were off limits. They refused to offer any ready-made components related to the weapon's nuclear core. The lack of Chinese willingness to supply all the necessary parts may have been part of the reason Khan ordered his agents to buy parts in Europe.

Soon after the Chinese started giving bomb designs to Pakistan, that information was picked up by British intelligence. In an intelligence coup, British spies stole the Pakistani blueprints for the newly acquired bomb design in 1981 from one of Khan's operatives in Europe, and quickly informed the Americans. The drawings were forwarded to Lawrence Livermore National Laboratory, a U.S. government lab in California that helped build America's nuclear arsenal. Researchers were flabbergasted by how much technological know-how had fallen into Pakistani hands, but by then Khan's plan was in motion.[64] By 1983, Pakistan had enough weapon-grade uranium to make a nuclear explosive.[65] Throughout 1984 and 1985, Pakistan conducted a series of "cold tests," an important technique whereby the weapon absent the weapon-grade uranium is detonated to test that it will work. On December 10, 1984, Khan wrote a letter to General Muhammad Zia-ul-Haq, the president of Pakistan. Zia had seized control of the country in a coup and Islamized the nation's system of Anglo-Saxon laws. Khan proudly declared that Pakistan was "now in position to detonate a device, a nuclear device on least notice."

Khan's procurement efforts were a remarkable accomplishment in an industrially backward country, producing highly enriched uranium for a deliverable nuclear weapon in less than a decade. Khan's achievement of putting together a centrifuge plant depended most importantly on his international procurement network. Although some of the members of the procurement team would move on to different work, most of them would work with Khan for the next two decades. The glue for this enduring network was huge sums of easy money and little chance of getting caught by the authorities, as the Pakistani government typically refused to cooperate with prosecutors abroad. When the Netherlands finally prosecuted Khan in absentia in 1983, Pakistan likened the charges to slander and categorically denied stealing centrifuge information. Khan was convicted of attempted espionage and sentenced to four years but he was acquitted on appeal due to a technicality. Khan heralded this acquittal as vindication that he had developed Pakistan's centrifuge indigenously.

Khan and his partners continued to equip Pakistan's nuclear weapons program, but later branched out to become suppliers to other countries. Several nations, such as Iran, Iraq, North Korea, and Libya, would create their own national smuggling networks that, in some cases, connected with Khan's partners who would become deeply involved in helping other countries proliferate. But who were these men? Why were they so important to Khan's business? And how did they make the world a much more dangerous place?

It's Just Business

Olli Heinonen, the IAEA's lead investigator, was hoping to penetrate the upper echelons of the Khan network when he met with German engineer and businessman Gotthard Lerch on March 31, 2004, in Zurich, Switzerland.[1] Lerch was known to have had extensive contact with Khan over the years, and was now suspected of being one of Khan's main buyers for Libya's secret nuclear effort. During the meeting, Lerch said he didn't know key members of the network, and had only a passing acquaintance with B.S.A. Tahir, Khan's chief aide who for years ran the nuclear trafficking operation from Dubai. Lerch claimed he had traveled to Dubai once to buy a computer and had met Tahir at one of his stores. (In addition to nuclear trafficking, Tahir ran a legitimate business selling computers with his brother.) If Heinonen was looking for insight from Lerch into a career of selling nuclear technology that dates back to the 1970s, he'd find none.

The Germans planned to have better luck when they asked Swiss authorities to arrest Lerch in November 2004 on suspicion of treason. Though he had lived in Switzerland since 1985, he remained a German citizen and was extradited to stand trial.

Lerch maintained he broke no laws. He didn't do business in seedy smugglers' dens but in office buildings and over fine meals in expensive restaurants. With his profits, he financed real estate projects in a number of countries, including South Africa, China, and the United States.[2] Was his business legitimate, as he claims? Or were the Germans onto something by calling it treason?

———————

LERCH'S LEGAL TROUBLES have made him among the most well-known and internationally recognized of Khan's inner circle. Lerch's activities show just how sophisticated nuclear trafficking has become over the last three decades, and how critical it has been to the global proliferation of nuclear weapons programs.

His career in selling secret technology goes back to the 1970s, when he was a rising star at Leybold-Heraeus in Hanau, Germany. A former Leybold-Heraeus employee who knew Lerch well then described him as a "well dressed, good-looking fellow."[3] His only deficiency at the time was that his English was "terrible," a problem for an international salesman. Earlier, he had worked at the German firm Dornier, which helped develop the German gas centrifuge for URENCO. Lerch understood the intersection between vacuum and nuclear technology, making him an invaluable addition to Leybold-Heraeus in an era where nuclear energy was widely expected to take off worldwide. President Jimmy Carter, for example, was a former nuclear engineer who wanted the United States to build two hundred nuclear power plants (almost none of which were ever ordered as nuclear power's appeal faded).

When Khan took over the centrifuge program, Lerch was

manager of the nuclear group in Hanau. This group was charged with selling large systems or "turnkey" facilities that used the vacuum equipment Leybold-Heraeus produced. Their construction required a high degree of specialized knowledge.[4] To fill these contracts, Lerch obtained equipment from many other suppliers. As a result, he knew highly qualified experts and subcontractors throughout Europe.

Lerch's fate became deeply entwined with Khan as a result of Otto Heilingbrunner, a Bavarian in charge of sales in Leybold-Heraeus's Cologne branch. His territory covered the "Near East," which included Pakistan, Iraq, Iran, Libya, South Africa, and Taiwan. According to a former colleague, Heilingbrunner was a "wheeling-dealing" salesman ready to travel to remote areas to make a sale. Heilingbrunner hired commercial agents in Pakistan, Iran, and South Africa who played key roles in funneling a wide range of items to their secret nuclear programs. Heilingbrunner's success in finding agents in remote areas of the world is one of the reasons why Leybold-Heraeus's equipment ended up in many nuclear weapons programs.

A key part of Heilingbrunner's job was to find local agents that would either sell the company's products or find potential customers whom Heilingbrunner would contact directly. In 1974, Heilingbrunner hired the firm Arshad, Amjad, and Abid (the first names of the owner's three sons, or "Triple A" for short) to be Leybold-Heraeus's agent in Pakistan. Heilingbrunner said many of his company's sales to Khan's centrifuge program went through Triple A.

By 1976, Khan's centrifuge project was buying vacuum equipment directly from Leybold-Heraeus.[5] Heilingbrunner's first major contact at the Pakistan Atomic Energy Commission, Dr. Fakhrul Hasan Hashmi, a metallurgist educated in Britain who would become an important aide to A.Q. Khan, purchased Leybold-Heraeus vacuum equipment. Later, Hashmi and Dr. G.D. Alam, another senior official in Khan's centrifuge program, would become crucial Leybold-Heraeus contacts. Pakistani officials, including Dr. Alam, regularly visited Leybold's branches in Cologne and Hanau.

Heilingbrunner's contact with Hashmi surprisingly didn't help Leybold-Heraeus in doing business with Munir Khan's Pakistan Atomic Energy Commission, which was focused on acquiring and developing plutonium. When France stopped supplying a reprocessing plant in Chashma in 1978, PAEC officials took Heilingbrunner to visit the facility and asked him if Leybold-Heraeus could help finish the plant. Heilingbrunner described the site as being in a state of "large ruin," and as Leybold had no expertise in plutonium separation equipment, he rejected the offer. Since then, Pakistan has struggled to finish the Chashma reprocessing plant.

Lerch's group in Hanau was hungry for business, since at the time there was "not much activity in Europe," according to a former Leybold-Heraeus official.[6] After reading Heilingbrunner's reports on his Pakistani visits, Lerch went to Pakistan seeking business with Khan. An ex-colleague of Lerch said about the Hanau office: "Engineers were easily seduced by interesting, complicated projects. They were glad if a salesman sold their skills and kept them busy." Khan eventually trusted Lerch, who secured major sales to Pakistan's centrifuge programs in 1977.

The Hanau group won contracts to build a critical part of the Kahuta gas centrifuge plant called a feed and withdrawal system. Each centrifuge enriches only a small amount of uranium gas. A large number of centrifuges are needed to reach the desired level and quantity of enriched uranium. A collection of centrifuges linked together by pipes is called a cascade; a centrifuge plant comprises many cascades. A specialized piping system carrying the uranium gas leads into and from the cascades.

The plant starts with an oven, called an autoclave, which heats a tank of natural uranium hexafluoride. At room temperatures and pressures, uranium hexafluoride is a solid. The autoclave turns the solid material into a gas, called the "feed," which then travels through pipes to the cascades. After passing through the cascades, the gas, now enriched, goes through another set of pipes to equipment that cools the gas and deposits solid enriched uranium hexafluoride, called the "product," into a transport tank. A third set of pipes leads to equipment to cool and collect the uranium waste, called the "tails." Collectively, the feed and withdrawal system represents a major part of an enrichment plant. Without it, a gas centrifuge plant cannot operate.

Although not as technically demanding as building thousands of centrifuges, this auxiliary equipment was also outside Pakistan's ability to design and manufacture. Pakistan's feed and withdrawal equipment would also rely on URENCO designs, although Khan did not steal such designs while at FDO. Instead, Leybold-Heraeus organized the acquisition of suitable designs and their production. Because the cascades operate under a vacuum, providing these finished systems to the Kahuta enrichment plant could be highly profitable for Leybold-Heraeus.

By August 1977, Lerch's group was preparing preliminary designs for a feed and withdrawal system for Pakistan at Kahuta, which they called the V 3A vacuum plant (a current Leybold employee suggested "V 3A" could stand for Vacuum, Triple A, Leybold's agent in Pakistan).[7] Lerch was deeply involved in Kahuta's construction from the beginning, and he had many discussions with Khan about the contract, according to a former colleague who was present at several of Lerch's meetings with Khan.[8] The contract was complicated, involving many engineers and technicians in Hanau who had to prepare engineering drawings of the feed and withdrawal system, establish technical specifications, and develop cost estimates. Other Leybold-Heraeus engineers also visited Pakistan to further develop the facility. Because of the large number of people involved, Leybold-Heraeus instituted greater secrecy measures than normal, actions that became essential when they sought to hide their activities from authorities.

Exactly how Leybold-Heraeus acquired the URENCO feed and withdrawal technology confounded European investigators for years, and Leybold maintained total silence on the issue. When German prosecutors finally felt they had enough evidence to charge Lerch and Heilingbrunner with stealing the information from URENCO in the 1980s, they alleged that Leybold-Heraeus obtained the URENCO information and blueprints during the process of bidding to manufacture equipment for a new URENCO centrifuge plant to be built in Gronau, Germany, near Almelo. Lerch and Heilingbrunner in turn were alleged to have illegally used the information to build duplicate facilities for Pakistan.

The commercial bidding process is a potential weak link in the leakage of sensitive information. Admittedly, Lerch was thoroughly familiar with URENCO's bidding process, and gained a wealth of sensitive URENCO information, but in fact, Leybold-Heraeus had simply bought the information for the feed and withdrawal system and the right to use it from Comprimo, a Dutch subcontractor to URENCO that had originally developed the information for the Almelo gas centrifuge plant.[9] As a URENCO contractor, Leybold-Heraeus could have had access to this information as part of a bidding process, but it paid Comprimo at least 230,000 deutsche marks from the end of 1977 until August 1978 so that it could have free use of the information.[10] URENCO labeled the information proprietary, not classified, leaving Comprimo within its rights to sell it. Whether Comprimo ever notified Dutch URENCO of its sale of the information to Leybold is unclear. Had British or German URENCO known that Leybold-Heraeus's intended customer was Pakistan, it would likely have opposed Comprimo's sale.

The Comprimo designs were for the production of low enriched uranium for nuclear reactors. In collaboration with Khan's experts, the Hanau branch modified these designs so they could make weapon-grade uranium for nuclear weapons. But that was just the start of Hanau's involvement. Leybold's Cologne branch and a French subsidiary could provide some equipment, but the company did not make many of the items needed in a feed and withdrawal system, such as heating and cooling equipment, and large numbers of sophisticated valves. Khan and Hanau looked to Switzerland for suppliers.

They found a partner in the Swiss company Vakuum Apparat Technik (VAT), located in St. Gallen, and Cora Engineering AG in Chur.[11] Khan's associates had approached VAT in the winter of 1976 looking for several thousand vacuum valves.[12] VAT also regularly supplied sophisticated valves to Leybold-Heraeus, making VAT a natural partner for this new project. Friedrich Tinner, then a chief salesman at VAT, would become another close associate of Khan's, bringing his sons Urs and Marco into the business and working with Khan until all three were arrested in 2004 and 2005.

Using Hanau's designs, Cora Engineering quickly finished manufacturing feed and withdrawal equipment, which Khan then had transported on three Pakistani Air Force Hercules transport aircraft in June 1978.[13] Internal documents suggest that Hanau took the lead in assembling all the equipment at Kahuta. In August 1978, the Hanau branch produced a quote for Khan's front company, the Special Works Organization, for planning the assembly of the V 3A vacuum plant, including a purification system.[14] The offer may have been a prelude to assembling the equipment delivered by Pakistani aircraft in June 1978 and other major equipment arriving at Kahuta from other European suppliers.

The next year, correspondence between Hanau and Triple A showed that Khan wanted a larger feed and withdrawal system. A Mr. Aslam of Triple A conducted numerous negotiations with Hanau about the size and cost of the plant, which was called in their correspondence a "Special Gas Handling Unit." A former colleague of Lerch noted that the Hanau project directors were "creative in creating names of projects" which concealed their real purpose.

This turnkey contract eventually covered the supply of a larger feed and withdrawal system, including all the miles of piping needed to connect the system to thousands of centrifuges. It also featured an electrical control system to run the plant. All of this equipment was destined for a new centrifuge building at Kahuta. The equipment was also redesigned to be modular, simplifying its shipment and erection on-site. The cost would eventually reach over 33 million deutsche marks, an amount which represented about one-quarter of the Hanau division's annual income in the late 1970s.

Following further discussions with Aslam, Leybold-Heraeus made a November 1980 offer for the Special Gas Handling Unit that refers to a "100 ton per year separation work plant." This could suggest the ultimate capacity of the centrifuge plant that Leybold-Heraeus intended to supply, which would have been immense, far larger than most would have expected Pakistan to build at the time. A 100 ton per year separation plant could hold up to 50,000 P1 centrifuges and make several hundred kilograms of weapon-grade uranium per year, enough supply for more than a dozen nuclear weapons.

Enjoying a good profit, Cora Engineering continued to make feed and withdrawal equipment for Kahuta despite at least two diplomatic protests from the U.S. government in 1979 and 1980.[15] In 1981, someone decided that diplomatic channels weren't sufficient. On February 20, a bomb exploded in the garden of Cora's managing director's house.[16] The mysterious "Group for Non-Proliferation for Southeast Asia" called Cora after the bombing and warned them not to continue sales to Pakistan. In November of that year, another bomb went off in Heinz Mebus's front yard. Mebus ignored such warnings and continued to work with Khan.[17]

To this day, the bombers have not been identified, but speculation has often settled on Israel, which was known to be carrying out attacks against those aiding the nuclear ambitions of countries in the Middle East. On June 7, 1981, Israel attacked the Osirak nuclear reactor southeast of Baghdad in an effort to delay that country's nuclear weapons program. These attacks fueled concerns in Pakistan that Israel or India would attack the Kahuta enrichment plant and its other nuclear facilities.

Soon afterward, Cora announced the suspension of all deliveries to Pakistan, despite having already received a payment of 6.4 million Swiss francs.[18] Pakistan went to court to get its money back, forcing Cora to declare bankruptcy. Khan settled for the repayment of about one-quarter of this amount.[19] For a brief period, European suppliers were frightened of doing business with Pakistan's nuclear weapons program, but the bombings did not deter Leybold-Heraeus and Lerch since their association with Cora was not common knowledge. When the news media finally caught up to Leybold-Heraeus's sales to Pakistan, the company either denied or ignored the reports.[20]

The bombings and media scrutiny led Leybold-Heraeus to take extra precautions to keep their Pakistani exports secret.[21] Employees in Cologne were kept in the dark about the actual destination of the large amounts of vacuum pumping equipment in these orders. If an order for vacuum equipment manufactured at the Cologne branch was exceptionally sensitive, it would be handled as an internal company order from Hanau and shipped there. From Hanau, it would be shipped onward to Pakistan. Hanau also used Leybold-Heraeus's French subsidiary as a false destination to get the goods out of Germany and to Pakistan. "Colleagues in Hanau were the masters of camouflage," said one Leybold official.

With Cora in bankruptcy, Hanau needed a new company to make feed and withdrawal equipment while keeping Leybold-Heraeus's role in the project hidden. They again turned to Switzerland, which was still lax in policing its exports. Lerch and Heilingbrunner visited the Swiss firm Metallwerke Buchs AG

(MWB) in Buchs on June 29, 1983, and quickly made a 2 million Swiss franc deal.[22] Helmut Eder, owner of Praesidial-Anstalt, a holding company in nearby Vaduz Liechtenstein that owned MWB, and Anton "Toni" Schoeb, MWB's director, welcomed the business, although Schoeb would later become worried about the potential illegality of the deal.[23] A few months later, Eder received a set of drawings and specifications for making feed and withdrawal equipment, including steel containers to hold uranium hexafluoride, autoclaves for heating uranium hexafluoride into a gas, equipment to cool the uranium gas after leaving the cascades and put it into tanks, special pipes, and electrical control equipment. Eder called the documents "top secret" and promised the Germans that they would not leave MWB's premises. Many of the documents were marked with the logo "CB," likely used to hide the original markings of Comprimo or URENCO. Eder told Schoeb that any questions should be forwarded to Lerch.

Despite these instructions, MWB personnel soon sent a query to the German company Maschinenbau Scholz near the Dutch border in Coesfeld, Germany, about buying some of the components which it could not make itself. Included in the query were blueprints of what were called a vessel or tank. The company was a URENCO contractor, and its officials quickly recognized that the drawings were actually for an autoclave used by Uranit, at the time the name of German URENCO. They immediately informed Uranit headquarters that MWB had its blueprints. On January 18, 1984, Hagen Fink, Uranit's chief lawyer, wrote to the president of the board of MWB, asking how their documents ended up at MWB and who provided them with this material. Fink assumed the documents had been stolen and was totally unaware of Comprimo's secret sale to Leybold-Heraeus.

Although the plans were not state secrets under German law, they were proprietary information and allegedly could not be transferred from Germany to Switzerland without an export license. Fink suspected that another case of industrial espionage had occurred.[24]

When Uranit's letter arrived at MWB ten days later, panic ensued. Eder collected all the documents and called Lerch and Heilingbrunner in Germany. The next day Heilingbrunner and Lerch flew to the Zurich airport and met Eder and Schoeb in the afternoon at the Kloten Hilton Airport Hotel. In an intense discussion, they agreed that the documents had to be sent to Uranit, but they needed a plausible explanation of how the documents ended up at MWB.[25] Despite having bought the documents legally from Comprimo, they did not want the authorities to learn of their involvement or their sales to Pakistan.

Heilingbrunner thought of a solution that would keep Leybold-Heraeus's involvement secret and protect MWB.[26] They would invent an imaginary businessman who had given MWB the documents. They settled on a "Dr. M. Kotari" who was a member of an engineering group that had passed through the Zurich airport in September 1983 and wrote several businesses seeking bids for equipment for the group's projects. Heilingbrunner took paper from his briefcase and started to write the letter by hand in English: "Dear Sir, I am a partner in an engineering group handling high technology projects in the Middle East area.... To check the capability of your company, I have attached a documentation about a vessel. Should you be able to quote, there is a good chance for business." The letter emphasized that "[f]or the moment, I have to ask for you for competitive reasons to treat this matter as confidential." Heilingbrunner ended the letter by stating that Kotari was traveling with no fixed address, but would phone in January to discuss the deal in more detail.

Heilingbrunner said that the letter needed to be typed at MWB and the handwritten letter and typewriter disposed of afterwards. Eder was too panicky to handle the details so Schoeb calmly said that he could procure stationery from the Hilton hotel. If the police ever searched MWB, the authorities would find the letter but no evidence that it was prepared at MWB. On January 30, Schoeb instructed his secretary Margrith Lippuner to type Heilingbrunner's handwritten letter onto the Hilton hotel stationery and then to get rid of the typewriter. She stamped the letter as if it were normal incoming mail, backdating it to September 30, 1983. She then created an official file with Kotari's name on it and put the letter and drawings in it. But instead of dumping the typewriter, she gave it to Spass Dagarov, an engineer at MWB, who gave it to his son to use. To protect himself, Schoeb kept Heilingbrunner's original letter and copies of the CB documents.

MWB returned the drawings to Uranit and fed them the fictitious Kotari alibi. Uranit lodged a complaint with German prosecutors, who filed a case against Kotari. With prosecutors and Uranit temporarily thrown off the trail, Heilingbrunner and Lerch were faced with a bigger problem. How would they make the feed and withdrawal equipment and get paid?

At this point, former colleagues believe that with increasing German government scrutiny, Lerch came to doubt that the business with Pakistan could be handled from Leybold-Heraeus.[27] Lerch tried to quit Leybold-Heraeus at the beginning of 1984, but the company's CEO persuaded him to stay another year.[28] The CEO had personally hired Lerch, and despite Lerch's growing notoriety, still had high expectations for him. When Lerch finally left Leybold in 1985, he took the Comprimo information with him, a violation of company policy and possibly a copyright infringement, but not a major crime.

In addition, Lerch was finding it harder to conduct his profitable business from Germany. A Leybold official remembered, "It was too hot for Lerch in Germany," particularly if he wanted to sell centrifuge equipment subject to export controls.[29] Leybold-Heraeus was under growing scrutiny by German officials about its dealings with Pakistan's nuclear weapons program. The U.S. government was sending diplomatic requests or démarches to the German government, complaining about Leybold-Heraeus's steady business with Pakistan. Leybold did not view the démarches as a serious attempt by the U.S. or German governments to stop German companies from selling to Pakistan and other sensitive countries; nonetheless, they were putting the company under greater pressure to act.

Throughout 1984, Pakistan continued to press for delivery of the feed and withdrawal equipment.[30] In 1985, Lerch established a new contract with MWB. Along with leaving Germany, he also took a position in the spring of 1985 as head of the small Swiss firm Apparate, Verfahren und Engineering AG (AVE), while continuing to represent Leybold-Heraeus until the end of 1985.[31] AVE was owned by Eder's company Praesidial-Anstalt and conveniently located across the street from MWB in Buchs. Lerch also moved to the nearby town of Grabs, Switzerland.

Armed with the designs again, MWB got to work filling the order (the initials "CB" did not appear on the designs).[32] Security at MWB was increased, with all employees receiving identification cards and being sworn to secrecy. Visitors were required to register at the entrance. Spass Dagarov, the engineer at MWB who had given the Kotari typewriter to his son, was told in case of questions he was free to call only two Leybold-Heraeus officials in Hanau, one of whom was an engineer who had been involved in the design of the feed and withdrawal equipment at the Almelo uranium enrichment plant.[33] No other Leybold-Heraeus officials were to be contacted.

MWB had to rush to finish the order by the end of 1985. It had learned that a new law, taking effect January 1, 1986, would make it illegal to export the equipment to any unsafeguarded nuclear facility like the Kahuta plant. This new law reflected the changes made by the multinational Nuclear Suppliers Group in early 1984, when it added centrifuge components and equipment, including the feed and withdrawal equipment being made by MWB, to the list of items requiring an export approval. Swiss government scrutiny of these sales would quickly reveal that the end user was Pakistan.

Workers raced to get the equipment ready for shipment prior to the deadline. Just before Christmas, the order was completed and several shipments left the factory for the Merimpex Company in Liechtenstein, which then shipped the containers to various front companies in Dubai, Saudi Arabia, and the Grand Turk Islands. Another batch of goods was transported by trucks from Switzerland to France and by Air France to Dubai, then onward to Pakistan.

Despite MWB's precautions, Swiss customs authorities stopped a shipment of three autoclaves, declared falsely as "steel pressure vessels," on December 30, 1985, and held them because of the lack of an export license. The police raided MWB but found little incriminating information. However, they interrogated

Schoeb, who had left MWB after a fight with Eder following the Kotari episode. Schoeb voluntarily turned over the Kotari correspondence and the "CB" documents to the police that he had kept despite company orders. He also led the investigators to the typewriter and agreed to cooperate with the investigation in exchange for not being charged. The police interrogated Lerch in late February and seized documents at AVE, including various bids, plutonium separation documents, and uranium enrichment records, according to court documents. MWB and Merimpex were found guilty of export violations and fined. MWB filed for bankruptcy in July 1988.

While the Swiss never filed charges against Lerch, German prosecutors reopened their investigation into the source of the Uranit documents, focusing initially on Lerch. A series of groundbreaking German television reports in late 1986 then led the prosecutors to identify Heilingbrunner's role in this effort. Lerch told Swiss investigators that Heilingbrunner was his superior and by implication responsible for the sales. Heilingbrunner said he saw it as an unfair attempt by Lerch to shift blame onto him.

Lerch and Heilingbrunner both tenaciously fought the charges, delaying a trial for years and forcing the prosecutor to reduce the charges. The German prosecutors faced a problem that has plagued many illicit nuclear trade cases—a lack of cooperation between different countries' prosecutorial teams. The Swiss courts ruled that the Germans could use the documents acquired by Swiss authorities from witnesses and at AVE only on condition that they would be used in a prosecution of illegally giving away business secrets. They could not be used to prosecute Heilingbrunner and Lerch for violating export control laws. This was a severe blow to German prosecutors since they believed that was the charge most likely to stick.

In 1992, Lerch and Heilingbrunner finally went to court in Cologne. By that time, the prosecutors had such a weak case that some of their own witnesses resisted attending the trial, viewing it as a waste of time. On the eve of the trial, Schoeb and Dagarov, two of the key state witnesses, complained to the prosecutor about attending the trial after they learned that the charges were confined to unfair business practices and not illegally selling classified nuclear technology. Whether Lerch and Heilingbrunner violated export laws was ultimately never determined by a court, and because the accused could show that Leybold-Heraeus had bought the rights to these designs in the 1970s, the court acquitted the two of even this minor charge of industrial espionage.[34]

Lerch wouldn't stay out of the spotlight for long. IAEA, German, and Swiss investigators continued to probe his activities with Khan and Libya. Lerch had worked with Khan since the 1970s and largely kept his business dealings secret from authorities. That was no longer possible. Swiss authorities finally arrested Lerch in November 2004 at Germany's request, but bringing him to trial turned out to be not the end of the story but the beginning of a much more labyrinthine one (Lerch's trial is covered in greater detail in Chapter 10, "Busting the Khan Network").

———■———

ONE MIGHT THINK that businesses confronted with tougher laws and the threat of prosecution would opt out of selling to Khan or other proliferators. Faced with weak or unenforced laws, many found the potential rewards too lucrative to resist. Lerch's success was due to his determination to continue doing business with Khan and other proliferators no matter what the dangers were, and his dogged pursuit of new clients. In 1985, when his business with MWB was still proceeding smoothly, a new customer interested in buying centrifuge technology visited Leybold-Heraeus—Iran.

FOUR

Khan's First Customers— Iran and Iraq

A t the height of the bloody war between Iran and Iraq that would eventually kill up to one million Iranians, engineer Masud Naraghi was in no position to decline a senior position in his country's gas centrifuge program. He had already used his expertise to renovate military equipment including radar vacuum tubes, a critical part in short supply because of Iran's international military embargo. Despite his lack of background in centrifuges, his superiors in the Atomic Energy Organization of Iran (AEOI) believed his expertise in vacuum technology qualified him to play a key role in evaluating centrifuge designs and making overseas acquisitions for this program. His initial visits to Germany in 1985 for the program would start a chain of events that would lead to A.Q. Khan's first sale of centrifuge technology to another country. Without Khan's assistance, Iran's gas centrifuge program would pose little threat to the region or the United States today.

In the 1970s, Shah Mohammad Reza Pahlavi launched an ambitious nuclear energy program with plans to build twenty nuclear power reactors and obtain the industrial capability to separate plutonium. The shah also wanted the ability to quickly build nuclear weapons using plutonium from these facilities, if the need arose. After the Iranian revolution in 1979, the new theocratic rulers curtailed most nuclear activities at the Tehran Nuclear Research Center, where Naraghi was head of the prestigious Plasma Physics Department. Iran's ruling clerics had a change of heart about the center's work, though, during their protracted war with Saddam Hussein. It was during the war that the regime's leaders began thinking about acquiring nuclear weapons. Iraq had widely used chemical weapons against Iranian troops and attacked vulnerable Iranian cities with ballistic missiles. Rumors were rife that Iraq was seeking nuclear weapons. If Iraq could threaten to use nuclear weapons against Iran, its regime would risk total annihilation.

Naraghi has said little about why Iran wanted to develop gas centrifuges, but during an interview with the Japanese television network NHK, he cited military use as one of the reasons. Officially, the Iranian government denies that it has ever considered building nuclear weapons, making the dubious claim to the International Atomic Energy Agency (IAEA) that in 1985—during the height of the war with Iraq—it wanted to enrich uranium using gas centrifuges solely for peaceful purposes. In fact, in April 1984, then president of Iran, Ali Hoseyai Khamenei, had announced to top political and security officials at the Presidential Palace that the supreme leader Ayatollah Ruhollah Khomeini had decided to reactivate the nuclear program as the only way to secure the very essence of the Islamic Revolution from the schemes of its enemies, especially the United States and Israel.[1] President Khamenei declared during the meeting that a nuclear arsenal would serve Iran as a deterrent in the hands of God's soldiers.

It's unclear why Iran's rulers decided on gas centrifuge technology for enriching uranium. The actions of the Iranian centrifuge program's early leaders remain shadowy. Iran has chosen to hide a considerable amount of information from this era from the IAEA, insisting that few documents still exist about its early efforts. Recollections of key Iranian participants are incomplete and contradictory, save for the almost universal agreement that Iran had, up to that point, no experience in building gas centrifuges nor did it possess any secret centrifuge designs upon which to base its program. As Naraghi put it, Iran "could not do nuclear by itself."[2]

Following the example of its neighbor Pakistan (whose exploits were well known at the time), Iran probably reckoned that gas centrifuges could be acquired faster than other technologies. It had also had limited success with its nascent laser enrichment program, a more technologically demanding program that was started in the 1970s under the shah. (The regime later secretly restarted its laser enrichment program as well.) Iran's leadership in the 1980s also had little chance of buying a nuclear reactor to make plutonium for nuclear weapons. Construction at Bushehr of reactors the shah purchased from Germany had come to a halt during the war. Iran likewise understood how vulnerable a nuclear reactor could be to attack after Israel's strike on the Iraqi Osirak reactor in 1981 and the Iraqi attack on the Iranian Bushehr reactor site in 1985. A gas centrifuge program would be easier to hide and keep safe than a reactor.

Iran's first procurements for its centrifuge program are difficult to track down. Either the AEOI or Iranian military organizations may have started to buy centrifuge equipment prior to 1985, the formal start date declared by the Iranian government. In 1983 and 1984, Iran Electronics Industries, a front company for the military, may have bought equipment for an experimental centrifuge rig from European suppliers, including Leybold-Heraeus, in an attempt to perform some initial studies of centrifuges before formally deciding to acquire them.

In 1985, Iran acquired key "flow-forming" equipment, useful in forming steel and aluminum centrifuge tubes, from the German firm Leifeld. At least one Leifeld flow-forming machine is still used in Iran's gas-centrifuge manufacturing complex. Leifeld personnel could have also instructed Iranians about flow-forming centrifuge components as they did for Iraqi engineers in 1988 when they sold flow-forming equipment to Iraq's newly established gas centrifuge program.[3] While Iran declared to the IAEA that it conducted its first phase of P1 centrifuge research and development from 1987 to 1993, devoting only limited financial resources and three researchers to the program,[4] these earlier procurements and Naraghi's activities prior to 1987 raise serious questions about the veracity of Iran's statements.

Iranian authorities have been more forthcoming on the methods that they used to overcome their technical shortcomings. They told the IAEA that the regime decided in the mid-1980s to acquire uranium enrichment technology on the black market.[5] This is where Naraghi played a critical role. With a doctorate from Case Western Reserve University in the field of plasma science, Naraghi had years of experience in vacuum technologies, much of which he gained in the United States while working on projects, including some at NASA. Over the years, he developed excellent overseas connections with key companies, particularly in Germany. Naraghi has denied being leader of the centrifuge program, saying the head of the program was a more senior official and that many decisions were made by the head of AEOI and senior leaders of the government. He denies making crucial decisions for the centrifuge program or for other parts of the nuclear program, such as the effort to develop the capability to make uranium hexafluoride, a vital material for the production of enriched uranium.[6] Yet a man with his experience as head of the Plasma Department at the AEOI undoubtedly played a central role in launching the centrifuge program.

Before the 1979 Revolution, Naraghi bought vacuum equipment from Otto Heilingbrunner, Leybold-Heraeus's salesperson responsible for both Iran and Pakistan. Seeking to renew business, Heilingbrunner visited Tehran in 1984.[7] When he visited Naraghi's office at AEOI this time, Naraghi's secretary would no longer shake hands with him and avoided eye contact, per the regime's new edicts. Naraghi, however, had not lost his interest in buying vacuum pumps. As was the custom at the time, Heilingbrunner did not ask Naraghi about the end use of the Leybold-Heraeus equipment, though he now believes that at least some of the equipment could have been intended for the centrifuge program.[8]

In 1985, Naraghi traveled to Leybold-Heraeus in Cologne.[9] One of the few companies in the world capable of making equipment sophisticated enough for a centrifuge program, Leybold-Heraeus was probably the top vacuum equipment manufacturing company in the world.[10] Naraghi would have known about Leybold-Heraeus's work for URENCO and also likely knew about Pakistan's centrifuge program.

Heilingbrunner met Naraghi in 1985 in the brick T-shaped administration building at the Leybold-Heraeus vacuum equipment manufacturing complex in south Cologne. When Naraghi visited, the corporate climate was far different from today's. Leybold-Heraeus was a much larger company engaged in a variety of high-tech enterprises.[11] Outside the administration building sat a van de Graaff accelerator and nearby, the VIP employee restaurant, where the CEO and other top management took their lunches.

Despite the open atmosphere toward clients like him, Naraghi was cautious in his initial approach. He did not explicitly tell Heilingbrunner that he wanted to buy items for a centrifuge program, instead saying he wanted "to have something spinning very fast," like in a certain type of sophisticated vacuum pump called a turbomolecular pump.[12] Naraghi told Heilingbrunner he wanted to turn that type of pump into a centrifuge.[13] Heilingbrunner told him that was not possible since the rotating part of the pump spins much slower than a centrifuge rotor. Neither pressed the issue further.

Heilingbrunner and Gotthard Lerch, who soon joined these meetings, were sophisticated enough to guess the purpose of Naraghi's orders. Despite visiting the Hanau branch, Naraghi did not order any turnkey systems. He limited himself initially to asking for items only from the company's extensive catalog. He also acquired parts for other Iranian programs. In the freewheeling 1980s, such sales were legal or, if questionable, easy to skirt under lax government rules and procedures.

Lerch had an uncanny ability of knowing when Naraghi would be in Europe,[14] and Naraghi remembers Lerch being particularly aggressive in trying to sell him equipment during his frequent shopping trips to European companies. He said Lerch also often visited Iran, contacting him and more senior officials for business. Lerch showed Naraghi videos and movies of nuclear programs to interest him in buying a range of items for the Iranian nuclear program.[15] "To this day, it is not clear whether the initiative for the first nuclear deal with Iran originated from Naraghi or from Lerch and his Pakistani business partner Abdul Qadeer Khan," says Olli Heinonen, who met with Naraghi twice. "They point the finger at one another."[16]

According to Naraghi, Lerch brought a sample list to Iran

of what would later become the first centrifuge offer. Lerch's note had five or six parts, or "phases." The first phase was just a blueprint of a centrifuge, the next a document for a cascade of ten or twelve centrifuges.[17] Subsequent phases involved more enrichment equipment. Compiling this offer would have required Khan's close cooperation.

Senior IAEA officials believe that by late 1986 or early 1987, Lerch and his colleague Heinz Mebus met Naraghi in Switzerland, possibly at the Zurich airport, and made an offer for a complete gas centrifuge plant, along with the equipment to turn the resulting highly enriched uranium into metal bomb components. The offer included delivery of a disassembled sample P1 centrifuge machine, complete with drawings, descriptions, and specifications for production; drawings, specifications, and calculations for a complete plant; materials for two thousand centrifuges; auxiliary vacuum and electric drive equipment; and uranium reconversion and casting capabilities. The latter included equipment to convert uranium hexafluoride into metal, furnaces to melt the uranium metal, and equipment to cast the uranium. This equipment would be used for making HEU and natural uranium metal components for nuclear weapons. Iran denies buying this equipment, although the offer shows that the Khan network was willing to provide assistance in building nuclear weapons right from the start of its export business.

The offer was reviewed at the highest levels of the Iranian government. In a confidential communication dated February 28, 1987, AEOI's President Reza Amrollahi, with the subsequent agreement of Prime Minister Mir-Hossein Mousavi, confirmed the decision to acquire centrifuge technology. The communication indicated that the activities "should be treated fully confidentially."[18] Soon afterward, Naraghi traveled with colleagues to Dubai to finalize the deal. It's suspected that his colleagues included a man named Azadi who later ran Kalaye Electric (or "Electric Goods," which suggests the name was chosen to hide its true purpose, that of a primary centrifuge research and development facility),[19] and a man named Allahdad, who was likely an administrator involved in handling money for the program.[20] Lerch attended the meeting, as did Mebus and S. Mohammed Farooq from BBE, along with Farooq's nephew and assistant Tahir. Dr. M.Z. Niazi, a dentist and long time associate of the Bhutto family, might have also attended the meeting. According to Heinonen, Farooq represented Khan's network.

The meeting led to agreements about the items supplied, the costs of the items, and their delivery. According to Naraghi, he and his colleague had two hours to examine the set of drawings, although they had already decided to buy the documents. He said that they were not able to examine the documents carefully, as there were "people sitting around us very impatient to finish this thing."[21] However, he could tell that the package of drawings was not a complete set.[22] Some of the drawings looked like copies that the original owners had rejected.

Naraghi could also tell from the way the drawings were formatted that they came from Pakistan, although he says Khan's name was not mentioned.[23] He said that while more senior Iranian officials probably knew that Pakistan was the source of the documents, he knew from leaks from Western intelligence agencies in the media at the time that Lerch, Heilingbrunner, and Mebus were suspected of selling items to Khan's secret Kahuta enrichment plant. Khan's agents also offered Iran the design of a P2 centrifuge.[24] Owing to its simpler design, Iran opted only for the P1 designs,[25] buying a set of P1 centrifuge drawings and a few sample, disassembled P1 centrifuges. Iran maintains that it bought two P1 centrifuges, but neither had all of its components.[26] Iran paid between $5 and $10 million for the package. Up to six people reportedly split the money, including Farooq, Khan, Lerch, Mebus, and perhaps Niazi.[27] Lerch earned the largest share, possibly for initiating the contact with Naraghi. Iran received specifications, documents, and manufacturing instructions—in essence, a starter kit. "All they had to do was copy this technology," Heinonen said.[28] With detailed designs in hand, Iran could leap over many difficult research steps which it might have lacked the experience to discover on its own.

Both the Pakistani government and its military have insisted Khan acted on his own authority. Yet the deal occurred the same year Pakistani president General Zia-ul-Haq reportedly approved a secret peaceful nuclear cooperation agreement with Iran.[29] A former senior scientist in Pakistan's nuclear program told *The Washington Post* that Iranian scientists had expressed interest around that time in "non-peaceful nuclear matters."[30] A Pakistani investigator said Khan had told General Mirza Aslam Beg in 1991 he had transferred nuclear equipment to Iran. Khan said Beg was "probably . . . under the impression that material and knowledge being transferred to Iran would not enable them to produce enriched uranium" because he told Beg he was not giving Iran the latest equipment.[31] This suggests Pakistani authorities wanted Khan to cooperate with Iran on a limited basis but that he exceeded this mandate.

The documents Iran acquired in 1987 date from the 1970s and early to mid-1980s. One attracted the IAEA's special interest because it was a ten to twelve page report for making natural and enriched uranium metal hemispheres, the shape and chemical form of uranium used in nuclear weapons. This report looked identical to a report in a large, detailed collection of documents that the Khan network had assembled for its customers on how to enrich up to weapon grade, and chemically convert the weapon-grade uranium into metal components for use in nuclear weapons.[32] Did Iran have the entire collection of documents? Did Iran, like Libya, also receive nuclear weapons designs? Iran says no, but questions remain about what exactly Iran acquired.

To get answers, the IAEA shared this short report with Pakistan in the fall of 2007 in the expectation that Pakistan would communicate their questions to Khan.[33] In April 2008, Pakistan confirmed that an identical document exists in Pakistan but did not shed any new light on how Iran obtained it or its role in Iran's nuclear program.[34] This time-consuming method is the only way the IAEA can seek answers from Khan and his associates as they are not allowed to interview them directly. The Pakistani government has repeatedly refused to allow the IAEA or foreign governments to directly question former members of Khan's network.

Another mystery is whether other Iranian groups, perhaps associated with the military, were also independently working on centrifuges. Naraghi suspected that two or three other groups were working in addition to his group at the AEOI. After the drawings and documents arrived in Iran in 1987, Naraghi had to wait at least a month to get them.[35] When they arrived, he could tell that the set had been photocopied. Iran has denied any military involvement in the centrifuge program and insisted that no other institution other than the AEOI was involved in the decision making or the implementation of the centrifuge program.[36] The IAEA continues to seek answers to these crucial questions.[37]

Ultimately, Iran bought few items from Khan's agents. Part

of the reason may have been a shortage of funds (what Naraghi referred to as cash shortages for his programs) as a result of the costly war with Iraq. Additionally, since Naraghi's group had already established a successful procurement network in Europe, the Iranians had little need to pay commissions to Khan's agents to acquire key equipment and materials technology in Europe and elsewhere. Tehran may have believed its scientists and engineers could deliver the centrifuge equipment and components necessary to build a plant, now that they had acquired the critical know-how. It may have also been suspected that Khan could not deliver all the items in the offer, or would not be able to keep the transfer secret.

With Khan's starter kit in place, Naraghi and his team went back to Europe to procure a wide range of critical items for the centrifuge program. He told suppliers he represented the Iranian company Kavosh Yar, a subsidiary of the AEOI based in Tehran on Africa Avenue. One supplier remembered Naraghi showing a business card from this company. His cover story was that he was buying for the Sharif University of Technology. He wrote checks worth millions of deutsche marks (DM), issued by a Frankfurt bank, to buy a wide range of equipment.

The program's priority was buying equipment to make centrifuges and assemble small cascades of them. A large number of orders were placed with European companies, but by the late 1980s and early 1990s, many of the items Iran wanted were now loosely regulated by national or international export controls. Iran had acquired many items legally, at least in the sense that suppliers did not knowingly break the then-lax export control laws, and government bureaucracies did not scrutinize the exports for their actual purpose. In other cases, however, company officials were well aware of the end use and knowingly falsified shipping documents to facilitate the export.

Some of these orders were for centrifuge parts. In late 1988, using a drawing derived from the information from Khan, Naraghi requested fifty P1 molecular pumps from Leybold.[38] These pumps are typically cylindrical pieces of aluminum with grooves cut into them. They have no moving parts, but the spinning rotor creates an upward force that prevents uranium hexafluoride from leaking out of the top of the centrifuge into the region between the spinning rotor and outer casing. This component was invented by the Russians after World War II and enabled centrifuges to maintain a vacuum in this critical region, reducing the chance of rotors breaking. On German export documents, Leybold officials called this crucial centrifuge component a "molecular pump stator" and included a detailed drawing prepared by Leybold. Despite the similarity in wording, German customs authorities approved the export in September 1990, which was valued at DM 164,500. This oversight demonstrated the ineffectiveness of the government's controls at the time.

Naraghi also paid Leybold DM 676,681 for 120 specialized valves prepared for use with uranium hexafluoride for a "high vacuum plant." Iran actually wanted these valves to build a small centrifuge cascade but soon learned that such high quality valves were not needed. Lesser quality valves ordered straight from the company's catalog would work well enough and would not trigger the need for an export license or cause unwanted scrutiny from suspicious government officials looking for tell-tale signs of a secret gas centrifuge project. Iran, Pakistan, and undoubtedly many other countries used this ruse for years.

Some countries, however, didn't need such elaborate ruses, but were offered these materials directly.

IN EARLY OCTOBER 1990, a Pakistani associate of
A.Q. Khan's named Zahid Malik approached Saddam Hussein's
government on Khan's behalf, offering secret assistance to Iraq in
building nuclear weapons aimed at deterring the United States
and its allies. Khan must have thought that his offer would find
a receptive audience. Faced with the worldwide threat of a military counterattack following his invasion of Kuwait in August
1990, Saddam Hussein ordered a "crash" program to build a
nuclear weapon. His atomic scientists were desperate to finish the
weapon.

For security purposes, Malik hand carried the offer. He told
the Iraqis he was employed by a Pakistani company owned by
Abdul Qayuum Khan, the brother of A.Q. Khan. Malik had
been seeking lucrative contracts from the Iraqi intelligence
agency Mukhabarat. John Vidalis, a Greek arms dealer who had
supplied Iraq during the Iran-Iraq war, vouched for Malik to the
Technical Consultation Corporation (TCC), the Mukhabarat's
procurement organization.[39]

When Malik met Aala al-din Hussein al Samaraae, the director general of TCC in Baghdad, he handed over a piece of paper
titled "Project A.B." Al Samaraae immediately understood that
A.B. stood for "atomic bomb." "Pakistan had to spend a period
of ten years and an amount of 300 million U.S. dollars to get it,"
began the five-point offer. "Now with the practical experience
and the world-wide contacts Pakistan has already developed, you
could have A.B. in about three years' time and by spending about
150 million U.S. dollars."

The memo continued, "We will provide the detailed design
and actual blueprint of A.B." at a cost of $5 million. Khan and
his associates were prepared to help Iraq establish a program to

enrich uranium to weapon grade and manufacture nuclear weapons. They committed to undertaking the procurement of all the vital components and materials from European suppliers via "our Dubai office," which is believed to be Bin Belailah Enterprises, where Abdul Qayuum Khan worked during the 1980s and which was then controlled by S. Mohammed Farooq.[40]

Khan's group would procure all the vital components for the Iraqis through its Dubai office at a 10 percent commission (no commissions would be charged on purchases made directly by the Iraqis). This arrangement could generate millions of dollars in commissions. In addition, all technological assistance would be provided free through Khan's Dubai office. "Meetings between the two top persons could be arranged" every three to four months to review the project. If necessary, two to three Pakistani scientists would be persuaded to "resign and join the new assignment."[41]

Malik requested a preliminary technical meeting to present the documents he was offering to sell. Both sides realized that given the tense international atmosphere, a meeting with Khan was not possible at that time. They discussed setting up a meeting in Greece with Vidalis and an intermediary. As was the practice, al Samaraae forwarded a classified summary of the offer on October 6, 1990, to Dhafer Rashid Selbi in the nuclear section codenamed 15S in Petrochemical-3 (PC-3), the secret name for the Iraqi nuclear weapons program.[42] "Exotic" offers received by the Mukhabarat were sent to PC-3 for evaluation and guidance about how to proceed. Members of PC-3 and the Mukhabarat would also meet periodically to discuss these offers.

Al Samaraae's memo, stamped "Top Secret and Personal," listed five points, the first of which was, "He is ready to give us the drawings of the nuclear bomb." On the bottom right corner of the memo, Selbi or one of his colleagues handwrote a note to Jaffar Dhia Jaffar, the head of PC-3 and a deputy minister in the Ministry for Industry and Military Industrialization, recommending that the Mukhabarat be asked to arrange to get samples relating to drawings of the nuclear bomb. Then PC-3 could assess "their real capabilities."

Given the demands on Jaffar's crash program, the most important part of Khan's offer was the nuclear weapon drawings. The Iraqi weapon designers were having trouble reducing the size of their nuclear warhead design from about 1,200 millimeters to about 800 millimeters so that it could fit on the Al Hussein ballistic missile, the most reliable nuclear delivery system Saddam possessed. Khan's weapon design would have gone far in helping the Iraqis solve this urgent problem.

Saddam Hussein already possessed enough highly enriched uranium (HEU) to make a nuclear weapon. This HEU was dedicated to civilian uses under IAEA inspections, but Saddam Hussein ordered its diversion to the crash program. The HEU had originally come from France and Russia in the form of fuel for two civil research reactors. One of them was the Osirak reactor that Israel bombed in June 1981 out of fear the reactor could be used to produce nuclear weapons. Israel missed the reactor's HEU fuel, though, a potentially deadly mistake. Iraq had stored this fuel for years, knowing that it might someday be needed for a nuclear weapon.

Jaffar had little interest in pursuing any offer for an enrichment plant. Iraq had its own enrichment plants under construction. Jaffar was heading the effort to build two plants north of Baghdad based on the electromagnetic isotope separation (EMIS) process developed by the United States in the Manhattan project during World War II. The first atomic bomb dropped on Hiroshima depended on HEU from this process. Although this process was archaic, it was largely declassified, and Iraq could build an EMIS plant with its limited indigenous technical capabilities. Jaffar's EMIS effort completely escaped detection by intelligence agencies until after the Gulf War. Iraq also had a gas centrifuge program run by Mahdi Obeidi, who himself was receiving a steady stream of classified centrifuge documents, equipment, and centrifuge parts from a group of European suppliers, including top-of-the-line German gas centrifuge experts, evidently with no connection to Khan.[43] He had received detailed drawings of the German URENCO's excellent G1 centrifuge, which is a smaller precursor to the G2 centrifuge stolen by Khan, several G2 drawings, and a few drawings of the significantly more advanced TC-11 centrifuge.

Jaffar and Obeidi were rivals to see which program could first produce enough HEU for a nuclear weapon. Obeidi was sure he would win that race, but neither program could produce enough HEU for several years. Thus the crash program would have to depend on diverting the civil HEU. Jaffar also still faced a formidable challenge in building a nuclear warhead for Iraq's missile. Although Jaffar's weaponizaton program started working on a nuclear design in 1987, it had progressed slowly. After the invasion of Kuwait, Jaffar had accelerated the work, yet by October 1990 he was still many months, perhaps a year, from building a miniaturized nuclear weapon. Khan's offer could have significantly sped up that time table.

Jaffar was cautious. Was Malik's offer a sting operation? He was always worried about attempts by foreign intelligence agen-

cies to discover Iraq's secret nuclear programs. He selected the
EMIS process partly because it was easier to build in secret and
less dependent on foreign procurement of sensitive dual-use
equipment, presenting fewer opportunities for detection. Jaffar
responded to Selbi on the same day, reminding him that, in the
past "we used to avoid such contacts because hostile bodies still
adopt a policy of embroilment." Jaffar's memo to Selbi shows,
however, that he was clearly interested despite his impatience
that the Mukhabarat had not already obtained more details from
Malik in order to judge the offer's authenticity.

Selbi's handwritten note on the al Samaraae memo said
that the Mukhabarat "does not see the need for this precaution [against a sting operation]." Iraqi intelligence evidently
trusted Malik because he was recommended by Vidalis, who
had supplied Iraq since around 1987 and had provided Iraq with
sophisticated equipment including encrypted communication
equipment. Nonetheless, Selbi proceeded cautiously, answering al
Samaraae in a letter dated October 15, 1990, marked "top secret
and confidential and to be opened personally."

He asked al Samaraae to obtain a sample of the bomb design.
Selbi warned against the risk of a sting operation and the exposure of Iraq's secret nuclear weapons effort, suggesting that
"your circles could mislead" Khan's intermediary to ensure that
they are not able "to see how the land lies." When asking for a
sample of the bomb design from the intermediary, Al Samaraae
was asked to include the following specific English text: "A
specimen of the detail design and its accompanying calculations procedure to produce the detail design." In short, Jaffar
wanted both a sample drawing and information on how that
drawing was produced. His own nuclear weapon experts could

then determine if the offer was genuine and useful to Iraq's effort.

Iraq did not receive this sample because the war started shortly afterwards and there was not enough time to arrange another meeting with Malik. After Iraq's defeat in 1991, the U.N. Security Council imposed a cease-fire agreement requiring Iraq to dismantle its nuclear weapons programs and come clean about all its activities to seek nuclear weapons (along with ballistic missiles, and chemical and biological weapons). Under U.N. Security Council authority, the IAEA established an action team and charged it with the task of overseeing and verifying Iraq's nuclear disarmament. Hans Blix, then director general of the IAEA, appointed Italian Maurizio Zifferero to be leader of the IAEA's action team. Although not involved previously in nuclear inspections, Zifferero was one of the few senior IAEA officials at the time with any detailed knowledge of the Iraqi nuclear program. Within weeks, his inspectors discovered hints of a vast, secret nuclear weapons effort that would take years to fully understand and dismantle.

Action team inspectors quickly uncovered a large international smuggling ring that had illegally obtained large quantities of technology, equipment, and materials for Iraq's nuclear programs from a range of countries including Britain, Germany, Switzerland, Austria, Japan, Brazil, and the United States. Zifferero used the extraordinary powers granted by the Security Council to launch an intensive multiyear investigation to uncover Iraq's black market smugglers and the items Iraq obtained.

That investigation was still not finished when Zifferero found the Project A.B. document in 1995. He was startled, particularly since he had not discovered any significant link between the traffickers supplying Iraq and those that helped Khan. The memo was in a huge collection of documents about Iraq's prohibited weapons programs that had been hastily assembled and turned over to the inspectors by Iraqi authorities in August 1995 after the defection of Hussein Kamel, Saddam's powerful son-in-law and head of Iraq's WMD programs. The Khan offer, written in English, stood out in this collection of Arabic documents.

Zifferero initiated an intensive search of the collection and with the help of a staff member capable of translating Arabic, discovered the three key documents written by al Samaraae, Selbi, and Jaffar discussing the offer. After collecting and translating the documents, Zifferero produced a report outlining the contents of the documents and the need for follow-up. He sent it to the "P-5," the five permanent members of the United Nations Security Council: Britain, China, France, Russia, and the United States. He also sent the report to two additional key countries, Israel and Germany, which often received action team information.

The response was tepid. The U.S. government wrote Zifferero that it did not have any information that further identified Zahid Malik. It supplied two possibilities—either he was Khan's personal Pakistani biographer, or another Pakistani who worked in a nuclear weapons-related area in Pakistan. The United States did not offer any concrete assistance in tracking down Malik. Zifferero was able to identify Vidalis, who had died a few years earlier, but learned little from the Greek government about any connection between Vidalis and Malik. Zifferero's April 1996 letter to the United Arab Emirates' (UAE's) mission in Vienna elicited only promises to investigate Bin Belailah Enterprises but no follow-up.

Zifferero became gravely ill with cancer in early 1997 and passed away within six months. Many were saddened by his death. I had cooperated with the action team since 1992 under Zifferero's guidance. He applied a rigorous and fair approach to understanding Iraq's nuclear weapons program. Without Zifferero's diligence, Khan's offer of nuclear weapons to Iraq would have likely been considered a far-fetched hoax.

Garry Dillon, Zifferero's British deputy and successor, picked up the investigation. He thought that the amount of money discussed was too small for such important information and therefore was a money-making scam. Nonetheless, he doggedly believed that this offer had to be fully investigated. If it were true, to whom else could Malik have offered the bomb design?

Although the Iraqis had become more forthcoming after Kamel's defection, they did not reveal the Khan offer to the inspectors, despite volunteering information about a large number of illicit procurement cases. When Dillon confronted Mohammed Saeed al-Sahaf with the documents Zifferero found, he was unhelpful and his denials unconvincing (hardly a surprise—in 2003, he would become internationally known during the Iraqi invasion as "Comical Ali" for his farcical statements denying that the U.S. invasion was succeeding).

Dillon approached Pakistan's embassy in Baghdad in 1998 and asked if any prominent Iraqis had gone to Pakistan in late 1990. Pakistani officials claimed that they needed instructions from Islamabad before they could cooperate. Dillon also questioned several Iraqis in Baghdad who were involved in producing the memos discussing Khan's offer, but the results were again disappointing. Jaffar tried to dismiss the Khan offer out of hand, telling Dillon that he had never heard of the offer before and

believed it a fake. After much prodding, al Samaraae remembered that Malik had come to Baghdad with his offer in October
1990, while Selbi admitted that "possibly someone did offer us
a ready made bomb." He said that if left to his own devices, he
would have been more adventurous and moved to get these types
of exotic items, but they insisted that the Mukhabarat had not
gotten to the stage of contacting Malik.

Dillon learned that an English-speaking TCC staff
member named Mizar Toma Boutros al Jazrawi interpreted for
al Samaraae and Malik, because al Samaraae could not speak
English and Malik did not know Arabic. Dillon was told that
Toma, a communications engineer, had left Iraq after the war but
the Iraqis were unwilling to help find where he went. Dillon insisted on interviewing Toma's relatives and discovered that Toma
had moved to Australia with his wife. He contacted a colleague
in the Australian government for help in finding him but the official told Dillon it would take time to locate him.

Meanwhile, in 1998, John Barry at *Newsweek* learned of
Khan's offer and published a short account about it.[44] Before publishing his article, Barry sought a comment from the Pakistani
government about the alleged offer. Pakistan quickly launched a
multipronged attack on the story in Washington, Vienna, and Islamabad. On April 30, 1998, the Pakistani embassy faxed Barry
a notice claiming that the story was "absolutely preposterous, totally baseless, and mischievous in nature." The fax stated that the
IAEA had asked Pakistan to investigate this case in March 1998
and in response, Dillon had sent the government a copy of the
memos and letters found in Iraq with explanatory notes on the
translations. According to the Pakistani facsimile, "This investigation conclusively established that no Pakistani scientist, sci-

entific or research establishment or any Government official was ever involved directly or indirectly in any activity related to the alleged offer." Given that the investigation had lasted little more than a month, few believed that Pakistan had actually conducted an investigation at all, let alone a thorough one, but no one was willing to tell that to Barry.

Earlier, on April 30, the Pakistani ambassador in Vienna met with a member of the action team. The ambassador accused the team of being Barry's source. He said that this leak had caused serious harm to the IAEA and its relationship with Pakistan and insisted that the team issue a statement condemning the allegation and contact Barry directly to tell him of the inaccuracy of the story. His government, he said, "finds it extremely regrettable that the good name of Dr. A.Q. Khan has been impugned by the reputed offer." Dillon and others at the IAEA, all of whom denied being Barry's source, were taken aback by the ambassador's aggressive stance.

After the *Newsweek* report appeared, public condemnation from Pakistan was swift. Khan was predictably outraged. His biographer, Malik, read Barry's report and assumed he was accused of being the middleman in Iraq. In his subsequent biography of Khan, he charged that he had been made a scapegoat because of his closeness to Khan. He railed against this conspiracy to discredit Khan and Pakistan's nuclear weapons program.[45] He assured readers that the nuclear program was in the hands of the Pakistani military and safe from any such transfers. Yet in a passage that perhaps reveals that he knew more than he acknowledged, he added, "And it is a fact that had it been in my control, I would have certainly transferred the nuclear technology to Syria, Iraq, Iran, Libya, or any other country that may stop Israel's expansionist designs in the Middle East."[46] But no one could establish that this Malik was the one who made the bomb offer in Baghdad.

Despite Pakistan's vehement denials that there was any truth to the allegations, Dillon continued to investigate. In April 1999, his Australian colleague contacted him by email and told him his government had finally located Toma, living under another name with his wife in Sydney. The Australian government sent two officials to interview Toma in October 1999, but Toma denied all knowledge of Project A.B. and angrily refused to speak to IAEA officials or answer their questions. He said he would leave the country if they kept bothering him. The Australian officials believed that he was hiding something and was likely frightened for his family, but Toma had become a citizen a few months earlier, and the Australian government was unable to pressure him to cooperate. This exhausted the leads of the action team, which by then had left Iraq and was not to return until December 2002, shortly before Iraq was attacked by the United States and its allies.

Dillon remained troubled about this case. "Project A.B." was one of the earliest and strongest indications that Khan was selling dangerous nuclear assistance to enemies of the United States. Yet as in many other cases during the 1980s and 1990s, there was no international outcry or concerted action either to stop Khan or to force Pakistan to fire or at least seriously investigate him. In an important 1997 report to the U.N. Security Council, Dillon made certain that the action team listed this case as one of the few outstanding nuclear issues remaining about Iraq's pre-1991 nuclear weapons program. Faced with Pakistan's aggressive denials, U.S. diplomatic protests remained ineffective. The

United States decided to downplay the evidence publicly rather than risk confronting the Pakistani government openly about Khan.

Nawaz Sharif, who was prime minister during the IAEA investigation of these documents, told the BBC in the spring of 2008 that he did not see any evidence of proliferation while he was in office.[47] His and other high-level Pakistanis' coddling of Khan was one of the reasons why the CIA and MI-6 would ultimately need to take such drastic action to stop the Khan network.

———■———

WHILE IRAQ'S ATTEMPTS to deal with Khan ultimately proved fruitless, during the late 1980s and early 1990s Masud Naraghi and his Iranian colleagues succeeded in buying a long list of centrifuge equipment from European companies. The equipment inspected in Iran's centrifuge facilities by the IAEA in 2003 and 2004 included many vacuum pumps from Leybold and its competitors Pfeiffer and Alcatel, capable of running numerous centrifuge cascades. The German firm Schenk sold Iran horizontal and vertical balancing machines, critical to assembling the finely balanced centrifuge rotors. Balzers sold Iran a mass spectrometer and from the Hanau branch of Leybold, Naraghi ordered a range of vacuum furnaces for the centrifuge manufacturing program. Welding equipment was purchased from Messer Greisheim. Suppliers trained Iranians in the use of critical equipment and taught them associated technologies needed in a centrifuge program. Iran also acquired high-strength aluminum for centrifuge rotors, maraging steel for bellows, special uranium hexafluoride resistant oil, aluminum piping, and many computer-numerically controlled machine tools, and flow-forming machines.[48]

Around 1991, Kavosh Yar stopped ordering for the centrifuge program, likely as a result of Iranian concern that European and U.S. authorities had discovered the true end user of Yar's purchases. That didn't stop purchases for the centrifuge program. Iran appears to have started using different front companies. New orders, including equipment to detect leaks from a vacuum and sophisticated turbomolecular vacuum pumps, appeared from the German trading company ARC Mondial. In 1991, ARC requested items in the name of the military-owned Physics Research Center (PHRC) in Tehran for delivery to Sharif University of Technology. PHRC placed many orders in Europe during the early 1990s and perhaps up to mid-decade that looked to be for a centrifuge program. This company would show up later at the Lavisan site, which Iran mysteriously ripped down in 2004. The IAEA still wonders if this site housed centrifuge development work.

By 1993, Iran had acquired many of the items it needed to make a small centrifuge plant, but it still could not make reliable P1 centrifuge components or operate P1 centrifuges.[49] Complicating the situation, the P1 was "not error free," according to Khan.[50] Adding to Iran's woes, Germany tightened its controls on the export of dual-use equipment. In 1992, Germany placed Iran on a blacklist that essentially halted its relatively open purchases there. As a result, Iran began purchasing items secretly through even more disguised front or trading companies.

Iran had also lost one of its centrifuge leaders. During the Iran-Iraq war Naraghi remained dedicated to his work, but became disenchanted after the war. He expressed frustration that decisions were made at a more senior level without consulting him. Adding to his disenchantment, his wife died and he became worried about the future of his three sons, sending one of them to study in Europe.

Naraghi made plans to leave Iran, selling his house and a factory he owned that refurbished television tubes.[51] His superiors learned of his plans, causing him to feel "like a dead mouse in a throat—they swallow or throw it out," but they didn't prevent him from leaving.[52] His frequent business trips to Europe allowed him to obtain a visa in Switzerland for his family to move to the United States. The CIA debriefed Naraghi when he moved to the United States which he says happened in 1989, although it could have been as late as 1992.[53]

His first task was convincing the CIA that he was not coming to the United States as an agent to export sensitive items to Iran. Naraghi claims he did not seek asylum and was willing to fully cooperate with the CIA, telling them about Iran's laser and gas centrifuge enrichment programs along with identifying several key aspects of the Iranian centrifuge program, including the crucial fact that Pakistan sold centrifuge designs to Iran. He fingered many of Iran's suppliers, some of whom were already known to U.S. intelligence. Little of this information was acted upon, and he has often wondered why the United States did not take more aggressive action against the Khan network.[54]

In 1989, Naraghi founded Torr International, located in New Windsor, New York, a company that retrofits and sells used vacuum equipment and is in operation to this day. Now a U.S. citizen, he has no interest in publicity.

With Naraghi gone, Iran's centrifuge program might have ground to a halt. Instead, the Khan network was once again its

savior. Iran told the IAEA that the Khan network initiated an
offer for further assistance in 1993. (It denies reaching out to
Khan first.) The Iranian company Dadeh Perdazi, established to
purchase computer software and hardware for an Iranian government agency, received a comprehensive proposal, which included
components for five hundred P1 centrifuges and P2 centrifuge
drawings. The company relayed the offer to the government
agency's head, leading to the notification of the AEOI's president, who decided to renew contacts with the network.[55]

The meeting to finalize the deal took place in Dubai during
1993 or 1994 at the Al Khaleej Holiday Hotel, a few minutes'
walk from Khan's luxury apartment.[56] Khan's Dubai-based aide
Tahir, and most likely Khan himself, were at the meeting with at
least two Iranians. The Iranians bought the components for five
hundred centrifuges (minus their motors) and auxiliary equipment. They also received a more complete set of P1 design and
manufacturing documents. This set included instructions on
establishing a quality assurance program—a necessity for centrifuge manufacturing, making individual components, and assembling the centrifuges.[57]

The offer did not include new centrifuges. By this time, Pakistan had replaced its P1 centrifuge with the more advanced P2
centrifuge so Khan sold off the surplus P1 components which
Pakistan no longer needed. As part of that offer, Khan sent Iran
15,000 used bellows. Many were visibly damaged; others were
filthy. Some still had traces of a special resin used to seal the
bellows and rotor tubes. Khan told Azadi, the project leader of
the Iranian centrifuge program, to have his experts sort through
them and they would find 1,500 good ones. Azadi refused and
reminded Khan that he had promised 1,500 good bellows. Khan

was obligated to send them, and they finally arrived in 1997. It took Iran another ten years before they finally sorted through the other 15,000 used bellows looking for good ones as it scaled up its enrichment program at Natanz.

The need for increased secrecy and security led to a decision in 1995 to move the centrifuge program from the Plasma Physics Building at the Tehran Nuclear Research Center. This building, which was built by a foreign company, would have served as a good centrifuge research and development facility, including building small cascades.[58] The program was moved to Kalaye Electric, which is where Iran finally succeeded in enriching uranium in small P1 centrifuge cascades.

Iran claims that in 1996 it received *gratis* from Khan a full set of general P2 centrifuge drawings at a meeting in Dubai as compensation for the poor quality of the P1 centrifuge components. Azadi told inspectors that the P2 designs sat in an office at Kalaye Electric until about 2002, when an ambitious Iranian engineer named Fard convinced the president of the AEOI that he could develop the P2 centrifuge. He had joined the small staff of professional engineers and technicians at Kalaye Electric around 1998 instead of performing his mandatory stretch of national military service. One of his research areas was trying to understand why the P1 centrifuge kept failing. When Fard eventually set up his own company, Imenista Andish, he received a contract to develop a modified P2 centrifuge that he would base on an advanced carbon fiber rotor. To produce the necessary carbon fiber rotors, Fard contracted with a military factory near the Lavisan site in the suburbs of Tehran, an area with many high-technology military institutes.[59] He worked on this project until June 2003, at which point he still had a considerable amount of work to do.

Iran continued to receive assistance from the Khan network after 1996. Meetings with a Khan intermediary continued and included discussions on technical issues. According to Iranian information, thirteen official meetings took place with the clandestine supply network between 1994 and 1999. It's unclear whether any meetings took place after that.

U.S. intelligence agencies did not detect Khan's transfers in the 1990s. The focus of the intelligence community had shifted to stopping Iran from buying nuclear equipment from China or exploiting weak controls over the nuclear assets in the former Soviet Union. U.S. intelligence believed Iran was still investigating centrifuge designs and looking to build a pilot plant.[60] There was little concern about Pakistan spreading additional centrifuge design knowledge to Iran.

The Clinton administration was further distracted by Russia's decision to supply Iran with nuclear facilities, including a gas centrifuge plant. They feared that Iran would extract plutonium from the reactor's irradiated fuel for nuclear weapons or use the reactor project as a cover to obtain secret Russian help to build a covert enrichment plant. Although Clinton convinced President Boris Yeltsin to stop the supply of the centrifuge plant in 1995, he could not convince him to cancel the sale of the nuclear power reactor at Bushehr on the coast in southern Iran.[61]

In hindsight, former Clinton administration officials have expressed reservations about their decision to press Russia instead of Pakistan over Iran. One former official said that the administration "picked the wrong guy."[62] Robert Einhorn, former assistant secretary of state for nonproliferation, said that, in the late 1980s, the United States learned that Pakistan "had export tendencies," and Khan had provided some centrifuge assistance to Iran.[63] The

United States was also aware of Iran's shopping excursions in Europe for its centrifuge program. However, U.S. intelligence agencies erroneously concluded that Iran was not that interested in P1 centrifuges or additional Pakistani assistance. Einhorn blamed a "lack of imagination" for the failure to anticipate that Khan would offer more assistance to Iran and other countries.

The lack of U.S. action against Pakistan was particularly troubling because Khan's group, armed with an entire package to make nuclear weapons, presented a nightmarish scenario. Shrewd businessmen in Europe and Dubai teamed up with nuclear weapons experts based at a secret gas centrifuge plant in Pakistan, with the goal of selling the capability to make nuclear weapons to developing countries. The convergence of easy money and weak controls on the sale of high tech equipment created a perfect storm that Khan and his associates exploited.

The U.S. government correctly concluded that a developing country wanting nuclear weapons would need to obtain both the know-how and equipment. That assessment underpinned the strategy of persuading countries such as China not to pass nuclear weapons designs to Pakistan, and for Germany, Russia, China, and Switzerland to tighten their export control laws. The United States believed that tightened export controls in the major supplier states could inhibit and significantly delay efforts in proliferating states. But a transnational network providing centrifuges and key classified technologies and equipment could easily sidestep that strategy, especially if it could create a key "node" to operate from, a country despised by the international community, impervious to U.S. diplomatic pressure, and in the midst of manufacturing its own nuclear weapons. Khan's network would find all of these things in one country: South Africa.

Finding a New Hideout—South Africa

After Swiss officials seized the three autoclaves made by MWB at the end of 1985, Gotthard Lerch realized that finding Swiss companies to make feed and withdrawal equipment was unlikely. He needed to look elsewhere. His old contacts at Leybold-Heraeus would prove invaluable in this search. Within months, Lerch found a trio of ideally qualified individuals in South Africa to make the equipment for a large feed and withdrawal system. Although they failed to sell gas centrifuge technology to South Africa, over the next decade, Gerhard Wisser, Daniel Geiges, and Johan A.M. Meyer created a crucial link in the Khan network, becoming a secret supplier of centrifuge equipment to Pakistan, Libya, India, and possibly Iran and North Korea.

Wisser was a German citizen who had relocated to South Africa in the 1960s and had been hired by Otto Heilingbrunner in 1975 as Leybold-Heraeus's South African agent.[1] In 1984, in an application to carry a semiautomatic pistol, Wisser stated he had a "very intensive relationship with the nuclear industry as well as the armaments industry" in South Africa and often carried "highly confidential and classified documentation."[2] Wisser's contacts in South Africa's illicit nuclear industry ran deep. To his former colleagues, Wisser appeared to enjoy the "money and adrenaline" his dealings generated. Before becoming an agent for Leybold-Heraeus, Wisser was head of Krisch Engineering, located in the suburbs of Johannesburg, and an agent of the German firm AEG Telefunken. Krisch Engineering was a major supplier to South Africa's nuclear program, including its secret uranium enrichment program at Valindaba, west of Pretoria, which was struggling to make highly enriched uranium for nuclear weapons.[3] Wisser and Leybold-Heraeus employees generated false documentation to conceal the recipient of exports to South Africa from German authorities because of laws banning such sales to the nuclear programs of the pro-apartheid regime.[4] Krisch also supplied Khan in the late 1970s with frequency converters that it bought from AEG Telefunken via its South African sales office. In a demonstration of how small the world of nuclear trafficking was at that time, Wisser had met Gotthard Lerch several years before becoming Leybold-Heraeus's agent. He would develop a close working relationship with Lerch that would last for almost thirty years.[5]

Geiges, a Swiss citizen, joined Krisch Engineering in 1978, seeking a freer lifestyle in South Africa than that offered in his native country. He had first met Lerch in the early 1970s when Geiges obtained Leybold-Heraeus equipment for South Africa's uranium enrichment program.[6] Geiges also traveled to Leybold-Heraeus in Germany to work on specific nuclear projects for South Africa.[7] Later, he became Wisser's chief engineer.

Meyer met Wisser and Geiges while working at South Africa's nuclear program at Valindaba in the 1970s. By 1980, Meyer formed Roxound Engineering Works at Vanderbijlpark, about an hour by car from Johannesburg. One of the company's first contracts was making "process piping" in 1980 for South Africa's enrichment plant, a contract valued at 5 million rand.[8] His firm was one of the few in the world that could make sophisticated equipment for enrichment plants, adding greatly to his value for Wisser and Geiges.

During 1984 and 1985, however, Krisch Engineering lost a substantial portion of its business with the South African nuclear establishment. The large nuclear construction projects at Valindaba were coming to an end, and the government, suffering increasingly from international sanctions, was cutting back its funding for all types of nuclear projects. As a result, Wisser and his colleagues needed new contracts. They looked abroad and connected with their old friend Lerch.

Years later, during the prosecution of Wisser and Geiges, the South African prosecutor Chris Macadam, a former member of the Scorpions, an elite commando unit, stated in a court document that after Lerch left Leybold-Heraeus, Lerch, in conjunction with Khan, Wisser, and Geiges, "decided to supply gas centrifuge technology to countries developing nuclear weapons."[9] Lerch's long-time colleague, Farooq, and his nephew Tahir, at BBE in Dubai, played critical roles in staging and facilitating this illicit trade. Their motivation was "purely financial" and their "previous work stood them in good stead" to accomplish their goal.

In hindsight, Lerch's choice of South Africa was inspired. Its government was an international pariah, in the midst of manufacturing its own nuclear weapons at the covert Armscor Circle facility west of Pretoria, using highly enriched uranium produced at the Y-Plant at Valindaba. These programs had depended on an extensive nuclear smuggling network which included Krisch Engineering. South Africa was unlikely to pass any laws inhibiting nuclear smuggling for its own programs. Tensions were high between the U.S. and South African governments, making it likely that a U.S. protest, or démarche, about sales to Pakistan would fall on deaf ears. Lerch and Wisser, seasoned in the art of maintaining secrecy and deniability, could avoid arousing any governmental qualms about helping Pakistan's or any other country's nuclear weapons program.

Wisser and Lerch got to work right away filling Khan's original order for feed and withdrawal equipment. According to Geiges, Wisser told him that Lerch sent down the designs for autoclaves and piping and that the intended customer was Pakistan.[10] Some of the designs still had the "CB" logo on them that had been on the original set Lerch sent to the Swiss firm MWB. A document seized by South African authorities after the arrest of Wisser in 2004 showed that by November 1986, Krisch was ordering components from Leybold-Heraeus for three autoclaves. The three finished autoclaves were sent to Pakistan via Dubai sometime around 1986 or 1987.

This group's second major contract was for a large piping system for the feed and withdrawal system. Most of these items were made by Meyer's company Roxound Engineering. Its archived website from the early 2000s notes a 1988 export of "process piping for an atomic enrichment plant," for which it charged 2.5 million rand.[11] Although the website calls the customer's project an "export" in a table of "turnkey projects completed," it does not hide the fact the export was sensitive, and possibly unlawful. In fact, a note states that customers listed as exports in the table represent sales to "sensitive countries or customers," and if a reader is interested in more information, they should "please contact the managing director." Meyer did not appear to be trying to hide his overseas customers, although many of his sales were carefully camouflaged.

From 1986 to 1989, this transnational team supplied key components for the large feed and withdrawal system to Pakistan. They evidently finished and perhaps enlarged the order that started in the late 1970s while Lerch was still at Leybold-Heraeus. In all of these transactions, a general pattern was followed. The orders from Khan were transmitted to Farooq, or later Tahir, who then placed an order to Lerch's company AVE, or in some cases Wisser's German company GEWI that he had established earlier to facilitate orders to South Africa's nuclear program.[12] Then AVE or GEWI would place an order with Krisch Engineering. Often, Meyer's companies would execute the orders through local manufacture, such as at Roxound, or Krisch itself would procure the finished items directly from other companies. The finished items were then sent to one of Tahir's companies in Dubai. From there, he would ship the items to Pakistan. Krisch charged AVE for all expenses; AVE then obtained the funds from Pakistan, often via Dubai. No one stated on the official export documents that the items were for nuclear facilities, but they all knew full well the true purpose of the finished items.

The transactions did not always go smoothly, and there were fights over payments. In a 1986 meeting in Dubai, for example, Lerch argued with Farooq about being owed 2 million Swiss francs.[13] In other cases, the filling of orders slowed as Lerch and his colleagues sought cheaper suppliers, trying to stay within Khan's budget while maximizing their own profits. Despite the problems and competitive relationships, Lerch and his collaborators never turned down an opportunity to expand their business.

In early 1988, Lerch ordered Wisser and Geiges to attempt to sell to the South African nuclear program, the Atomic Energy Corporation (AEC), the "know-how for ultra centrifuge and system engineering for complete enrichment plant," excluding some of the electric and electronic equipment to drive the centrifuges, for $13.8 million dollars.[14] The AEC operated a small gas centrifuge program, and Wisser was well known to its leaders, for whom he had procured in Europe critical ring magnets used in their centrifuge's upper bearing. Wisser also knew that South African nuclear officials were instructed to pick up sensitive information whenever they could. This time, though, the head of the AEC, Waldo Stumpf, saw the offer as too expensive and balked.

Undeterred, about a year later, Wisser offered the centrifuge program a complete set of drawings for the "electro-motoric drives" for centrifuges and "double-stage" centrifuges for 6 million Swiss francs. The term "double stage" referred to a P2 centrifuge, instead of a P1 centrifuge, which was the type sold to Iran in 1987. Again, Stumpf rejected Wisser's offer.

In September 1990, the original package was reoffered but with the "electro/electronic drive." This time the South Africans asked to see the equipment built from the designs, a request Wisser denied because "the know-how will not be acquired via official channels," shorthand for shady acquisition. Instead, Wisser gave them samples of the data being offered, including drawings of cascades and feed and withdrawal systems. (These documents corresponded identically to those that Geiges gave Meyer when they received a contract to build a centrifuge plant for Libya several years later.) Stumpf, however, convinced that Lerch had unlawfully obtained the plans, turned down the offer because he was unwilling to accept stolen property.

In 1988, South Africa was developing its own centrifuge and a "large amount of knowledge of these designs was in the public domain."[15] Interestingly, these South Africans in the Atomic Energy Corporation called their maraging steel centrifuge the "S2," using similar nomenclature as URENCO and Pakistan. It had the same diameter as the German URENCO centrifuges (and the P2 centrifuge), although its rotor was double the P2's length.

The use of the term "public domain" is perplexing. Did the South African engineers use this term broadly, including the acquisition of design information available on the grey or black markets? A former senior official of the South African centrifuge program said that he believed that security at the "German URENCO was very loose; it had lots of subcontractors and information has easily spread."[16] They were picking up in Europe or elsewhere any URENCO information that could help them advance their own centrifuge design. Part of the problem with Wisser's offer was that his information would not significantly improve South Africa's more advanced centrifuges.

Ironically, President P.W. Botha's government had in 1985 decided to freeze its production of highly enriched uranium for weapons. F.W. de Klerk's government ended the nuclear weapons program in 1989. By 1988, the gas centrifuge was needed solely for the production of enriched uranium for nuclear reactors. A few years later, after South Africa's isolation had ended, the AEC determined that a South African gas centrifuge plant was unlikely to be competitive with existing URENCO plants, leading it to cancel its domestic centrifuge program in late 1991.

Wisser was more successful in selling items to India's gas centrifuge program, which was established in the 1980s to make highly enriched uranium for naval submarine reactors and thermonuclear weapons.[17] In the late 1980s and early 1990s, Wisser commissioned one of his employees, Len Harvey, to produce and deliver specialized measurement devices for India's centrifuge cascades that were hard to procure through legitimate suppliers.[18] After their delivery, these devices experienced problems, and Harvey and a colleague traveled to India to fix this equipment. Krisch Engineering may have provided additional sensitive items to the Indian centrifuge program, including feed and withdrawal equipment for centrifuge cascades. The full extent of Lerch's involvement in supplying India's nuclear program is not known, although when he was employed at Leybold-Heraeus, he may have been involved in starting up sales of vacuum equipment to India's gas centrifuge program. Leybold-Heraeus (renamed Leybold in 1987) continued to sell vacuum equipment to this program until the early 1990s.

The early 1990s saw many changes in South Africa, starting with the end of apartheid and the dismantling of South Africa's nuclear arsenal. President F.W. de Klerk also enacted strict export control laws in 1993 that banned many of the sales made by Wisser and Geiges. Criminalizing their activities did little to stop Wisser and his colleagues, though. Wisser and Geiges were already allegedly breaking a host of international laws and had learned how to hide their activities from domestic and foreign authorities. As citizens of Germany and Switzerland, they were also subject to the laws of those countries. Germany's Bundesnachrichtendienst (BND) suspected Wisser was supplying Pakistan and North Korea, but they lacked enough evidence or the means to collect any new evidence in South Africa to enable German prosecutors to formally charge him.

Krisch's steady sales to Pakistan's gas centrifuge plants continued throughout the 1990s. In 1994, three more autoclaves, made by Roxound, were sold in a contract worth 1.1 million rand. Once completed, Krisch sent four crates containing the autoclaves from Durban, South Africa, to the attention of "Mr. Junior" (Tahir's nickname), at BB Enterprises in Dubai. The bill was sent to AVE.

In February 1995, Lerch and Wisser hosted a summit meeting at Krisch Engineering to discuss Pakistan's further needs for its centrifuge program.[19] Khan sent his representatives Tahir and Dr. Hashmi, Khan's longtime aide and also chairman of the Karachi Peoples' Steel Mill, charged with secretly making advanced metals for Khan's program and serving as a front company for overseas purchases for the centrifuge program.[20] The group's priority was finding maraging steel, which was difficult to make or acquire, but was critical to Pakistan's centrifuge program.[21] Likely to that end, Hashmi needed specialized, hard-to-get furnaces, which Wisser could provide. Unknowingly, Wisser had several years earlier sold a Yemeni company several furnaces that Hashmi told him were actually for Peoples' Steel Mill.[22]

Hashmi also needed help in making maraging steel centrifuge rotors, likely equipment that could manufacture the rotors faster. Khan was building thousands of P2 centrifuges and envisioned soon building thousands of P3 centrifuges. In a promotional video about the Khan Research Laboratory found in Libya and in South Africa, Khan said the P3 is about double the length of the P2 centrifuge, leading IAEA inspectors to speculate that the P3 was modeled after the German G4 centrifuge. URENCO was just starting to develop this model in 1975, and Khan had access to information about this design. It has four maraging steel rotors connected by three bellows and an enrichment output almost double that of the P2.

Wisser convinced a member of South Africa's Atomic Energy Corporation to meet Hashmi to discuss helping make thin-walled rotors. The expert was shown drawings of centrifuge rotors, and Hashmi tried to convince him to travel to Pakistan and start a training program in making both maraging steel and rotors.[23] The expert was unwilling to help without approval from his superiors. This ended the discussions.

The Peoples' Steel Mill's role in Khan's program was largely unknown in the 1990s. In correspondence with European suppliers, its management denied any nuclear, even civil applications.[24] Because this mill's activities for Khan were secret and a relatively small fraction of its total business, it was difficult to prove during the 1990s that some of the company's overseas purchases were indeed for nuclear purposes. In a case in Germany, Peoples' Steel Mill hired German legal representation to help obtain the government's approval to import manufacturing equipment. Despite suspicions by the German government that the actual end use was for Pakistan's centrifuge program, the government was unable to muster a strong enough case to stop the export. Often, evidence of linkages is slim or subject to multiple interpretations. This ambiguity has been exploited by companies such as the Peoples' Steel Mill to obtain items for secret nuclear programs.

Lerch was also independently seeking a variety of items for Khan at Tahir's request using trading companies to hide both his own involvement and the ultimate end user. Once he placed orders for vacuum pumps at a Swiss company through a former, naïve employee, Fridolin Zahner.[25] Although the former employee had created a new company to sell safety technology, at the time he was glad for every order and uninterested in knowing the pumps' true purpose. Lerch told him which pumps to order, and to order them from Pfeiffer Vacuum Technology in Zurich. Zahner instructed Pfeiffer to send the pumps to a forwarding company, which, unknown to Pfeiffer, sent the pumps to one of Tahir's companies. Tahir sent back a wire transfer signed by "a customer" for 92,000 Swiss francs, covering the cost of the pumps and Zahner's profit of about 5,200 Swiss francs. Pfeiffer likely saw the sale as a domestic sale warranting little scrutiny, although a cursory examination of the forwarding company, particularly its lack of any involvement in vacuum technology, would have exposed it as a trading company buying items unrelated to its purpose.

Lerch could not get all the vacuum equipment he needed from Pfeiffer. Pakistan required new Leybold equipment to sustain its nuclear weapons program. It possessed a huge amount of Leybold equipment and needed spare parts and replacement equipment for its centrifuge plant. For years, Lerch had easily bought Leybold equipment. Starting in the spring of 1991, however, Leybold set a new course that clearly diverged from its past practices. Leybold enacted strict internal nonproliferation policies and rules and created an unprecedented set of corporate principals, the "Leybold Charter," placing the goal of the nonproliferation of nuclear weapons and their delivery systems over commercial interests. This meant that Lerch in particular was unwelcome at the new Leybold's export oversight headquarters, which was all too familiar with his Pakistan dealings.

Lerch had to find a way to trick Leybold into selling key equipment. He decided to ask another company to request equipment from Leybold, hiding his involvement in the transaction. In 1995, Lerch's company AVE placed four orders with the British company Kurt J. Lesker intended for Leybold. Lesker ordered the equipment from Leybold's British subsidiary. For many companies, this act would have been sufficient to hide the sale from the overseas headquarters. Moreover, officials in British Leybold were inclined to provide the equipment after receiving an AVE certificate pledging that the equipment was destined for Bulgaria and would not be reexported or used for any nuclear purpose. Even when AVE was reluctant to disclose its customer in Bulgaria, British Leybold officials accepted AVE's explanation that it needed to do so "out of fear of Leybold or Lesker dealing direct with their customer" and cutting them out of the business.[26]

Leybold, however, had instituted a centralized system as a key part of its reforms and such sales required the approval of the tough-minded and experienced Leybold trade control manager Ralf Wirtz. Immediately suspicious, he asked for more detailed information about the equipment, wanting to compare it to orders that had been denied to other customers, particularly Pakistani companies. Trying to track down the source of the order, Ralf called AVE and surprisingly ended up talking to Lerch. He told Lerch that he would "get nothing from Leybold."[27]

Undaunted, Lerch instructed Wisser in South Africa to purchase equipment directly from Leybold.[28] After it dismantled its nuclear arsenal in the early 1990s, South Africa was no longer viewed as a "sensitive country," becoming a so-called "white knight," a leader in international nonproliferation that major suppliers could trust. Because South Africa was now a member of the exclusive Nuclear Suppliers Group, Leybold, starting in 1995, did not need export licenses to sell there. Afterward, Cologne did little checking of exports to South Africa, particularly when Leybold's own agent asked for that kind of equipment.

Wisser's first order to Leybold was successful. In May 1995, AVE placed an order with Wisser for fifteen Leybold vacuum pumps and sensitive equipment to detect leaks of uranium from centrifuge cascades. To hide its nuclear use and ultimate destination in Pakistan, Wisser instructed one of his employees to forge an order from Electric Lamp Manufacturers of Southern Africa. The forged order used an earlier legitimate order placed by the company but the employee replaced that equipment with the items ordered by AVE. Wisser sent Leybold the forged order and a declaration that the equipment would be used to make only incandescent lamps and not for any nuclear purpose. After the equipment arrived in South Africa, Wisser illegally reexported it to Al Hadwa General Trading in Dubai, which, according to Tahir, was used by Khan as a front.[29] From Dubai, the equipment was diverted to Pakistan.

Shortly after the first order, AVE sent a larger order to Wisser for Leybold equipment. This time the order was split into three separate parts, making it harder to recognize that the order, in its entirety, was equipment intended for a centrifuge plant. Wisser needed to select another South African company to place the bogus order. He picked the respected company Integrators of System Technology (IST), located near Johannesburg, which had conducted legitimate business with Krisch Engineering. Using an official letter from the company containing its address and the signature of its executive director, Wisser copied the letter with the old order blocked out, then substituted the new orders from

AVE. The forged letter also stated that the equipment would be reexported to an unstated country, but IST would obtain the necessary licenses to export the equipment.

While maintaining a conspiracy to deceive Leybold, Lerch and Wisser also each sought to increase his own profit at the expense of the other. They negotiated over the price Krisch Engineering charged AVE for various Leybold vacuum pumps. Wisser wanted to ensure the largest possible commission, while Lerch wanted to obtain the equipment as cheaply as possible.[30]

Over at Leybold, Wirtz analyzed the orders placed by Krisch and recognized that someone had split the original order from Lerch to the Kurt J. Lesker company into several orders. He also knew IST housed former nuclear technicians from Pelindaba and Valindaba and was involved in South African nuclear projects. Wirtz refused to approve the delivery of the equipment to Wisser and reported the incident to Leybold's head. Leybold management blamed Wisser for not checking the order but did not suspect that he had concocted the forged letters. To protect himself, Wisser composed another bogus letter. In a letter dated August 30, 1995, on Krisch stationery, he addressed G. De Lange, the executive director of IST, and stated that Krisch could not provide the equipment because his company was not prepared to disclose the final destination of the equipment, as required under the Leybold Charter. But Wisser did not send the letter to De Lange, he sent it only to Leybold to mislead Wirtz and convince him that he was fulfilling Leybold's strict export policies. This letter saved Wisser's job as an agent. Leybold blamed IST and put a respectable customer on its blacklist. Although Wirtz remained suspicious of Wisser, he was not able to take any action against him and others at Krisch until the arrest of Wisser,

Geiges, and Meyer in September 2004 by the South African police.

For years, Wisser, Geiges, and Lerch outfoxed authorities and intelligence agencies on three continents. They managed to devote almost their entire careers to outfitting secret nuclear programs, getting caught only as they neared retirement. After their arrests, all denied any wrongdoing. Confronted with Meyer's and Geiges's testimony, Wisser pled guilty to a range of charges in September 2007 and was sentenced to eighteen years in prison. His jail time was suspended, and he was placed under house arrest for three years, forced to pay millions of dollars in fines. Geiges, after being diagnosed with terminal colon cancer, pled guilty in February 2008 after several postponements of his trial due to illness. He received a sentence of thirteen years, all of which was suspended, and forfeited over $100,000 held in Swiss bank accounts, a bitter blow as he had worked on salary, unlike Wisser and Lerch, who had earned enormous commissions. Geiges died in late 2008. Meyer was never charged because of his cooperation with authorities.

Wisser's and Geiges's activities had "all the hallmarks of sophisticated organized crime," according to Wisser's 2007 Plea and Sentence Agreement. Over the years, this transnational group developed sophisticated methods to execute its orders, including using subcontractors and businesses with suitable engineering expertise, and as the group carried out its activities, it stressed secrecy. According to Jeff Bedell, a senior nuclear expert from Los Alamos National Laboratory, they had also assembled "a large and complex body of very proliferation-sensitive applied engineering design and applied technical data pertaining directly to gas centrifuge plant and gas centrifuge machine design, construction, and operation."[31] Armed with this information and schooled in sophisticated procurement and manufacturing methods, they became a critical manufacturing unit of the Khan network and a supplier to other countries' secret nuclear weapons efforts.

One effort, though, stretched all of Khan's resources and talents. It was the pinnacle of his network's accomplishments. Its sheer scale would also lead to their undoing.

SIX

Libya: A Major Sale at Last

Throughout the 1970s and 1980s, Muammar Qaddafi sought nuclear weapons. In response to Qaddafi's contributing money to Pakistan's nascent cash-starved nuclear weapons effort, Khan raised the possibility of selling Libya centrifuge technology in January 1984.[1] Qaddafi's scientists were worried that Libya did not have the physical or scientific infrastructure to take up the offer.[2] This may help explain why at about that same time, Qaddafi recruited a European gas centrifuge expert to come to Libya and develop centrifuges.[3] Fired from the German URENCO contractor MAN New Technologies in Munich,[4] this expert brought his own equipment and designs to Tripoli in an effort to develop a gas centrifuge.[5] He left Libya in 1992 without ever getting one to work.[6]

Qaddafi had always found it difficult to expand his ostensibly civil nuclear infrastructure. Many countries have relied on such a foundation to develop nuclear weapons. Although he managed to buy a small Russian nuclear reactor in the 1970s, few countries were willing to sell him more nuclear facilities or train Libyans in the specialized arts of nuclear science and engineering. His military attacks on his neighbors, the 1988 downing of Pan Am

103 over Lockerbie, Scotland, and his broad support of terrorism united much of the world against him. By 1989, with Qaddafi still unable to launch a nuclear weapons program, Khan and his team once again stepped into the nuclear proliferation breach.

The details of who initiated the crucial meeting to establish the sale remain murky, but the IAEA does know that Khan renewed his contacts with Libyan officials starting in the fall of 1989, five years after the initial offer.[7] By early 1991, both sides had reached an agreement on the supply of P1 centrifuges, the same ones sold to Iran.[8] The Khan network's offer may have been similar in scope to the 1987 offer to Iran. Fairly quickly, Libya received a few P1 components and centrifuge designs.

Like Iran's, the P1 centrifuges would have come from Khan Research Laboratories (KRL), which was switching out the older P1 centrifuges and replacing them with the P2 model. Thousands of these machines were retired, starting as early as 1985. For Khan and his underlings at KRL, taking away hundreds or even a few thousand of these surplus machines was straightforward.

Since its founding in 1976, Khan Research Laboratories had grown into a small, self-contained industrial city, an extensive technical and manufacturing center able to build and operate tens of thousands of centrifuges. Behind KRL's security perimeter, Khan oversaw his primary business of enriching uranium for Pakistan's nuclear arsenal. This is where the true nexus of Khan's power lay within that "city" 's perimeter. Khan erected many factories and workshops, employing many thousands of skilled, well-trained Pakistani specialists and managers. In addition, KRL had branched out into making nuclear-tipped Ghauri missiles, conventional armaments, and a wide variety of equipment for Pakistan's military and industrial sectors. KRL had its own hospital, provided its workers with "colonies" of housing and schools, and even had a national cricket team.[9]

One former URENCO specialist said that KRL had more capabilities than URENCO facilities.[10] While URENCO could contract for most items and thus did not need such a large in-house capability, Khan did not have that luxury in underdeveloped Pakistan. KRL had centrifuge drawings, surplus centrifuges, test data and process calculations, all of which were derived from the information Khan had stolen in the Netherlands or obtained from key European suppliers. Khan had also overseen the training and development of a cadre of centrifuge experts who had the knowledge to solve centrifuge-related problems raised by customers. He had to use his network to create the industries to make centrifuge components and equipment, and keep them supplied with raw materials and spare parts.

The sale to Libya involved several other members of Khan's network. Friedrich Tinner, Khan's old colleague and supplier in Switzerland, contracted to manufacture a few "test modules," or small-scale feed and withdrawal systems.[11] He most likely used the same designs Khan had given him in the 1970s when Tinner worked with Cora Engineering. These test modules were needed for the operation of a single P1 centrifuge and cascades of nine, nineteen, and sixty-four P1 centrifuges. Libya needed to operate these cascades to develop the experience to operate a plant comprising thousands of centrifuges. Khan's old friend, Selim Alguadis, who headed 3E Endustriyel and its subsidiary EKA Elektronik Kontrol in Istanbul, agreed to produce six frequency converters, each of which could power many centrifuges. Gunes Cire, Khan's old university classmate and a close business associate of the Tinners who headed ETI Elektronik and its subsidiary Techno Elektrik in Istanbul, ordered a large number of P1 ring magnets from suppliers to make up part of the upper bearing of the P1 centrifuge.[12]

Khan's sale to Libya stalled when the United Nations Security Council imposed a total air and arms embargo on Libya in 1992 for refusing to extradite two Libyans accused of carrying out the bombing of Pan Am 103.[13] In 1993, the Security Council banned the sale of petroleum equipment to Libya. Faced with such harsh sanctions, Khan's network was stymied for several years.

Khan's network members had already fulfilled a portion of their contracts before the start of the UN embargo but had not yet delivered any P1 centrifuges or equipment to Libya. They wanted their payments, but Libya was not going to pay for un-delivered goods. Tinner had finished one test module and sent it to Dubai where it awaited shipment to Libya. He had also built a nine-machine test module that remained in Switzerland. Cire and Alguadis had likewise acquired ring magnets and made fre-quency converters.

Under pressure from his contractors and unable to get money from Libya, Khan devised a way to sell at least some of this equipment to Iran and KRL. When Iran decided to buy more centrifuges from the network in 1993, a network representative told them that centrifuge equipment stored in Dubai was for sale.[14] Based on member state information and interviews with Libyan officials and supply network members, the IAEA con-cluded that most of the centrifuge equipment offered to Iran by the network in 1993 had originally been ordered by Libya.[15] This equipment was in addition to the 500 P1 centrifuges Iran bought that had come directly from KRL.

Iran bought all the P1 magnets and one frequency converter. It did not buy Tinner's test modules. Khan's enrichment program bought the other five frequency converters. Iran again showed its resistance to buying very much from the network. As in the past, according to Olli Heinonen, it bought "bits and pieces" and then tried to use its own network to create an indigenous centrifuge capability.

After several years of trying, the Khan network appeared unable to seal a major deal. Libya was ensconced in sanctions and Iran was cherry-picking its offers. South Africa turned down the network's offer for centrifuge technology. Desert Storm began before a nuclear weapons deal could develop with Iraq. North Korea was a potential customer, although not many sales would ever develop. Many of these countries had nuclear complexes and could afford to turn down Khan or take only part of what he offered. Others likely suspected that Khan could not be trusted. Still other countries that Khan is believed to have approached, such as Egypt, are not believed to have bought centrifuges.[16]

Libya reinvigorated its efforts in July 1995, although sanctions would delay the actual restart.[17] According to Tahir, Libya formally asked Khan to supply a gas centrifuge plant in 1997 at a meeting in a café in Istanbul, Turkey.[18] Khan, accompanied by Tahir, met with Mohamed Matuq Mohamed, the senior Libyan government official heading the nuclear weapons effort, and a man named Karim, who was the head of the gas centrifuge program.[19] Matuq was secretary of the General People's Committee and secretary of the National Board of Scientific Research, which provided a convenient cover for Libya's nuclear weapons program.[20]

By this time, the thirty-seven-year-old Tahir was firmly in

control of the network's daily operations, having bought his uncle Farooq out.[21] Farooq took his cash buyout and moved to Singapore in 1992, where he has lived since.[22] Khan tells a different story. He said that in 1991 or 1992, Farooq cheated Tahir and fled to Singapore with all the money in their bank accounts, later trying to blackmail Tahir.[23] Whatever the exact circumstances of Tahir taking over, he ran the business differently than his uncle. Unlike Farooq, who was like a "servant" to Khan, Tahir had a stronger, more personal relationship with Khan. He sought a more powerful role in the network, increasingly using his own family's Dubai computer business, SMB Group (which included SMB Computers and SMB Traders Computers Division), as his base of operations. He injected new blood into the network and had Khan's complete trust.

By 1997, a few countries started to unilaterally loosen sanctions against Libya, and Qaddafi sent signals that he was interested in resolving Libya's role in the Lockerbie bombing. The orders resumed in 1997, and the network sent twenty preassembled P1 centrifuges to Libya, renaming them the L-1 centrifuge for Libya-1. The Khan network also sold Libya another two hundred unassembled P1 centrifuges, uranium hexafluoride cylinders, and frequency converters.[24] Khan sent most of the P1 centrifuge components on Pakistani Air Force C-130 cargo aircraft.[25]

Despite Libya receiving the P1 centrifuges ordered in the early 1990s, Matuq had by then realized that the P2 centrifuge was a better machine.[26] Moreover, Khan no longer had surplus P1 centrifuges, so he would need to find an offshore manufacturer to provide them. Matuq placed an order for a P2 centrifuge plant. He still wanted the two hundred P1 centrifuges, because the Libyans could use them while waiting for the manufacture of the

P2 machines to build up their expertise and experience in running centrifuges.

Matuq placed an initial order for 5,000 centrifuges and later expanded it to 10,000 centrifuges, enough to create a sizeable nuclear arsenal of tens of nuclear weapons. Khan had finally landed a major sale. Libya would pay $100 to $200 million for these centrifuges and associated equipment and materials, far outstripping what Iran purchased.[27] Key members of the network stood to earn enormous profits.

The sale to Libya represented the pinnacle of the Khan network's achievements. Not since the mid-1950s, when the Soviet Union offered to help its communist ally China build nuclear weapons, had a country received a proposition for such a massive infusion of nuclear weapon technology and know-how. Making the offer even more remarkable was that it came from Khan's transnational band of businessmen, smugglers, money manipulators, and engineers—a combine held together by the allure of large profits and fidelity to their leader. As George Tenet, former director of the Central Intelligence Agency (CIA), said, Khan was "at least as dangerous as Osama bin Laden."[28]

Even though the United States had bombed Libya in 1986, a small Libyan nuclear arsenal would have deterred almost any country from attacking it. Qaddafi would have also gained an immense amount of prestige in the Arab world and could threaten his neighbors with impunity, though he likely would have sparked a nuclear arms race in the area. He would also have been capable of spreading centrifuge technology to other countries, which would have had a profoundly destabilizing effect in the Middle East and in Europe.

Although Libya ordered 10,000 centrifuges, the planned centrifuge plant was designed to hold less than two-thirds of them. Given the likelihood that Libyan technicians would break many of the centrifuges once the plant began operating, the rest were intended as spares. The plant would contain 5,832 P2 centrifuges in thirty-eight individual cascades, all run by computers—four sets of cascades would be producing enriched uranium in stages up to weapon-grade:[29]

- Twenty-four "C" cascades, each containing 164 centrifuges, for a total of 3,936 centrifuges, would in parallel enrich natural uranium to 3.5 percent enriched uranium.[30]
- Eight "HC-01" cascades, each containing 164 centrifuges for a total of 1,312, would enrich the 3.5 percent uranium to 20 percent.
- Four "HC-02" cascades, each containing 114 centrifuges, for a total 456 centrifuges, would in parallel enrich from 20 percent to 60 percent material.
- Finally, two "HC-03" cascades, each containing 64 centrifuges for a total of 128 centrifuges, would enrich the 60 percent material to 90 percent, or weapon-grade.

Each of these blocks of cascades would have its own feed and withdrawal system. A small fleet of vehicles would carry the uranium hexafluoride canisters among the various stations.

When operational, the plant would produce approximately one hundred kilograms of weapon-grade uranium a year, enough nuclear material for several nuclear weapons a year.[31] The amount of weapon-grade uranium Libya intended to use in each nuclear weapon can only be surmised but a Pakistani document seized by authorities in South Africa, where much of the plant was designed and built, offers important clues. The document, taken in a raid of Meyer's company, Tradefin Engineering, detailed the rough casting of weapon-grade uranium metal hemispheres and the machining of the cast material into smooth, polished hemispheres. Each rough hemisphere contained fifteen kilograms of weapon-grade uranium, for a total of thirty kilograms. When finished, the final two hemispheres would have twenty-five kilograms, the rest removed during machining and polishing.[32] This quantity is very similar to the amount of weapon-grade uranium in the nuclear warhead design China supplied Pakistan and later Khan supplied to Libya. Nuclear bombs can require less weapon-grade uranium; Iraq's 1990 design called for fifteen kilograms of weapon-grade uranium.[33] The Libyan program appeared sized to produce at least four nuclear weapons per year, a small but formidable nuclear arsenal.

After the initial agreement between Khan and Matuq in that Istanbul café in 1997, Khan called together the leaders of the network to divide up the enormous work of supplying this large centrifuge plant. Friedrich Tinner, Gotthard Lerch, Tahir, and Khan agreed on who would supply various parts of the centrifuge plant.[34] Tahir, based in Dubai and Malaysia, was the coordinator of the project and main point of contact. If Khan was the president of "Bomb Inc.," Tahir was its managing director.[35] Tahir often stated to investigators that he is not an engineer; instead, he administered the project and controlled its financing, and served as the contact between Khan, the main network contractors, and the Libyans, principally Matuq and Karim. He had the responsibility to manage the band of contractors, often not an easy feat.[36] When necessary, Tahir would contact Khan for a decision.[37] Tahir would then relay the decision to the Libyans and contractors. The contractors sent progress reports to Tahir or Khan and requested payments for their work. After approving the requests, Khan passed the details to Tahir for payments to the contractors. Tahir then contacted Matuq for payment.

Tinner was the principal contractor to produce the centrifuge components. Khan had spent years establishing an indigenous capability to make P2 components, but he could not use this manufacturing infrastructure to supply P2 centrifuges to Libya without alerting Pakistani authorities to his secret sale. To fulfill this contract, Tinner involved his close knit family in this endeavor. The network made many modifications as it struggled to provide the more sensitive centrifuge components, and other network members had to get involved in acquiring centrifuge components.

Lerch agreed to produce the feed and withdrawal units of the main centrifuge plant. He subcontracted this work to his experienced South African colleagues, Wisser, Geiges, and Meyer. Selim Alguadis agreed to produce the frequency converters, each of which can power about two hundred centrifuges.[38] Gunes Cire, who was by then aided by his son Kursad, contracted to produce the centrifuge motors using designs supplied by Tahir.[39] They also agreed to obtain centrifuge ring magnets from European companies. Because of Turkey's proximity to Europe and its close economic relationship, this node had easy access to raw materials from European suppliers.

That Cire and Alguadis were still in business was a testament to the network's resiliency. Both had been supplying Khan's nuclear weapons effort since the 1980s. The Reagan administration had threatened to cut off assistance to Turkey because of their actions; however, Turkey was a crucial ally in the fight in

Afghanistan against the Soviet Union, and many did not want
to threaten that cooperation by pressuring the Turkish government to stop sales to Khan. A huge internal debate at the State
Department resulted, culminating in President Ronald Reagan
raising this issue in 1988 in a tête-à-tête with Turkish President
Kenan Evren, who admitted that "there had been nuclear enrichment exports from Turkey to Pakistan."[40] Evren added that his
government had "decided to prohibit the export of such materials." Many U.S. officials believed that the Turkish government
stopped Cire's and Alguadis's sales to Pakistan's enrichment
program, but that attempt, like so many others aimed at stopping
Khan and his gang, failed because the Turkish government did
not follow through on its commitment.[41]

Because centrifuges break and must be replaced, the Khan
network also agreed to sell Libya the capability to make centrifuges. According to Tahir, Peter Griffin and his son Paul, who
owned Gulf Technical Industries (GTI) in Dubai's Al Quoz
Industrial Estate, were in charge of acquiring machines for a precision manufacturing workshop that would allow Libya to make
its own P2 centrifuge components, variously called "Workshop
1001" or the "Machine Shop." Peter Griffin has admitted that
Tahir asked him to specify and supply machine tools for a general
maintenance workshop in Dubai for the manufacture of spare
parts and components for the oil and gas industry, yet he denies
that he knew it was for making centrifuge components. He said
that he learned only in 2002 from Tahir that the workshop was
destined for Libya. Tahir stated that all these contractors, including Griffin, "were fully aware that the equipment that they were
supplying was for the Libyan gas centrifuge program."[42]

In another brilliant move, Khan placed the network's logistical hub for the Libyan order in Dubai. Khan was a frequent visitor (maintaining an apartment there) as it was an important intermediate stop for his illegal purchases. An added benefit was Dubai's Jebel Ali Free Trade Zone.[43] Any item in this zone was considered in transit, meaning local authorities could search a facility in the zone only if they believed a crime had been committed.[44] By using Dubai companies as false end users for an order, the Khan network complicated the ability of the authorities or suppliers to figure out the actual destination. Moreover, using Dubai as the end user provided valuable deniability to the network's members. Although it is less a free-for-all zone today than prior to Khan's arrest, it remains an important transit point for smugglers from Iran's and Pakistan's nuclear programs.

Because of Dubai's importance, several Khan network members maintained companies there. Tahir's cover business, SMB Computers, was a flourishing wholesale computer company that Tahir ran with his brother. Tahir's warehouse of computers was one hectare long (100 meters by 100 meters), while a separate warehouse held the network's orders before Tahir rerouted them to Libya.[45] Tahir was also well connected to a number of Dubai companies that would serve as false end users for network suppliers. The network used a variety of local companies to ship proscribed nuclear-related equipment to Dubai and then onward to Libya and Iran.[46] Once an order arrived at one of these companies, Tahir could take control of the goods and send them onward to Libya, Pakistan, or other places with almost no risk of being arrested by UAE authorities. Until 2007, UAE did not even have an export control law.

The close-knit Tinner family owned Desert Electrical Equipment (DEE) Factory in Dubai. Urs Tinner supervised operations there during the late 1990s and early 2000s. DEE received goods, serving as a false end user, and arranged their transfer to Libya,[47] along with manufacturing, assembling, and testing centrifuge components[48] and training Libyans in how to manufacture various centrifuge components and balance centrifuge rotors.[49]

One of Tahir's major responsibilities was paying members of the network while hiding these cash transfers from the authorities. Tahir convinced two of his friends, Syed Fareed al Habshi and Shah Hakim Shahnazim Zain, to use their offshore accounts to receive funds from the Libyans and then transfer the money to contractors.[50] In an account Meyer opened at Credit Suisse in Switzerland, he assigned the Libyan project the code name "E-Projects." Tahir's two friends made deposits into this account from their offshore accounts listing this code name as the transfer's purpose.

At the heart of Libya's deal was a set of detailed centrifuge plans and drawings. These were based on Leybold-Heraeus drawings and documentation, combined with Pakistani drawings and documentation, test results, and various calculations.[51] In total, they embodied years of knowledge and first-hand experience. The architectural plans for the layout of the centrifuge plant were so complete they contained instructions on where to install toilet paper holders in the bathrooms.[52]

Since Libya would assemble the centrifuges, operate the plant, and build more centrifuges itself, it received an extensive set of centrifuge drawings and documents for both the P1 and P2 centrifuges on a hard drive and a pair of CD-ROM discs. One disc contained a full set of P1 centrifuge drawings, together with manufacturing, assembly, and test instruction manuals. A second disc contained similar data for the P2 centrifuge. Providing the materials in an electronic format was a relatively new innovation; however, it was a convenient one given KRL's large library of centrifuge designs, detailed manufacturing manuals, and nuclear weapon designs. While this made dissemination easy, it also makes it impossible to gauge with any certainty who else might have made copies of this highly classified information.

To give Libya a preview of what its completed facilities would look like, the Khan network provided a KRL promotional video. The video showed a large cascade hall at KRL, which held about between eight and ten thousand glistening P2 centrifuges in cascades dedicated to making low enriched uranium, like the "C" cascades in the Libyan order. Much of the video showed the manufacture of P2 centrifuge components in KRL workshops. Many specialized, computerized machine tools were shown making high-precision centrifuge components. According to the narrator, the workshops could achieve an accuracy of one-tenth of a micron, which is roughly one hundred times smaller than the diameter of a human hair. Undoubtedly, KRL's Foreign Procurement Division acquired much of this equipment under false pretenses abroad.

The video also proudly featured the Ghauri missile, Pakistan's first nuclear-tipped missile. It was shown on a mobile launcher in a large, high-ceilinged building which appeared to be where the missile was assembled. Since a nuclear weapon must be mated with a delivery system that has a good chance of reaching its target (aircraft are too easy to attack on the ground or shoot down), it's reasonable to assume Khan planned to eventually sell Libya plans to make its own version of the Ghauri missile, or the capability to make a nuclear warhead that could be tipped onto one of Libya's less capable missiles. After acquiring the missile's technology from North Korea in the early 1990s, KRL rapidly developed it, conducting its first flight test in April 1998 just before Pakistan's and India's underground nuclear tests. The Ghauri missile, named after a twelfth century medieval Afghan Muslim invader of India, is Pakistan's response to India's nuclear-tipped Prithvi missile. Prithviraj Chouhan, a powerful Hindu ruler of northern India, initially defeated Shahab-ud-Din Ghauri, but Ghauri eventually returned with a bigger army and triumphed over Prithviraj. To play up the symbolism of a Muslim warrior successfully invading Hindu India, Khan organized the construction of a memorial tomb to Ghauri. (India contends its missile is not named after Prithviraj but rather means "earth.")[53]

Filling the Libyan order was a massive undertaking for the Khan network. A centrifuge plant with ten thousand centrifuges requires the production of more than one million high-precision components. The network would have to organize the construction of a centrifuge plant comparable to an early URENCO facility in secret, with a complicated set of suppliers and manufacturers stretching around the world. From procurement to production to shipment, members of the Khan network had to manage a network of interconnected businesses and oversee the movement and storage of raw materials, equipment, and manufactured items in Asia, Africa, and Europe.

Because of the immense effort required, many experts and government officials didn't believe a Khan-type transnational network could build an enrichment plant. Yet since Libya had essentially unlimited funds to buy the facility, and was in obviously no position to complain if there were price increases in supplies or major delays in securing the requisite materials, the Khan network had a realistic chance of succeeding. Khan created his supply chain in the 1970s; by the time they were ready to supply Libya, its members had accumulated extraordinary procurement skills that had weathered many investigations and prosecutions. The Libyan plant was a duplicate of what had already been built at KRL, meaning they could incorporate the lessons learned during the previous construction process and likely come out ahead with an increased profit.

Khan's network also benefited from technology's continuous improvement throughout the world. Many countries which were dismissed as developing nations had sophisticated manufacturing and machine tool capabilities. John M. McConnell, former U.S. director of national intelligence, testified before the Senate Armed Services Committee on February 27, 2007: "The time when only a few states had access to the most dangerous technologies has been over for many years. Dual-use technologies circulate easily in our globalized economy, as do the scientific personnel who design and use them."[54] The Khan network recognized this new reality as far back as the 1990s and exploited it at a time when few understood the threat it posed to world security.

The network's largest priority was organizing the manufacture of over one million P2 centrifuge components. A centrifuge is composed of rotating and nonrotating parts. Although the nonrotating components require precise machining and have stringent tolerances, they are easier to make than those that rotate. Those components, such as the rotor and bellows, must withstand spinning at high speeds and be precisely machined and balanced. In addition, many components are actually composed of several smaller pieces that must be carefully assembled. Sometimes this assembly is complicated and requires the creation of final assembly workshops. This in turn necessitates coordination among those responsible for each subcomponent.

Khan could not order these parts ready-made in KRL's workshops, and surplus P2 centrifuges did not exist. To supply the Libyan order, the centrifuge components had to be made outside Pakistan, a responsibility that fell to the Swiss Friedrich Tinner and his sons, Urs and Marco, "the Three Tinners." Khan had often visited the Tinner family at their home in Switzerland over the years and developed a high regard for Friedrich. He trusted this close-knit family to produce this essential part of the Libyan order.

To make many of the components, the Tinners used their family-owned companies, including PhiTec AG, Cemeq AG, and Traco Schweiz AG based in eastern Switzerland. Friedrich was the unchallenged patriarch of the family while Urs and Marco, known in intelligence circles as the "Brothers," carried out most of their family's contractual obligations. Friedrich's wife, daughter, and her husband, also worked in the family businesses, mostly involved in the more routine day-to-day operations of the companies.[55]

In 1998 or 1999, the Libyans received the two P1 test modules that Tinner had made in the early 1990s but which he could not sell to someone else. He also sent two larger modules that he manufactured under the new order. According to Swiss investigators, Tinner contracted for most of the items from other companies, who were oblivious of the true end use of the items.

Sometime in the mid to late 1990s, Urs and his younger brother Marco started playing a more central role in the Tinner family's day-to-day work on the Libyan contract, as well as operating family businesses in Switzerland and Dubai. Neither has a university education. Urs had difficulty in school and reportedly got into trouble with the law after leaving home. Nonetheless, he became a very skilled technician. His father asked him to go to the United Arab Emirates in 1998 to help with the family business. He settled in Ajman, next to Dubai, where he started running the family's overseas operations to supply Libya.

Marco was quiet and mentally quick. He studied electronics, but later developed expertise in financial management. Based in Switzerland, Marco focused on the deliveries and financial aspects for the family. He also served as an intermediary between suppliers and Khan. If a Swiss supplier had technical questions, he faxed Marco, who would in turn fax Khan for an answer, often using fake names and aliases.

Friedrich operated PhiTec, which sold engineering services, vacuum valves, and vacuum systems. Cemeq was a partner company of PhiTec. In addition to helping outfit Libya and Pakistan in the 1980s and early 1990s, Friedrich filled orders for the Iraqi gas centrifuge program. He even sold Iraq goods after it invaded Kuwait in direct violation of a U.N. Security Council embargo. According to Mahdi Obeidi, the former head of Iraq's gas centrifuge program, Tinner provided valves and piping for a fifty-machine cascade as part of its program to build nuclear weapons. Because of the embargo and the war, these items were detained in Jordan, where U.N. inspectors eventually discovered them. Since the items never reached Iraq, Friedrich was never prosecuted.

To order the parts for Libya, the Tinners received complete sets of centrifuge drawings and manufacturing manuals from Tahir.[56] Because modern machine tools are automatic, depending on computers programmed with precise instructions, digitized engineering drawings were needed. The Tinners digitized these drawings in order to produce computer-aided design (CAD) drawings, which were easier to alter (they erased any traces on the original drawings that could expose Pakistan or Khan as the source) and share among themselves and manufacturers. As they likely had an incomplete understanding of centrifuges, each time they changed a centrifuge drawing they sent the new drawing to Khan for approval.[57]

While the Tinners decided to make some of the centrifuge components in Switzerland, many of them could not be made there without undue risk of detection. An opportunity developed in Malaysia, a stable country without export controls and with a fast-growing high-tech sector, eager for business with the rest of the Muslim world.[58] Starting in the mid-1990s, Tahir cultivated social and business relations in Malaysia. When in late June 1998, he married the daughter of a former Malaysian diplomat in a lavish wedding, Khan, who often treated Tahir as a son, was an honored guest and a celebrity in the wake of Pakistan's nuclear tests just a month earlier.[59] Important members of the network, including Henk Slebos, Peter Griffin, and several senior KRL officials, also attended the wedding.

Tahir mixed with Malaysia's elite, growing close to Kamaluddin Abdullah, the son of future prime minister Abdullah Ahmad Badawi. Kamaluddin appointed Tahir a director of his privately held investment company. Later, Tahir's wife replaced her husband on the board. Kamaluddin's investment company in turn controlled the major share of Scomi Group, a respected Malaysian chemical, oil, and gas trading and manufacturing company poised to expand its business in Thailand, Myanmar, Qatar, and the UAE. Its chief executive officer was Shah Hakim Shahnazim Zai, Kamaluddin's school classmate and the other major shareholder and co-founder of Scomi Group. Tahir said Shah Hakim later helped him disguise payments from Libya to the network's contractors.

In the first half of 2001, Tahir brokered a two-year, $3.42 million contract with Scomi Group to manufacture fourteen centrifuge components. This contract represented at the time 26 percent of Scomi's total turnover; another 12 percent was with Malaysia's Ministry of Defense.[60] As Scomi did not have the facilities to make these components, it purchased a single-story, 33,000 square foot production facility in an industrial park in Shah Alam twelve miles southwest of Kuala Lumpur.[61] The company was initially called Prisma Wibawa Sdn. Bhd., before being renamed Scomi Precision Engineering Sdn. Bhd., or SCOPE for short, in December 2001. SCOPE's roughly thirty-person-strong workforce, under general manager Shamsul Bahrin bin Rukiban, was excited about the contract and optimistic that more work would follow this initial contract.

Urs moved to Malaysia in 2001 to help set up the workshop where he oversaw production of the components.[62] Tahir, who among Urs's contractors was nicknamed "sponsor," remained active in SCOPE, making key decisions about orders and authorizing payments. However, there was friction between Urs and Tahir, who treated Urs in a condescending manner.[63]

Urs procured high-precision machine tools for the new workshop by dealing with well-known European and Japanese suppliers.[64] Swiss export records show that Traco Schweiz sent SCOPE several pieces of manufacturing equipment in 2001 and 2002. The Japanese company Mitutoyo sold SCOPE six precision measurement machines, of which at least one ended up in Libya's gas centrifuge program.[65] Traco Schweiz's machines were used to cut and shape parts, while Mitutoyo's machines would measure the dimensions of a piece, ensuring it was acceptable to use in a centrifuge. (Japanese police arrested senior Mitutoyo officials in 2006 on suspicion of violating foreign trade control laws.)

To make the nonrotating components, Urs had to find a supplier of over one hundred thousand raw aluminum tubes and rods, or "preforms." Each piece corresponds in length and width to the finished centrifuge part. The high-precision machines would cut and shape these preforms into their finished form. Urs found a reliable aluminum supplier in Thorsten Heise, who had just established Bikar Metal Asia Pte Ltd, a Singapore subsidiary of the German metal dealer Bikar Metal. Urs believed that Bikar Metal would supply higher quality aluminum than Malaysian companies.[66]

In the fall of 2001, Rukiban and Urs, representing Prisma Wilbawa, signed a series of sales agreements worth over $1.5 million with Bikar Metal Asia for a large order of preforms. Many of the aluminum preforms came in lots of 10,100 pieces, corresponding closely to Libya's order of 10,000 centrifuges.[67] Bikar Metal Asia acquired these preforms from at least four companies—its German parent company, the Swiss sales agent Aluminum Silicon Mill Products (ASMP) representing the SUAL group of Russian aluminum producers, the Slovakian producer Impol, and an unknown Italian company.[68] Many of the shipments went to Singapore, some by airline but most by sea, and then were shipped by sea to Malaysia.

A company called KUMZ, a member of SUAL, sold SCOPE about 300 tonnes of aluminum tubes slated for the outer casings. The tubes, valued at about $1 million and Urs's single biggest purchase, traveled to Singapore and then to SCOPE during

2002.[69] The outer casing contains the rotor assembly, or the spinning parts of a centrifuge. Operating at speeds that exceed the speed of sound, a rotor that fails can explode into deadly shrapnel and must be surrounded by a nearly one-inch-thick casing wall to prevent injury to anyone nearby.

For arranging these orders, Urs wanted commissions from Bikar Metal, in essence getting paid twice: once for arranging the supply of raw materials for these parts, then again for putting the parts together. To funnel commission payments to Urs for his orders to Bikar Metal Asia, Urs and Thorston Heise together founded in an adjacent office the company Engineering-Trading-Asia-Consulting (ETAC).[70] Later, ETAC started to make parts of vacuum valves, even participating in a vacuum equipment sales exposition in Germany in 2004 and sharing a booth with PhiTec.[71]

After receiving the aluminum preforms, Urs used the digitized centrifuge drawings to program SCOPE's newly imported computerized machine tools. For security reasons, he removed any design information from the machine after the component was finished.[72] Each part had an ID number and underwent quality assurance to make sure that the part met the required standards.[73] The components were then carefully packed in boxes with a packing slip and sent to Libya via Dubai in four separate shipments from December 2002 to August 2003.[74]

Most of the aluminum is believed to have ended up in finished parts. However, questions remain about the fate of the unused preforms. About ten thousand pieces, or about 5 to 10 percent of the total, are unaccounted for. Were these leftover preforms destroyed by the network? Or did they end up in the hands of other customers?

Back in Switzerland, the Tinners were organizing the production of another thirty-two centrifuge subcomponents. The total order was valued at 3 million Swiss francs, or about $2.5 million at the time. The Tinners selected the Swiss firm Kirag, a machine workshop in Chur, to make most of these components. In late 2001 and early 2002, the Tinners arranged for Bikar Metal Asia to ship aluminum preforms to Kirag.

One major component made at Kirag was the motor housing. This part is in the bottom of the centrifuge and holds the motor that turns the centrifuge. Urs arranged for two shipments of about one thousand aluminum cylindrical preforms to Malaysia in November 2001. Subsequently, he ordered Bikar Metal Asia to send several more shipments with about eight thousand more aluminum cylindrical preforms directly to Kirag through April 2002.[75] The source of the aluminum was most likely Russia.[76] Bikar Metal sent invoices for these preforms, totaling about $270,000, to Marco at Traco Group International in Vaduz, Liechtenstein, a country with notoriously weak banking laws susceptible to exploitation by money launderers. Between late May and the end of July 2001, the network transferred a total of about $5 million via Malaysian financial institutions into Traco accounts held in Liechtenstein banks.[77] This was part of the money received to pay for the preforms and other costs associated with making the centrifuge components.

In the end, Kirag received enough preforms to make at least 9,600 motor housings. The first batch of 990 housings was ready for shipment in early 2002. The Tinners picked up the parts from Kirag and shipped them by truck to Istanbul, to Gunes Cire's company Tekno Elektrik Sayay ve Bicaret Lte, a subsidiary of ETI Elektronik. Six or seven more deliveries followed until

April 2004. Cire's company installed the motors it made into the housings, then transported the assembled components to Dubai, where they were declared as "transformers" on export documents and warehoused awaiting shipment to Libya.

Khan appointed Gotthard Lerch to make the feed and withdrawal system, which would ultimately net Lerch a profit of at least 3.5 million Euros, or almost $5 million at current exchange rates.[78] Lerch turned to Wisser (who didn't know the client was Libya until late 2001 or early 2002) to be the prime contractor responsible for procuring all necessary materials and for manufacturing the feed and withdrawal equipment for the enrichment plant.[79] Tahir provided Wisser with centrifuge drawings (some of which had Khan's signature), cascade designs, calculations on producing weapon-grade uranium, Pakistani data about the time necessary to produce a specified amount of weapon-grade uranium using P1 and P2 centrifuges, and information on converting weapon-grade uranium into nuclear weapon components.

Wisser appointed Meyer as his key manufacturer and assigned Geiges as the chief engineer of the project. To get sensitive equipment overseas, Meyer established a front company in Switzerland, buying vacuum pumps from the Spanish company Telstar and measuring equipment in Germany.[80] Wisser also involved Len Harvey, a consultant to Krisch Engineering, in initial designs of the feed and withdrawal system. Later, Harvey agreed to make specialized measurement equipment for use in these centrifuge cascades as Wisser and Geiges had both failed in their attempts to buy this equipment overseas.[81]

The feed and withdrawal system developed by Lerch and Khan was originally designed for P1 centrifuges, but could be modified for P2 centrifuges. Although P1 and P2 centrifuges are different, they have similar performance characteristics that allowed them to be used with the same feed and withdrawal system with straightforward modifications.[82] Any major changes in the original design required Khan's approval. For example, to compensate for being unable to bend stainless steel at Tradefin, Meyer requested some design changes in the piping, which Wisser sent to Dubai for approval. The changes were accepted although this modification meant that Libya would need to do considerably more welding during setup, further delaying the plant's start-up.[83]

Libya sent two engineers, identified only as Abdul and Ali, to inspect the feed and withdrawal systems at Tradefin. They appeared to have a comprehensive knowledge of gas centrifuges and evidently liked what they saw.

One of the preassembled P1 centrifuges was finally set up in 2000 at Al Hashan on the outskirts of Tripoli.[84] Libyan technicians then started to install three progressively larger cascades of P1 centrifuges. (None of the centrifuges enriched any uranium before Libya dismantled them in 2002.)[85] Fearful that the site would be discovered, Libya designed its centrifuge program to be mobile to lessen the chance of detection. Centrifuge buildings were also located far from Libya's declared nuclear research site at Tajura, outside Tripoli, where the IAEA would periodically inspect the Russian-supplied reactor located there. Qaddafi deliberately refused to sign the IAEA's Additional Protocol for fear that its more intrusive inspections would expose his secret centrifuge efforts. Under the Additional Protocol, the inspectors could more easily access Libyan sites and demand information if they had any suspicions of undeclared nuclear materials or facilities.

In 2000, as part of its switch to P2 centrifuges, Libya received two sample P2 centrifuges from Dubai.[86] These centrifuges were part of a set of as many as nine that network members received in Dubai slated for actual or potential customers.[87] Any good salesman would want to carry a sample of his wares as he visited customers, but no one had ever offered such samples to a customer—those which could assist in the building of a nuclear weapon production complex. Urs Tinner allegedly received two at the family-owned company Desert Electrical Equipment Factory in Dubai for shipment to Libya.[88] These centrifuges were not designed to become operational without undergoing additional manufacturing steps, but they contained all the necessary parts and provided a detailed look at this sophisticated and secret centrifuge.

After the network was discovered in 2003, network operatives told the IAEA that it destroyed four of these centrifuges to hide evidence, although the IAEA could not confirm their destruction. Up to three additional centrifuges may have remained in Dubai, but the IAEA could not locate them or confirm that they existed. In 1997, Iran may have received these three P2 centrifuges or other ones, although Iran denies this.[89]

By the time Khan finalized the Libya deal, he was lionized in Pakistan. His knack for self-promotion and publicity had already led many to think of him as single-handedly responsible for obtaining Pakistan's nuclear weapons. When Pakistan conducted its underground nuclear tests on May 28 and 30, 1998, Khan dropped his façade of humility. In the media and among the majority of Pakistani people, Khan became the undisputed "father" of Pakistan's nuclear bomb. To his biographer Zahid Malik, Khan was the "benefactor of Pakistan." Later, Khan called himself "second only to the founder of Pakistan, Mr. M.A. Jinnah."[90]

His personal website, not surprisingly, contains an appropriately modest biography: "It is rare that a person in [a] single life time accomplishes so much. This is done only by men who are endowed with special abilities by God."[91]

Khan shores up this god-like perception by seeking, whenever possible, to minimize the role of others in the creation of Pakistan's nuclear arsenal. In August 1998, he told the German journalist Egmont Koch that the process of creating a warhead required "no time, no money," implying that the only major contribution was the production of weapon-grade uranium.[92] Other contributions, many by those in the Pakistan Atomic Energy Commission, were critical in producing the centrifuge feed gas uranium hexafluoride and the nuclear weapon itself. Khan's relentless publicity machine, much of it paid for by Khan himself, led many Pakistanis to believe that Khan was a selfless, tireless worker who would never pass—let alone sell—nuclear secrets to other nations.[93] "We have not indulged in any proliferation," a stone-faced Khan told Koch. "We have not sent any scientists or engineers to any other country. If any Muslim country wants to [get nuclear weapons], they have to do it themselves. You cannot buy nuclear weapons; you cannot get nuclear weapons on a platter."[94]

The same year Khan gave the Koch interview, he took his first of up to five trips over the next four years to Africa. President Musharraf said part of the reason that Khan made these trips was to meet Libyan officials about the centrifuge deal.[95] But Khan might have used these trips to hide even more of his trafficking and proliferation.

On these trips, he was accompanied by an entourage of top aides, nuclear experts, and salesmen, including Slebos and Tahir.

They visited several countries, including Morocco, Mali, Sudan, and Niger. Three of these trips were chronicled by one of Khan's friends, the Pakistani accountant Abdul Mabood Siddiqui, in a little known book, *Timbuktu, City in the Middle of Nowhere.*[96] The book had only a limited English edition in Pakistan and is now hard to find. In the book, Siddiqui claims that all these trips by Khan were "vacations."

As innocent as their trips appear in Siddiqui's account, Khan, Tahir, and senior KRL personnel traveled so often that they could not possibly have been only on holiday.[97] They chartered airplanes, bought satellite phones, and were honored guests of several governments. On these travels, what hat did Khan wear—scientific advisor, government advisor, or smuggler? Were they just jet-setting? Or were they arranging black market deals under the cover of a vacation?

In the book, Siddiqui describes the group's fascination with the Islamic heritage of Timbuktu, Mali. This city was a center of a Muslim empire in the thirteenth through the fifteenth centuries that stretched from the Atlantic to current-day Nigeria. A center of finance, education, and culture, Timbuktu grew rich from straddling important trans-Saharan trade routes. Today it is a poor, desolate town with a mere fraction of the population it had in its heyday.

Despite this, Khan bought a small hotel there and named it after his wife. Hardly a typical place to make an investment, valued at $10 million, according to an assessment in an internal Pakistani government dossier.[98] After his arrest, Khan would disparage the property as barely more than a hovel, but in the late 1990s, Khan took the unusual step of ordering antique Pakistani furniture and flying it to this hotel in a Pakistani Air Force

C-130 aircraft. This same aircraft is suspected to have stopped in Libya and off-loaded centrifuge parts.

Siddiqui certainly appears to be naïve at best. He lived in Britain, earning his living as an accountant, and his son Abu Bakr Siddiqui, in partnership with Tahir, engaged in unlawful procurements for KRL. Abu Bakr was director of the British company Orland Europe Limited and diverted goods largely through the Dubai company Samu Machinery and Equipment.[99] He was arrested in July 1999 and convicted in 2000, but received a light sentence of one year, which was then suspended.[100] In correspondence about the orders he helped fill, Abu Bakr referred to Khan as Dr. Sahib, or D.S. One of the false end users for some of the shipments was the Peoples' Steel Mill, a company that often appeared as a KRL front.

Unlawful procurement might have been at the heart of their several trips to Sudan, ruled by the brutal dictator President General Omar Hassan El-Beshi.[101] During a trip in February 1999, Khan was joined by Tahir, Slebos, and Dr. Fakhrul Hasan Hashmi, Khan's second-in-command and the head of Peoples' Steel Mill. They flew first to Khartoum where the minister of education met them, and stayed in the State guest house. They then traveled to several other countries, including the usual visit to Timbuktu. After they returned to Khartoum, Khan and Hashmi met the president. During a later trip, the group, including Khan, Tahir, and Slebos, again stopped in Khartoum.

Were these trips related to Sudan's purchase from 1997 to 2001 of about half a billion dollars of high-tech, dual-use equipment from European and former Soviet Union suppliers, much of it routed through third countries to Sudan?[102] A portion of these goods, including some used in manufacturing missile parts, were so sophisticated that their use in Sudan was not plausible, and Sudan is suspected to have shipped these goods onward to other countries.[103] In the run-up to the 2003 Iraq war, many intelligence analysts believed that Iraq was the recipient of this equipment. However, none of it was found in Iraq after the fall of Baghdad. Nor was any of this equipment found in Libya.

Khan's many travels to Sudan, accompanied by procurement experts like Hashmi and Slebos, heightened suspicions that Khan arranged purchases of at least some of this equipment on the visits Siddiqui chronicled. Did Khan arrange the purchase of these goods for Pakistan, Iran, North Korea, or someone else? It remains unknown.

———————

UNTIL HIS HOUSE arrest in 2004, the Pakistani government aggressively defended Khan against criticism or prosecution from other countries. The government certainly defended and encouraged his illegal procurements for KRL and its remarkable network. The smuggling group inside KRL, called the Foreign Procurement Division (FPD), was enormously successful in outfitting KRL. FPD formed the basis of Khan's acquisitions for KRL, and that role continues today. Its success also laid the basis for Khan's export operation. To understand better how Khan's export operation worked, it is useful to examine the FPD and its overseas suppliers and middlemen.

To outfit all the factories at KRL, a small army of FPD procurement specialists under the leadership of the Pakistani Dr. Mohammed Farooq shopped around the world looking for essential equipment that could not be obtained in Pakistan. Because KRL was well known as a covert nuclear weapons site, few responsible countries would knowingly allow any exports there. As a result, FPD personnel had become masters at obtaining items without arousing suspicions among suppliers about their true end use.

Khan described his *modus operandi* in an interview with Egmont Koch: "If you want to buy a thing, you place the order directly and you get it. If you don't give me [the item] for one reason or another, I ask Tom, Dick or Harry [for] this item. Could you please buy it for me? Okay, no problem. It is a commercial deal. The guy buys from you. You are not willing to sell it to me, but you are willing to sell it to Tom. So, Tom buys from you. He takes ten or fifteen percent and he says to me that this is purely a business deal."[104] In response to Koch's challenge that this type of deal was illegal, Khan retorted, "Maybe in your eyes it is illegal."[105]

Khan knew many "Toms." Over the years, one of the most loyal was his friend Henk Slebos, the Dutch businessman who had worked with Khan since the mid-1970s. As a close confidant, he was a reliable supplier of a myriad of items for Pakistan's nuclear, missile, and other military programs. His main companies, Slebos Research and Bodmerhof B.V., routinely received requests for a wide variety of merchandise from KRL.

Sales records seized by Dutch investigators at Slebos's companies in the early 2000s provide a glimpse into that secret world. Ashraf Atta, a senior official at KRL, placed many orders, often signing them with his initials, A.A. When Slebos got a request from Khan, he listed him in these internal records under the alias "Peter."[106]

During the late 1990s and early 2000s, Slebos received hundreds of orders from FPD by fax, phone, or hand delivery, involving millions of dollars of goods and large markups for Slebos. To hide their true end use, Slebos sent the items and invoices to a number of KRL fronts. Sometimes, Slebos sent items to Belgrade where they could then be routed secretly to Pakistan or Dubai. If an export required an official end user statement, Slebos would seek to avoid delicate questions by finding a credible false end user in Pakistan or in more sensitive cases, a destination in a third country that would not arouse suspicion. Payments were routed through banks like the Pakistani Habib Bank Limited in Dubai to help hide their origin at KRL.

This system was not foolproof. On November 30, 1998, one of Slebos's companies, Bodmerhof B.V., received a faxed order from Atta for special devices used to make key measurements in gas centrifuge cascades. He asked the company to purchase these devices from the German subsidiary of the U.S. vacuum company MKS Instruments, which sold many such devices to URENCO each year. Slebos's chief assistant called the Dutch MKS subsidiary that same day, which immediately sent to Slebos Research a faxed offer for six devices. Slebos subsequently obtained six of the devices from MKS's subsidiary in Germany. The invoice from MKS clearly stated that the devices were subject to export controls if they left the European Union. Slebos ignored the warning. He even had MKS Germany send the equipment directly to the Dutch shipping company ACE Peterson, which promptly sent the devices by air to the KRL front Institute of Industrial Automation. MKS officials told investigators later that they were unaware that the export was intended for Pakistan. The case highlighted how easily a clever exporter could evade governmental controls within the European Union. In the end, Dutch authorities, tipped off by the United States, eventually prosecuted

Slebos successfully for this illegal sale. When finally convicted by a Dutch court in December 2005, Slebos received a few months' jail time and a relatively minor fine.

Slebos has not been directly incriminated in any sales to Libya or Iran. Nonetheless, he received some orders from FPD for centrifuge subcomponents that could have been for the Libyan or Iranian centrifuge program.

An FPD order in November 2000 asked Slebos to order 10,000 tiny steel balls from Team Industries near Stuttgart, Germany. FPD's selection of Team Industries was surprising. Team Industries had done business with KRL since the 1970s, but its former managing director, Ernest Piffl, had been sentenced in 1998 to three years in jail for illegally providing KRL with centrifuge subcomponents. As part of his defense, Piffl said that he was an informant for the German BND, and he had provided information about Pakistan's military procurement efforts.[107] Despite his defense, the prosecutor convinced the judge that any spying for the BND did not excuse his violations of German export laws.

Soon after the sentencing, Khan called Piffl's conviction hypocritical, claiming the German government "used him, then misused him."[108] Khan's defense of his longtime friend highlights how intelligence agencies were more interested in following the activities of Khan's accomplices, receiving information from them whenever possible, than in actually arresting the smugglers. A senior BND intelligence official with long experience tracking the Khan network said that when intelligence agents question smugglers like Piffl, they rarely provide more than a small part of the entire story. Often they limit their revelations to their competitors' activities while hiding their own. In some cases, smugglers deliberately keep in contact with intelligence agencies as a way to sense a possible prosecution. If an agent was unwilling to meet, or acted distant during a conversation, it could mean that a prosecution was imminent. Khan himself may have been aware of, or at least suspected, his smugglers' need to provide some information to intelligence agencies to keep them at bay. Piffl's spying served as a way to protect himself from the authorities and continue his lucrative sales to KRL, while revealing only a partial picture of Khan's true operations.

———————

QADDAFI HAD TAKEN his ambition of acquiring nuclear weapons as far as a despot can single-mindedly pursue an idea when, in 2003, he changed his mind. In exchange for the United States and Britain agreeing to end the domestic and international sanctions that were strangling Libya's economy, he abandoned his quest for nuclear weapons.

IAEA inspectors who examined all the evidence during the program's dismantling concluded that Libya was still about three to four years from starting the centrifuge plant when it ended its nuclear weapons program in late 2003.[109] Libya would have also needed to train more engineers and technicians to operate such a large centrifuge plant.[110] Despite several problems that would have likely delayed the start of the plant, the Khan network had created an impressive supply operation.[111]

One of the remaining mysteries was how Qaddafi was going to build nuclear weapons out of the highly enriched uranium. Libya said it had not started any weaponization work, a statement verified by the IAEA, but Matuq, the head of the weapons program, revealed that Khan had given them a set of nuclear weapon drawings and manuals in late 2001 or early 2002 during a meeting in Dubai. In that meeting, Khan told a senior Libyan official that when Libya was further along with enrichment, those documents could become very helpful.[112]

The designs provided were the same China had given Pakistan in the early 1980s. Although the documents did not appear to have come from Pakistan, they'd been transported in two white plastic shopping bags from Good Looks Tailor (whose Islamabad address was printed on the bags in red letters.) That tailor had made many safari suits for Khan in the past.[113]

The two white bags contained eight bound documents, each about fifty pages in length. Three of these bound packets were specifically about nuclear weapons. In addition, one bag contained a stack of about one hundred drawings and schematics, almost all of which were for weapon parts. The primary documents and all the drawings were in English. Many of the documents had the "samizdat" appearance of having been repeatedly photocopied. While Libyan officials claimed all the materials were relinquished and no other copies existed, the risk to international security was judged serious enough to fly the documents to Washington, where they are now securely stored.[114]

Khan has uncharacteristically downplayed his actions in Libya by saying that he had supplied them with "plans for a non-working nuclear device," but U.S. and British weapons experts judged the plans "very well engineered."[115]

As it turned out, Khan appeared to be willing to go a lot further than supplying technical blueprints and instruction manuals for the old Chinese designs. Khan laid down the basis for a second wave of assistance, a plan which only emerged in 2006 when the three Tinners were arrested and their computer hard drives seized.

Buried in these files was not only a digitized version of what Khan had handed over in that late 2001 or early 2002 Dubai meeting but also drawings for the components of two smaller, more advanced nuclear weapons. Although Pakistan developed its first miniaturized nuclear weapons from a Chinese-supplied design, its own scientists had gone further in designing several warheads that were lighter, smaller, and better able to fit on its ballistic missile. By 1990, Pakistan had developed "levitated" designs that compress the nuclear core more efficiently than a crude solid core design, such as the 1945 Trinity nuclear explosion.[116] A levitated design is analogous to swinging a hammer to hit a nail instead of setting the hammer on the nail and pushing it. This innovation allowed for a significantly smaller, lighter weapon. Khan might very well have turned over drawings from such designs to his network.

A senior IAEA official told the Pakistani government about what was found in Switzerland, and the response was genuine shock and dismay. What were on these computers were not secrets procured from other countries, but Pakistan's own secrets and innovations. Pakistan's national hero may have transferred his own country's most confidential and dangerous information for nothing more glorious than a profit. During subsequent questioning by Pakistani authorities, Khan acknowledged the existence of these drawings, saying he "may have had such stuff" in Dubai, but these advanced nuclear weapons designs could now have long since been sold off to some of the most treacherous regimes in the world.

What was Khan planning to do with these drawings? According to a senior official who saw them, the network looked like it was aiming to sell the finished drawings and manufacturing instructions. However, the plan might have gone further. It might have included selling the equipment and materials necessary to make the warhead itself. Such sales would be far more lucrative,

involving much larger contracts and commissions than just selling the designs.

The Tinners were scanning the drawings, turning them into
CAD schematics, and developing manufacturing instructions
for each part, according to the senior official. Missing in the set
of the more advanced drawings were those for high explosive
and uranium metal components. Other experts, likely Khan's
colleagues in the nuclear weapons program, would have had to
digitize these drawings and develop their manufacturing instructions. Their first customer was likely to be Libya. Once this package of drawings and instruction manuals was finished, however,
the network could have looked for other customers interested in
fitting nuclear warheads on ballistic missiles.

One of the more intractable legacies of the Khan network is
the ease with which digitized secret information about centrifuge
and nuclear weapons can be spread. The Internet is often erroneously cited in the media as a place where anyone can learn how to
build nuclear weapons. Considerable information about nuclear
weapons is online and the quantity of such information is growing, but it lacks additional design and experimental work that is
necessary on the part of the party attempting to build the device.
What's more, accurate and inaccurate information are often in-
termixed, with no easy way for a layman to distinguish between
them. Those behind the Iraqi nuclear weapons effort in the 1980s
independently checked any nuclear weapons data obtained from
open sources because as one Iraqi nuclear expert told me, he was
convinced intelligence agencies like the CIA were deliberately
putting bad information in the public domain to confuse those
seeking to build nuclear weapons.

On the black market, classified nuclear weapons designs might now be available to those who can afford to buy them, information that's far more dangerous than anything on the Web today. Complete nuclear weapons designs, manufacturing manuals, and detailed drawings of components might have slipped through the hands of law enforcement and intelligence personnel charged with rounding up members of the Khan network. It is no longer possible to know who might have this information or where they might obtain it in the future. A senior IAEA official doubted that the Tinners were the only ones who had the drawings found on their computers. Others were bound to have received the digitized information, he added, but who? And what would those clients do with the information? How can authorities recover these designs if they are not sure who has them? Could Iran or al Qaeda acquire these designs, or already have them in their possession? And could a setup like this be how North Korea got its start in the nuclear proliferation business?

SEVEN

North Korea

In 2002 North Korean officials were procuring equipment in Europe for an undisclosed site in Syria whose purpose was still unknown. Namchongang Trading Company (better known as NCG) headquartered in the Mangyong district of dreary Pyongyang, was seeking a component for a gas-cooled reactor that was intended for the site near the remote Syrian town of Al Kibar.[1] Unaware of these purchases in Europe, but aware of other suspicious NCG procurements, the German government issued a confidential early warning letter on North Korea to companies that manufactured sensitive equipment, listing NCG on its watch list of companies to avoid selling to. This letter contained a disturbing new item: "North Korean organizations are active purchasers for third countries."

The man behind NCG's purchases was Yun Ho Jin, a pleasant, former senior diplomat who was based in Vienna at North Korea's Mission to the IAEA throughout the 1980s and 1990s. His career shadowed North Korea's growing sophistication in unlawful nuclear trade.

While at the Vienna mission, Yun was part of North Korea's strategy to use its embassies and missions as bases to obtain

Western goods and technologies.[2] In the 1980s, the Korea Lyongaksan Import Corporation, headquartered in Pyongyang's Potonggang district, was a main importer for North Korea's military industries, disguising itself as an importer of civilian goods. Such foreign trade companies were crucial in circumnavigating long-standing sanctions on its nuclear and military industries.[3] Despite these sanctions, North Korea easily imported items for its military and nuclear programs. Yun organized North Korean trade delegations' visits to Europe to negotiate a range of purchases from German companies. Several of these purchases are believed to have ended up at the Yongbyon nuclear center, including the center's uranium fuel fabrication plant.

When not procuring items for North Korea's nuclear program, Yun was a diplomat who represented his country at the IAEA. He was at the center of heated discussions in 1992 and 1993 over charges that North Korea had secretly produced and separated more plutonium than it had declared to the IAEA.[4] Yun was North Korea's senior representative at a key IAEA board of governors meeting in February 1993 at which inspectors presented dramatic evidence, including high resolution U.S. spy satellite images showing North Korea disguising evidence of its secret nuclear activities at the Yongbyon site. He exploded after the presentation, denouncing the images as fakes and accusing the IAEA of acting illegally by using spy photos provided by a "third power."[5] As a way to ameliorate a year and a half of deteriorating relations between the United States and North Korea, the Clinton administration negotiated the 1994 Agreed Framework whose purpose was ultimately to end North Korea's nuclear weapons program in exchange for the provision of nuclear power reactors for civilian energy.

In 1994, Kim Jong Il had agreed to shut down his country's main nuclear reactor and its associated plutonium separation plant at the Yongbyon nuclear center, about two hours north from Pyongyang. The 1994 Agreed Framework capped North Korea's plutonium production before its engineers could build a nuclear arsenal. The agreement was negotiated by Ambassador Robert Gallucci, who in the 1970s and 1980s had fought hard to stop Khan's enrichment program. It was widely credited with suspending North Korea's nuclear weapons program and possibly averting a war on the Korean peninsula. However, the implementation of the agreement encountered numerous delays, and by 2001 many were frustrated with its slow pace. Overall, though, the agreement appeared to keep North Korea from producing more plutonium and building a nuclear arsenal that would threaten the United States and its allies South Korea and Japan.

Yun left Vienna in the mid to late 1990s; North Korea's diplomatic missions were under increasing scrutiny for signs of illicit procurements. When Yun started to work for NCG is unclear, but his activities there would be far less visible to foreign intelligence surveillance, and NCG agents were freer to contact suppliers and trading companies. Yun was still cautious, though. In a letter to a key German intermediary, who obtained over $1 million of equipment for NCG, he wrote: "I want to discuss certain matters with you by mail and not by phone. That is because letters are more reliable in a certain sense."[6]

By 2001, Yun was buying a range of items in Germany and other European countries. Yun sought out small private companies which placed orders for him from major suppliers. Through one small German company, Optronic GmbH in the Swabian town Königsbronn-Zang, Yun bought vacuum pumps, dial gauges, generators, gas masks, steel rotors and plates, and compressors, many of which were bound for North Korean military programs.

Suppliers sent the equipment either to NCG in Pyongyang, or if a North Korean destination worried a supplier, Shenyang Aircraft, a large Chinese operation which assembles fighter planes for the Chinese military. This company has cooperated with Airbus and Boeing, providing a civilian screen to any authorities that might raise questions. Conveniently, Shenyang had a subsidiary in the Chinese city of Dandong, which is linked to North Korea by the Friendship Bridge across the Yalu River. Unsurprisingly, Dandong was often just a transit point on the equipment's journey to North Korea.[7]

German authorities finally learned about NCG in September 2002. Yun had ordered aluminum tubes through Optronic. Its head, Hans Werner Truppel, approached German customs officials about whether he needed permission to export the tubes to NCG. Truppel was told not to export the tubes because of suspicions NCG was providing them to the North Korean nuclear program.[8] Despite this, Truppel exported the tubes anyway in April 2003. By the time the authorities found out, the tubes were on the French container ship *Ville de Virgo* bound for Dalian, a port in northwest China near North Korea. The owner of the ship was contacted, and he agreed to off-load the tubes at Alexandria, Egypt, where a special crew was waiting at the dock to ship the tubes back to Germany.[9] Meanwhile, Truppel had been arrested; in 2004, a Stuttgart court convicted him of violating export control laws, sentencing him to four years in prison.

Authorities showed the seized tubes to Horst Pütter, a centrifuge expert with long experience investigating secret gas centrifuge programs for the German government and the IAEA. He determined that these tubes appeared as if they would be used for outer casings of a P2 centrifuge. The dimensions of the tubes closely resembled the ones acquired by the Tinners for SCOPE in Malaysia. North Korea was undoubtedly working from P2 centrifuge designs provided by Khan. Documents seized during the official investigation showed that the North Koreans intended to acquire 220 tonnes of aluminum tubing from Truppel, enough for about 4,000 P2 centrifuges. During the same period, North Korea successfully obtained 150 tonnes of aluminum tubing (enough for 2,700 centrifuges) with these same dimensions through an unknown agent, possibly Yun, via a Russian company. Questions remain whether Khan network operatives had a role in this order.

In 2003, Yun disappeared from Germany, where he undoubtedly sensed the authorities were alert to his business. NCG, however, was still able to operate in Beijing's Chaoyang district, the city's prime commercial, entertainment, and shopping area, where more than eight thousand foreign companies were headquartered.[10]

NCG's *modus operandi* continues to be buying from other traders, who then buy items from suppliers. In China, it can effectively buy equipment from suppliers throughout the world, even Europe and possibly the United States, particularly if the suppliers have subsidiaries in China. When NCG buys an item from another company in China, the transaction can appear as a domestic sale. While NCG would then have to smuggle the item to its final destination, such as North Korea or Syria, controls in China against illicit exports have been easy to evade. Ironically, controls on exports to North Korea did tighten, at least for a few years. China cracked down and prevented many exports to North Korea several years ago, so many that Pyongyang formally complained to the Chinese government.[11] This crackdown did not stop NCG. Even international sanctions imposed on NCG by the U.N. Security Council in July 2009 might not lead Chinese authorities to stop exports by NCG, or whatever organization it will ultimately morph into. One European intelligence official who tracks NCG closely said that NCG was as active as ever and expressed frustration at China's failure to stop NCG's activities.

NCG, or persons associated with it, may also be operating in Myanmar, a country run by a military dictatorship that has in recent times strengthened its military ties to North Korea. Persons known to be from NCG have traveled to Myanmar to provide some type of technical assistance. Has Myanmar considered buying a reactor from North Korea? Several years ago, Myanmar tried to buy a nuclear reactor from Russia, but this project stalled, at least temporarily, due to international pressure and a high price tag. Or is Myanmar engaged in some other military or nuclear project? NCG's presence in Myanmar coincides with its receipt of a large amount of expensive, high-tech dual-use equipment from Germany, Japan, and Switzerland in 2006 and 2007. An analysis of the purchases by European intelligence services yielded that the equipment was multipurpose, running the gamut of possible uses from turbines in aircraft to nuclear. The declared purposes given to the European suppliers have many inconsistencies, and the equipment, some of which is extremely high-precision manufacturing machinery, is way beyond what intelligence analysts would expect to find in Myanmar. Adding to suspicions about Myanmar's actions, the head of that country's Department of

Atomic Energy was involved in these purchases under the auspices of a nonnuclear state educational department.

The fundamental question becomes: will North Korea stop its nuclear proliferation? As a source of proliferation, North Korea has nearly matched the Khan network. Michael Hayden, director of the CIA during the final round of six-party talks that ended with North Korea's temporary agreement to halt its nuclear weapons program, said: "North Korea asks only two things of its customers: first, can they pay, and second, can they keep a secret?"[12]

Khan, of course, was a natural person for North Korea to contact for help in overcoming its shortcomings in building centrifuges. There had been earlier reports from IAEA inspectors that North Korea was interested in gas centrifuges in the 1980s but had abandoned its effort because of technological limitations. In the autumn of 1993, second-time Pakistani Prime Minister Benazir Bhutto travelled to North Korea. With her were CDs, which she referred to later as "installments of computer disks" containing sensitive centrifuge data.[13] A key part of her 1993 visit was to negotiate with Kim Il Sung for missile assistance.[14] Khan had told Bhutto that Pakistan could get this much-needed missile technology from the Koreans if Pakistan assisted North Korea in developing centrifuges. The data on those disks was either a sweetener or intended as payment for missile technology. Publicly, however, Bhutto said that Pakistan paid for the missiles and did not obtain them in exchange for centrifuge assistance.

Pakistani President Pervez Musharraf revealed that Khan provided North Korea with nearly two dozen P1 and P2 centrifuges and measuring equipment that would permit trial enrichment.[15] A North Korean plane reportedly picked up the used centrifuges from Khan in 2000 after delivering missile components to KRL.[16] Musharraf confirmed that North Koreans were regular visitors to top-secret centrifuge facilities at the Khan Research Laboratories, receiving regular coaching on centrifuge technology.

In a December 10, 2003, letter from A.Q. Khan to his wife that aimed at defending his actions and was obtained by British journalist and Khan family confidant Simon Henderson, Khan states that he passed $3 million from the North Koreans to a senior Pakistani general, who had asked Khan to give drawings and centrifuges to the North Koreans. However, this letter reportedly omits key parts of this story, namely that North Korea had to pay off this Pakistani general, who wanted the money for a secret army fund, before he would authorize the payment of monies owed to North Korea for an earlier shipment of missile components to KRL's Ghauri missile project. A North Korean official approached Khan and said that North Korea would agree to pay this Pakistani general if they received help on uranium enrichment technology. It was in this context that this Pakistani general "approved" Khan's sending North Korea drawings and centrifuges.

Khan apparently did not need or seek approval when several years earlier he allowed North Koreans into Kahuta's two centrifuge-manufacturing workshops so that North Korean engineers could teach KRL technicians how to make missile components. Not surprisingly, the North Koreans became interested in centrifuge technology, and Khan did not stop these inquisitive engineers from spending considerable time in one of the workshops with a top Pakistani centrifuge expert, where construction of the most sensitive centrifuge components occurred and the P2 centrifuge underwent testing. Even Khan admitted that he knew that it was quite possible that this Pakistani expert explained details of centrifuges to the North Korean engineers.

In 2002, the Bush administration was confident that North Korea was undertaking a major expansion of its centrifuge program. In late October, Bush administration officials traveled to Pyongyang and accused North Korea of hiding a large-scale secret gas centrifuge program. Much of the evidence, as in the case of Iraq's alleged gas centrifuge plant that was then on the front pages, centered on the illicit procurement of aluminum tubes. According to a fact sheet distributed by the CIA to Congress on November 19, 2002, there was "clear evidence indicating North [Korea] has begun constructing a centrifuge facility." The CIA assessed that this plant could annually produce enough weapon-grade uranium for two or more nuclear weapons per year when it was finished and could be fully operational "as soon as mid-decade."[17]

It was not without some relish that this assessment was hyped as a means to attack the Agreed Framework, which many in the Bush administration deeply opposed. After being confronted with having a secret centrifuge program, North Korea at first waffled, suggesting that it might, or might not, have one. Later, North Korean officials in lockstep insisted that no such program existed, going so far as to deny receiving any centrifuges from Pakistan, and accusing Musharraf of lying, out of fear of the Bush administration.[18]

A tit-for-tat exchange ensued and by the end of 2002, the U.S.-North Korean Agreed Framework was in tatters. The collapse satisfied many in the Bush administration who thought that the deal merely rewarded the dictatorship in North Korea, but the result was that by the end of the year, the IAEA was forced to withdraw the last of its inspectors. North Korea proceeded to unfreeze its nuclear facilities, separate plutonium from irradiated fuel rods that had been under IAEA seal, build several nuclear weapons, and ultimately detonate an underground nuclear explosive in a test in October 2006.

Meanwhile, in a reversal reminiscent of the Bush administration's view of Iraqi WMDs, U.S. officials suddenly began to downplay the original assessment about the centrifuge plant. One former State Department official stated in 2004 that there were disagreements over the projected timetable for the centrifuge plant's completion. By November, a U.S. intelligence official said that the CIA is "not certain" a uranium enrichment plant exists. By 2007, many U.S. officials doubted the original CIA assessment about a large centrifuge plant under construction although few believed that North Korea had abandoned centrifuge development.[19] Yet this original preoccupation with an alleged North Korean centrifuge plant might have ironically helped blind U.S. intelligence to North Korea's growing nuclear proliferation efforts.

In the spring of 2004, Pakistan told the IAEA that North Korea was the source of 1.6 tonnes of uranium hexafluoride that the network sent Libya in February 2001 for use in centrifuges. A subsequent U.S. Department of Energy technical assessment concluded that North Korea had likely produced the uranium hexafluoride for Libya. This assessment included the detection of minute amounts of plutonium on the materials' shipping canister that Energy Department analysts linked to North Korea.

Over the next two years, the IAEA discovered several pieces of evidence that North Korea intended on becoming Libya's main supplier of uranium hexafluoride, in essence becoming a full-fledged state member of the Khan network. Lack of uranium hexafluoride was shaping up as a bottleneck in Khan's operation to provide Libya with a centrifuge plant and despite its best efforts Libya had failed to acquire its own facilities to make its own. In 1984, agents for Libya had bought a facility from the Japanese company Otsuka Iron Works that was needed to transform raw uranium most of the way into uranium hexafluoride gas.[20] Components for this facility were acquired from several other Japanese companies.[21] However, Libya failed to ultimately obtain critical equipment that would produce the finished uranium hexafluoride.

To run its centrifuge plant, Libya needed 30 to 40 tonnes of uranium hexafluoride each year. Libya told the IAEA that it planned to build its own plant to make uranium hexafluoride.[22] Yet it had become even more difficult to buy the key equipment for such a facility, casting doubt on Libya's ability to become self-sufficient.

As an interim step, Khan's network agreed to provide Libya with 20 tonnes of uranium hexafluoride.[23] The 1.6 tonnes of North Korean uranium hexafluoride already provided to Libya was part of this commitment. When confronted by IAEA investigators, Libya feigned ignorance of the uranium's origin in North Korea and denied cooperating with North Korea on nuclear technology (although they freely admitted cooperation on missiles).[24]

Some IAEA officials expressed skepticism that North Korea made the uranium hexafluoride.[25] They suggested that Khan could have diverted this amount of uranium hexafluoride from Pakistan's own nuclear program. Strict controls on Pakistani uranium hexafluoride would have made this unlikely. Khan's rival, the Pakistan Atomic Energy Commission (PAEC), made uranium hexafluoride, and many PAEC officials would have opposed Khan diverting the material. Further complicating such a transfer, Khan lost his position as head of KRL in the spring of

2001. President Musharraf, under increasing pressure from the United States, had not renewed Khan's contract, instead installing him as a special advisor with little authority to the prime minister. He thought Khan would be powerless to proliferate in this new position but later admitted he seriously underestimated Khan's ingenuity.[26]

Evidence soon emerged that Khan's network was helping outfit North Korea with equipment to produce uranium hexafluoride. Several years earlier, KRL had aided North Korea's effort to make sufficiently pure uranium hexafluoride. With North Korea interested in developing secret uranium conversion capabilities for its own gas centrifuge program, it may have decided to fund the construction of these conversion facilities by supplying uranium hexafluoride to Libya. In 2002, using Libyan funds, the network ordered "centrifuge-related equipment" and shipped it to North Korea.[27] Suspicion immediately arose that the equipment was to produce uranium hexafluoride for Libya.[28]

Another piece of evidence came from Pakistan, where it was learned that ten uranium hexafluoride transport canisters from the same batch as the one found in Libya had gone missing. Someone had transported them all out of Pakistan; the most likely destination was North Korea. Pakistan had purchased all these canisters for use in Khan's centrifuge program.[29] Khan and his associates might have sent these cylinders to North Korea to help them supply uranium hexafluoride to Libya.

Despite the evidence, the IAEA could not definitively determine the status of North Korea's uranium hexafluoride production capability or its relationship to the Khan network. North Korea continues to reject any such relationship. However, after the collapse of the six-party talks in 2009 that witnessed North Korea's launch of a long-range missile and another underground nuclear test, North Korea stopped denying it has a uranium enrichment program. In September 2009, North Korea announced that it had completed experimental enrichment and was entering into the "completion phase" without providing any details about its intentions. A European intelligence official noted that recently North Korea had illicitly purchased computerized machine tools to make centrifuge components. When it might finish, or even start, building a centrifuge plant is unknown. And given that intelligence agencies already assessed that North Korea at least had a centrifuge research and development program, North Korea's ambiguous announcement remains difficult to interpret.

North Korea remains committed to making deals that would result in much needed hard currency. It has often exported conventional weaponry and missiles to pariah nations but its clandestine efforts to help Syria build a nuclear reactor marked the first time it was willing to go beyond a straightforward "arms-for-cash" transaction. Because North Korea's proliferation networks remain largely unidentified, it remains unclear if North Korea was also supplying Syria with uranium fuel, the facilities to make the fuel, and a plutonium separation plant. Syria has likewise steadfastly denied that the site bombed by Israel in September 2007 was a nuclear reactor. Nevertheless, U.S. and Israeli intelligence communities identified the site as a gas-graphite reactor based on a North Korean design. Syria allowed IAEA inspectors to visit the site once in June 2008, where they found traces of natural uranium particles that could be associated with a nuclear reactor of the type found in North Korea.[30] However Syria, like Libya (before it renounced nuclear weapons), has refused to sign the Additional Protocol, making it difficult for the IAEA to come to any independent conclusions.

Construction of the Syrian reactor started in 2001. North Korea is believed to have provided reactor designs and expertise and reactor components, though their assistance fell short of providing a complete or "turnkey" facility, which is what Khan had promised to Libya. North Korea used its own trading companies, some with offshore offices, to illicitly buy items in one country for sale to Syria, in essence serving as smugglers for Syria's secret nuclear program. Syria also used its own smuggling networks to obtain some of the reactor components while both the United States and Israel pressured Russia and other civilian suppliers not to sell Syria a reactor. North Korea became a supplier of last resort.

Sometime between 2002 and 2003, Syria converted the shape of the building housing their reactor. Originally, the building was similar in appearance to the reactor building at Yongbyon. Then, Syrian engineers and architects went to astonishing lengths to conceal the building's true purpose.[31] The giveaway was a photo obtained by Israel that showed the top of the reactor core as it was undergoing construction in 2006. Its appearance was remarkably similar to a North Korean style reactor core. Another photo taken in Syria showed Ibrahim Othman, the head of Syria's Atomic Energy Commission, with a North Korean who the CIA believed was head of the Yongbyon fuel fabrication plant. IAEA inspectors knew this North Korean from their days of monitoring the Yongbyon facility in the 1990s. Was he selling Othman uranium fuel for the reactor or a fabrication plant to make the fuel? Or both?

Sifting through prior intelligence, the CIA pinpointed details it had unearthed in 2005 about Syria and North Korea being involved in a project in the province of Dayr az Zawr. An intensi-

fied satellite image search resulted in the discovery of a large unidentified building near the town of Al Kibar that appeared "odd
and in the middle of nowhere." U.S. intelligence analysts labeled
it an "enigma facility." Only with the Israeli pictures did the CIA
determine that the building was Syria's covert nuclear reactor.

Many other signs of nuclear cooperation were missed. Intelligence agencies were well aware that North Korea was providing
Syria with missile components and technologies. In pursuing its
sales, North Korea was known to disregard U.N. Security Council embargoes, as when it sold to Saddam Hussein's Iraq missile
components and conventional armaments. Yet these agencies
failed to appreciate that North Korean–Syrian nuclear cooperation stemmed from their cooperation over missile sales.

With hindsight, the CIA could finally make sense of some ambiguous information it had collected years earlier. Yet there's very
little room for hindsight when dealing with nuclear proliferation
among pariah nations. In fact, almost every organization that was
determined to get help with nuclear weapons and had contacted
Khan to do so eventually received it, one way or another.

All except one: al Qaeda.

EIGHT

Al Qaeda's Bomb

The image of Osama bin Laden discussing nuclear weapons around a campfire with two former senior Pakistani nuclear engineers is the stuff of movies. Yet it actually happened in August 2001, when A.Q. Khan's deal with Libya was in full swing.[1] Access to these Pakistani engineers was a major shortcut to possessing nuclear weapons. No one could dismiss the likelihood of nuclear terrorism again.

Bin Laden had thought seriously about acquiring nuclear weapons for many years. In the early 1990s, an al Qaeda agent unsuccessfully sought uranium in Sudan. In 1998, the year Pakistan tested its nuclear weapons, bin Laden declared that acquiring unconventional weapons was a religious duty.[2]

He apparently realized early in his quest that he would need help. In 1998, bin Laden's representatives approached the Khan network.[3] They tried at least three times, and each time were rebuffed.[4] A lack of funds might have been the reason, or resistance to share nuclear weapons expertise with terrorists who could be expected to use a nuclear weapon if they ever got one.

Bin Laden fared better with some of Khan's longtime rivals, Sultan Bashiruddin Mahmood and Chaudiri Abdul Majeed, two retired senior engineers at the Pakistan Atomic Energy Commission (PAEC) who were more willing to help bin Laden build nuclear weapons.

After retiring from the PAEC in 1999, Mahmood established Ummah Tameer-e-Nau (UTN), Reconstruction of the Muslim Ummah (community), a nongovernmental organization whose stated mission was to invest in industries and conduct relief work in Afghanistan. Majeed, who retired in 2000 from the PAEC's prestigious Pakistan Institute of Nuclear Science and Technology (PINSTECH), became one of UTN's key officials. UTN was also supported by Pakistani military officers who opposed President Musharraf and sympathized with the Taliban. One of the most important members was General Hamid Gul, former director of the Pakistani intelligence service, the Directorate of Inter-Services Intelligence (ISI). In Afghanistan, UTN was one of the few non-governmental organizations (NGOs) that had the approval of Mullah Omar, the Taliban head of Afghanistan.

In addition to its civil work, however, UTN had a darker side, providing a cover for helping al Qaeda build nuclear weapons and other weapons of mass destruction. UTN had global ambitions to spread nuclear technology. It approached the Libyans with an offer to provide nuclear as well as chemical and biological weapons assistance.[5] Yet Libya had little need of UTN's help because Khan was already providing much more than UTN could offer.

Mahmood, a fundamentalist, had even less compunction than Khan about proliferation, believing that spreading nuclear technology to other Muslim countries was his duty and viewing Pakistan's nuclear capability as "the property of a whole Ummah."[6] Conversely, Khan is not typically viewed as a fundamentalist, but his support is strongest among them. Pervez Hoodbhoy, professor of physics at Islamabad's Quaid-e-Azam University and a long-time Khan observer, said that Pakistani fundamentalists continue to "view Islam and the bomb together."[7] He added, "Their belief system revolves about Islam and Pakistan being besieged by powers outside, Israel and the United States. It's that paranoid mindset." Mahmood internalized this mindset; Khan was merely interested in exploiting it for profit.

Mahmood was an early recruit to Pakistan's nuclear weapons program. His son recounted that his father wept after India conducted its nuclear test in 1974 and vowed to make Pakistan an atomic power.[8] A few months after India's test, at a nuclear scientists' meeting called by President Zulfikar Ali Bhutto, Mahmood argued strenuously in favor of building nuclear weapons and recommended buying necessary items illicitly overseas.

In 1974, at age thirty-three, Mahmood became the first head of Pakistan's secret gas centrifuge program that was created to exploit Khan's ongoing espionage in the Netherlands. He played a pioneering role in establishing Pakistan's gas centrifuge project, including its focus on unlawful procurement, but he lost his job after Khan returned from the Netherlands and was pushed out in the summer of 1975.[9] Since he was determined to have Mahmood's job, Khan was a vocal critic of Mahmood's early leadership of the gas centrifuge program.

Mahmood's professional career continued, and his resume grew, like that of any accomplished nuclear engineer. He held many senior positions and became a successful nuclear project manager in a country at a tremendous technological disadvantage. Mahmood received several awards for his work in the nuclear program, including a gold medal from the Pakistan Academy of Sciences. He was elected president of the Academy in 1997, and in March 1999 was awarded the prestigious Sitara-e-Imtiaz award by the president of Pakistan, Muhammad Tarar, for his outstanding contributions to Pakistan's nuclear program. Yet his most prestigious assignment was designing and directing the first Khushab nuclear reactor, which went "critical" in April 1998.[10] This covert reactor project depended extensively on illicit overseas procurement. It can make enough weapon-grade plutonium for about two fission nuclear weapons each year. However, Pakistan has plenty of weapon-grade uranium to make fission weapons. With the operation of the Khushab reactor, and its ability to produce weapon-grade plutonium, Pakistan had, according to Mahmood, "acquired the capability to produce boosted thermonuclear weapons and hydrogen bombs."[11]

While Mahmood had a sterling list of accomplishments and contacts among Pakistani nuclear experts that any terrorist organization would be thrilled to exploit, he also had a bizarre fascination with the occult, writing a series of controversial apocalyptic reports based on pseudo-science and fundamentalism. In 1987, he published *Doomsday and Life After Death—The Ultimate Fate of the Universe as Seen Through the Holy Quran*, a 232-page treatise based on Islamic teachings. In one chapter Mahmood seeks to explain scientifically how the world will end and theorizes that his "scientific mind can work backward and analyze the actual mechanism . . . of the great upheaval before the Earth's Doomsday." In *Cosmology and Human Destiny*, published in 1998, Mahmood argued that sunspot activity has influenced human behavior and historical events, such as the French Revolution, the Russian Revolution, and World War II.[12] He concluded that governments across the world "are already being subjected to great emotional aggression under the catalytic effect of the abnormally high sunspot activity under which they are most likely to adapt aggression as the natural solution for their problems."[13]

Mahmood was inspired by Dr. Israr Ahmad, a prominent pro-Taliban radical Islamic cleric who became a patron of UTN.[14] From his headquarters in Lahore, Ahmad advocated the creation of a "true Islamic state." He believed that Pakistan and Afghanistan were the only two countries that had the potential to become the starting point for the global ascendancy of Islam, advocating their union to lay the foundations of a model Islamic system.[15] Since he argued that Pakistan's nuclear capability does not belong to only one country, but is actually the collective trust of the entire Muslim Ummah, Ahmad believes that in the event of U.S. military or economic sanctions, Pakistan should provide Muslim countries access to Pakistan's nuclear technologies in exchange for funds needed for national development.[16]

Mahmood was also a vocal critic of Pakistan constraining its nuclear arsenal, strongly opposing the signing of the Comprehensive Test Ban Treaty (CTBT).[17] In March 1999, Pakistan's intelligence agency recommended his transfer from the sensitive position of the director of the Khushab reactor to a desk job, sparking Mahmood's resignation.[18]

Less is known about Chaudiri Abdul Majeed's motivations for working with UTN. A former artillery officer, Majeed worked at PINSTECH, the premier scientific research and development center of the Pakistan Atomic Energy Commission. His nuclear competence appears more specialized than Mahmood's and might include expertise in plutonium separation—a vital step in producing weapon-grade plutonium for a nuclear weapon.

Soon after 9/11, the CIA learned of UTN's help to bin Laden from a friendly intelligence service.[19] Acting on an American request, on October 23, 2001 Pakistani authorities detained Mahmood and Majeed for questioning. They also detained all seven members of UTN's board of directors including Mirza Yusef Baig, an industrialist with the largest foundry in Pakistan and extensive ties with the Taliban regime.[20] Other members of UTN's board were retired military officers or engineers.

Many Pakistani officials, not surprisingly, tried to downplay what information Mahmood and Majeed could have provided to al Qaeda. The interrogations were largely ineffective. In late November 2001, CIA director George Tenet told President Musharraf that Pakistan's experts were wrong about how difficult it would be for al Qaeda to build nuclear weapons. He demanded a crackdown on the UTN scientists and "certain elements of the Pakistani military and intelligence establishment" that he said supported UTN.[21] President Musharraf had little choice but to act on the growing U.S. concern about UTN and nuclear terrorism.

This time, Pakistani interrogators (with American assistance) got their confessions. Searches in Afghanistan discovered disturbing evidence of UTN's and al Qaeda's work on weapons of mass destruction. After the fall of Kabul on November 13, 2001, the CIA searched UTN offices and houses looking for documentary evidence of its secret WMD work. The searches of UTN houses, located in Kabul's wealthiest suburb, revealed that while UTN did conduct charitable activities as claimed, they were also working on obtaining WMDs.

The U.S. government has released little information about UTN's activities in Afghanistan. However, Ingrid Arnesen, a seasoned CNN producer who arrived in Kabul soon after the Taliban withdrew from the city, visited several houses and offices linked to UTN and al Qaeda based on information provided in part by the Afghan police. These houses' inhabitants had fled, but in their haste many had left behind caches of documents.

Arnesen found documents and drawings showing work on biological weapons, including a series of illustrations scrawled over a white board in UTN's headquarters in Kabul that appeared to show plans to use high-altitude balloons to spread anthrax spores or cyanide.[22] These plans were evidently a reaction to Mahmood's false claims that the Northern Alliance had attacked Taliban soldiers with chemical and biological weapons supplied by the United States.[23]

Arnesen and her CNN crew were taken by Afghani police to a safe house in an upscale neighborhood known as Wazir Akbar Khan. Neighbors told CNN that "big Arabs" lived there. One of them was a member of al Qaeda known as Abu Khabbab al-Masri, an Egyptian expert in WMD and conventional explosives. At this house, which the Arabs had likewise fled in haste, CNN found a nuclear document titled *Superbomb* and a number of documents on making conventional explosives from easy-to-obtain ingredients.

Arnesen could tell with the help of her translator that the twenty-five-page *Superbomb* document, handwritten in Arabic, was an elementary primer on nuclear weapons. The text exhibits an understanding of basic nuclear physics and chemistry but lacks familiarity with nuclear weapons' design and manufacture, describing the complicated process of laser enrichment as a "simple" method to pursue, and presents several properties of plutonium and uranium but does not discuss the production of weapon components out of these materials.

Moreover, the document had errors. For instance, a hand-drawn diagram of a nuclear explosive appears unworkable. The crudeness of this schematic is difficult to understand when accurate schematics of fission weapons are easy to find online. Al Qaeda has searched the Web, too; a torn, partial document found at an al Qaeda safe house in Kabul was printed from a website discussing nuclear and thermonuclear weapons. While the bizarre site mentioned nuclear weapons, it also discussed the phony elements Jupiternium, Saturium, and Marisum. On an edge of the document underneath the fake elements, the word "bullshit" was written in Arabic.

The United States identified the Egyptian chemical engineer and explosive expert Mohammed Abdel al-Aziz al-Masri as a key figure in al Qaeda's nuclear weapons effort. Following Khalid Sheikh Mohammed's capture in Pakistan in 2003, Mohammed named Abdel al-Aziz al-Masri as the "nuclear CEO" of al Qaeda.[24] After Kabul fell, al-Masri fled to Iran, where he was placed under a loose form of house arrest. A senior al Qaeda operative told the CIA that Abdel al-Masri conducted experiments with explosives to test the effects of producing a nuclear yield.[25] These experiments were likely rudimentary ones in using high explosives to implode an object.[26] Such experiments are necessary for building an implosion type nuclear weapon out of plutonium or highly enriched uranium. An implosion design is complicated to master and would require an extensive, time-consuming effort. While al Qaeda invested considerable resources into developing its explosive capabilities, its nuclear program might have started only a year before the fall of Kabul.[27] Nonetheless, according to the after-action assessment by the Commission on the Intelligence Capabilities of the United States Regarding Weapons of Mass Destruction, the intelligence community underestimated al Qaeda's fast-growing unconventional weapons capabilities and aggressive intentions.[28] Documents found and detainees interviewed after Kabul's fall in 2001 demonstrated that al Qaeda had a "major biological effort" and had made "meaningful progress on its nuclear agenda."[29]

As a major force in Afghanistan, organizing a range of commercial projects that would draw upon the private and governmental resources of Pakistan, UTN was well suited to help al Qaeda make progress on its nuclear agenda. With offices in Kabul, Lahore, and Islamabad, UTN was growing into a large organization. In conjunction with the Baracat Islami Investment General Trading and Contracting Co. Ltd. (BTC), a suspected al Qaeda money laundering front company, UTN and BTC had drafted a memorandum of understanding to establish a close working relationship to promote the relief, rehabilitation, and reconstruction of Afghanistan.[30] The memorandum was signed at Kabul on May 15, 2001, by Ghali Atia Alshamri, president of BTC, and Mahmood himself. They agreed to establish joint projects and to share all their financial, technical, and human resources in all disciplines such as commerce and industry, agriculture, banking and finance, health education, social welfare, communications, energy, minerals and mining, and research and development. Mahmood was so confident about UTN's potential that one day before his arrest in October 2001, he bragged that if the United States had not attacked Afghanistan, the country would have developed, with his help, into a strong industrial country during the next ten years.[31]

Many of UTN's commercial projects needed large loans from investors and the Pakistani government. UTN's strategy was to obtain permission from the Taliban regime for a project and then seek a loan to fund the initial stage of construction. Local companies would use materials and equipment imported from or through Pakistan. In return for finishing the first stage, Afghanistan would furnish UTN with cash and minerals that could be easily sold. After selling the bartered commodities, UTN would furnish another payment to the local companies for the next stage, and so on, until the project was completed. Mahmood referred to this approach as "investment recycling." Such an investment strategy is consistent with Islamic economic principles advocated by UTN that oppose the charging of interest on loans. Revenues earned from the sale of the commodities would also be used to cover UTN's costs. After paying back the initial investments, any surplus revenues would represent profit for the investing parties. UTN was certainly not opposed to seeking large profits for itself and its investors.

As it grew more successful, UTN was also growing more dependent on the Taliban regime and indirectly on al Qaeda for the approval of its commercial projects.[32] Mahmood and Majeed reportedly told their interrogators that Pakistan's intelligence agency had sanctioned both their charity activities and their meetings with Mullah Omar.[33] UTN's growing dependence on the Afghan government would have made it increasingly difficult for Mahmood and his associates to say no to Taliban or al Qaeda requests for nuclear assistance, but given Mahmood's pro-Taliban views, he was inclined to help in any case.

Over two or three days in August 2001, Mahmood and Majeed had long discussions with Osama bin Laden, Ayman al-Zawahiri, and two other al Qaeda officials about the development of weapons of mass destruction, providing detailed responses to bin Laden's technical questions about the manufacture of nuclear weapons.[34]

Mahmood and Majeed described bin Laden as intensely interested not only in nuclear, but in chemical and biological weapons.[35] Mahmood provided information about the infrastructure needed for a nuclear weapon program and the effects of nuclear weapons (which led the CIA to derisively refer to Mahmood as "bin Laden's nuclear secretary.")[36] One senior al Qaeda operative shared his ideas of constructing a simple firing system for a weapon using commercially available supplies and in response Mahmood provided a rough hand-drawn bomb design.[37]

Al Qaeda also wanted Mahmood and Majeed to help with making radiological dispersal devices (RDDs), or "dirty bombs." Farhatullah Babar, who had known Mahmood for many years and was a media advisor to the Pakistan Peoples' Party, said U.S. interrogators were unable to prove that work on a RDD progressed much beyond an agreement in principle.[38] Babar added that Mahmood would have been willing to make a RDD, but the September 11 attacks ended all their plans, this in spite of the fact that a senior Pakistani intelligence official described both scientists as "very motivated."[39]

Mahmood and Majeed were not the only Pakistani scientists in contact with the Taliban and al Qaeda. Several other Pakistani nuclear scientists were contacted by representatives of the Taliban government and al Qaeda seeking assistance to create a nuclear program inside Afghanistan. Out of those, two unnamed Pakistani scientists who were veterans of Pakistan's nuclear weapons complex and associates of Mahmood and Majeed were amenable to al Qaeda's overtures (one of the two was already under suspicion for trying to sell weapon designs).[40]

Although President Musharraf detained many UTN officials for questioning, often at the request of the United States, he limited the ability of U.S. interrogators to question them. Pakistani officials accused the United States of using these interrogations to learn secrets about Pakistan's nuclear weapons program. Behind the scenes, these interrogations unsettled the leaders of Pakistan's nuclear weapons program. For the first time, concern over the potential threat of losing classified secrets because of the actions of Pakistanis employed in the nuclear programs superseded concern over Indian or Israeli attack or sabotage.

In response, the government implemented systematic checks to ensure its nuclear scientists were reliable. This tougher stance didn't apply to Mahmood and Majeed.[41] Pakistan announced in late January 2002 that it would not press criminal charges against them. They were released from detention and put under house arrest with a limit placed on their communications (code language for being forbidden to talk to the media or other governments).[42] Musharraf's tepid punishment against Mahmood and Majeed furthered doubts that Pakistan had truly fixed its massive security breach.

There is little doubt that if Musharraf had not joined the United States in fighting al Qaeda, UTN officials would have probably provided extensive and ongoing assistance to nuclear efforts in Afghanistan. UTN's civilian projects could have served as a front for illicit procurement of items from Pakistan or other states with inadequate or nonexistent controls. Under the cover of civil industries, medical facilities, and universities, UTN or al Qaeda agents could pose as legitimate buyers. They could connect with suppliers and transnational smuggling networks unlikely to sell overtly to terrorists but willing to break or exploit loopholes in the U.N. embargo on Afghanistan. Much of this assistance would have occurred in secret and could have transformed al Qaeda's primitive nuclear effort into a much more serious threat.

Shielded by the Taliban government, al Qaeda would have been able to create secure bases of operation to seek plutonium or highly enriched uranium, conduct secret, long-term research and development work on nuclear weapons, along with building crude facilities to both make and test nuclear weapons components. Al Qaeda was well positioned to create a smuggling network to seek nuclear explosive material and key dual-use items for producing nuclear weapons. Al Qaeda's activities in Afghanistan demonstrate that a subnational group operating relatively freely within a weak, nonindustrialized state could, with determination and patience, develop its own nuclear weapons program.

A central lesson of Afghanistan is that nuclear terrorism is possible even in the most remote locations. According to Rolf Mowatt-Larssen, former director of the Office of Intelligence and Counterintelligence at the Department of Energy and former head of the Central Intelligence Agency's WMD and terrorism efforts, "There was an assumption within the intelligence community that nuclear material was too hard to acquire and that even if they had material, nuclear weapons are too sophisticated to be built without an industrial complex supporting the effort."[43] Easing its task, he added, a terrorist group does not need the "surety and consistency" that a state desires as its weapon can be far less safe and reliable, forgoing certain hard-to-make components that would give a state pause.

Few believe that a terrorist group has a nuclear weapon today or that acquiring one would be easy. However, nothing suggests that al Qaeda or similar groups have given up on their hopes to attack the United States or its allies with a nuclear weapon. In May 2003, al Qaeda obtained a *fatwa* from a radical cleric that approved the use of WMD against civilians if they are killed during an attack aimed at defeating an enemy. Al Qaeda spokesman Suleiman Abu Ghaith said that al Qaeda had the right to kill four million Americans, including one million children, in retaliation for Muslim deaths that al Qaeda blames on the United States. Abu Ayyub al-Masri, the leader of al Qaeda in Iraq, issued a public call for help in September 2006 from "people of distinguished skills and high levels of expertise, particularly nuclear scientists and explosives engineers."[44]

Over time, the chance of al Qaeda succeeding in recruiting experts is almost certain to increase. One place they could come from is Pakistan. Richard Holbrooke, special U.S. advisor to Pakistan and Afghanistan, warned in September 2009 that al Qaeda was publicly asking nuclear engineers to provide Pakistan's nuclear secrets. There remain Pakistani nuclear scientists and engineers with radical views who could be open to helping al Qaeda or another terrorist group build nuclear weapons. Pakistani government officials regularly state that no Pakistani scientists could now leak sensitive information, but how can we have confidence that they would know a breach had taken place? Even today, U.S. intelligence officials believe Pakistan's vital nuclear technology is not as secure as its government wants us to believe.

Theft and smuggling of nuclear explosive materials by terrorist groups remain a deep concern. The IAEA's head, Mohamed El Baradei, said in 2004, "We are actually having a race against time which I don't think we can afford. The danger is so imminent not only with regard to countries acquiring nuclear weapons but also terrorists getting their hands on uranium or plutonium."[45] So far, the IAEA has confirmed about fifteen incidents of theft and smuggling of plutonium and highly enriched uranium.[46] These cases involve relatively small amounts of material, typically by smugglers with material, or access to material, but no buyers. Yet according to Charles Allen, former undersecretary for intelligence and analysis at the U.S. Department of Homeland Security, these cases also suggest that "an organized trafficker with access to both materials and qualified buyers might escape detection."[47] His comment implies what many already believe—some nuclear explosive material is already missing.

A nuclear weapon requires just fractions of a percentage of the huge quantities of weapons-usable plutonium and highly enriched uranium stored or transported around the world.[48] Russia possesses hundreds of thousands of kilograms of nuclear weapons–usable materials as does the United States. Europe and Japan at any one time have almost 150,000 kilograms of weapons-usable plutonium in their civilian nuclear industries. China has about 30,000 kilograms. India has almost 2,000 kilograms and Pakistan has well over 1,000 kilograms.[49] Over the next fifteen years, hundreds of thousands of kilograms of weapons-usable plutonium are slated for transport on the world's highways and sea lanes. With such large quantities dispersed through so many parts of the world, protecting this material is vital to stopping nuclear terrorism.

A breakthrough in learning to make an implosion-type nuclear weapon could stimulate a terrorist group to more aggressively seek nuclear explosive materials. This type of crude nuclear explosive is very difficult to make, but from a materials standpoint, an implosion type has advantages for a terrorist group compared to the simpler-to-make gun-type device. First, an implosion device can use all nuclear explosive materials, including plutonium and highly enriched uranium, rather than just highly enriched uranium (or the rare element neptunium) as in the gun-type. Second, an implosion-type device needs far less highly enriched uranium than a gun-type. An implosion weapon needs less than 6 kilograms of plutonium or 20 kilograms of weapon-grade uranium. In contrast, a gun-type device requires about 50 kilograms of weapon-grade uranium.

Another consideration is that terrorist groups devote considerable resources to training explosives experts, a focus that gives them a considerable advantage in building a nuclear weapon. Abdel al-Aziz al-Masri showed that a terrorist group can work on developing the ability to set off a nuclear explosive with high explosives under crude conditions. Achieving a capability to implode a nuclear core with high explosives might represent an ominous threshold at which point a terrorist group feels it can actually succeed in detonating a nuclear explosive, particularly if it has a recipe for a nuclear weapon. It might find innovative ways to ease its task of building a nuclear device, sacrificing the size of the nuclear explosive yield or the device's reliability and safety.

Despite the improvements in intelligence since 2001, terrorist work on nuclear weapons is incredibly difficult to discover. The head of the Department of Energy's intelligence office, Rolf Mowatt-Larssen, stated in Congressional testimony in April 2008, "The task for the intelligence community is not easy. We must find something that is tactical in size but strategic in impact. We must stop something from happening that we have never seen happen before."[50] Beyond some basics, he added, "We do not know what a terrorist nuclear plot might look like."

Mowatt-Larssen warns, "In the early years of the twenty-first century, we will likely be tested in our ability to prevent non-state efforts to develop and detonate a nuclear weapon."[51] Stopping terrorists from detonating a nuclear explosive is a crucial challenge. Mahmood and Majeed represent a true nightmare, but they should also be an urgent wake-up call.

Uncovering Iran's Illicit Gas Centrifuge Program

A round 2001, Iran was ready to greatly expand its centrifuge program. Its successful nuclear smuggling combined with its own progress on developing the P1 centrifuge had brought it to a critical stage. The Atomic Energy Organization of Iran (AEOI) secretly ordered ten thousand P1 centrifuges from its centrifuge manufacturing complex and started construction of a vast underground complex near the town of Natanz to house those centrifuges. This decision, to move ahead with centrifuge enrichment, put Iran squarely on the path toward possessing nuclear weapons. A nuclear armed Iran could threaten Israel's existence, bully its neighbors, set off a regional arms race, and establish itself as an untouchable regional hegemon. It could also place it on a path toward nuclear confrontation with the United States. So how was it that its plans were temporarily but significantly derailed not by military force, but by weapons inspectors?

Iran's progress, along with Pakistan's vital assistance, was exposed by the International Atomic Energy Agency (IAEA). Its inspectors took the initiative to confront the powerful Iranian regime and prevail. The IAEA's victory demonstrated the value of having nuclear inspectors empowered with robust investigatory capabilities inside a country, a "boots on the ground" approach that focused on peacefully uncovering secret nuclear sites and those who assist them.

The story starts in the late 1990s. Iran, and especially its nuclear program, has always ranked as a "hard target" for intelligence gatherers who have found the autocratic state difficult to penetrate. Those responsible for Iran's nuclear program took great precautions to keep its progress secret. The centrifuge program was initially operated by a subsidiary of the AEOI called the Kalaye (which in Persian means "goods") Electric Company.[1] The AEOI bought Kalaye, once a watch factory, and kept the company's innocuous name. This facility, a stretch of unremarkable looking buildings on an alley off a main road out of northern Tehran, was ideal for concealing Kalaye Electric's new activities from U.S. spy satellites. Once the facility opened in 1997, Iran's centrifuge program continued to make steady progress. It was here that Iran first enriched uranium in its centrifuges and gained the expertise to scale up its operations at Natanz.

One of the first signs that the Natanz facility was being built was the excavation of a huge seventy-foot-deep hole. At one point during construction, this site required almost all the cement produced in Iran.[2] The Natanz main enrichment halls were constructed underground, covered by about twenty-five feet of soil, concrete, and cement. No other gas centrifuge program in the world can boast of such an arrangement and for good reason. Iranian defense planners knew that the site's discovery would alarm the international community and perhaps spark an Israeli military strike.

The IAEA knew Iran had a gas centrifuge program but was

unsure about its current status or its location. In either 2000 or 2001, safeguards inspectors obtained an old order from Masud Naraghi in the late 1980s for fifty molecular pumps for P1 centrifuges. Senior inspectors viewed this information as a dramatic confirmation that Iran was hiding a centrifuge program, but the procurement order did not list any locations of Iranian centrifuge facilities. Without that information it was difficult for the IAEA to confront Iran. Naraghi had purchased the parts in the name of an Iranian company, Kavosh Yar, in Tehran, which was certainly not where the order was headed. Kavosh Yar is a large company involved in a broad range of activities, including nonsensitive sales of nuclear equipment. The German company Leybold had approached German authorities for approval of the export, unaware themselves about the real nature of the parts. Government officials did not know then that Kavosh Yar was also a front for the growing Iranian centrifuge program and approved the export.

Any uncertainty came to an end when the National Council of Resistance of Iran (NCRI) called a press conference in Washington, D.C., on August 14, 2002, and publicly identified two secret Iranian nuclear sites near the cities of Natanz and Arak.[3] Initially the media coverage was limited. NCRI was affiliated with the Mujahideen-e-Khalq based in Iraq, an Islamic-Marxist insurgent group with cult-like overtones that is reviled by the Iranian regime and considered a terrorist group by the U.S. government. It had disseminated inaccurate information about Iran before. This time, their information was correct, and their revelations started a chain of events that led to an international outcry.

Olli Heinonen, who had recently taken over the IAEA's Iran portfolio, immediately suspected Natanz as being the gas centrifuge site his inspectors had struggled to locate for several years. Several months earlier, the IAEA had received information from the United States on the precise geographical coordinates of the two suspect locations at Natanz and Arak but the information did not conclusively point to a centrifuge plant.[4] After NCRI's revelations, the IAEA's analysis depended on both a process of elimination and U.S. intelligence in order to conclude that Natanz was most likely an enrichment site.[5]

Iranian officials never denied having an enrichment program, though when asked by the IAEA during informal meetings in Vienna in the summer of 2002, they likewise never volunteered the location of any enrichment plants or admitted that one existed.[6] Iranian officials usually confined their remarks to plans to build a wide variety of fuel cycle facilities.[7]

Despite the new analysis, the IAEA did not believe it had enough information to accuse the Iranians of hiding a gas centrifuge plant at Natanz. Its sources were solely American and the IAEA had been embarrassed earlier by U.S. intelligence about suspect Iranian facilities. In 1993, IAEA inspectors visited several suspicious Iranian sites but found no indications of undeclared nuclear activities.[8] Bruno Pellaud, then deputy director general of Safeguards and leader of the inspection team, said that the CIA had given them "disturbing indications of procurement, but that was about all."[9]

In its August 2002 release, NCRI pointed to a physical location that had a good chance of being a nuclear site. Heinonen wrote a letter to the Iranian government asking that the IAEA be allowed to visit the site to either confirm or deny these allegations. The request caught the Iranians off guard. They had hinted to the IAEA for months about having a larger than acknowledged nuclear program, but they admitted later that they did not intend to reveal the existence of the plant until a time of their choosing. Part of the reason Iran resisted was obvious. Secrecy eased Iran's task of building the facility, since most states would not believe sketchy intelligence from only Israel and the United States. Admitting the existence of the facility would confirm that information, leading to international calls to close it. Exposure would also complicate Iran's overseas purchases of essential items for this plant. In a worst case scenario, Israel or the United States could build international support to bomb the facility, a possibility Iran worried about in the run-up to the 2003 Iraq war.

Iran did not want to publicly refuse the IAEA's request, but it was not anxious to accommodate it either. Gholamreza Aghazadeh, the vice president and head of the AEOI, told the IAEA in September 2002 that the visit could happen in October.[10] The visit was cancelled and rescheduled several times.[11]

At ISIS, where I am president, we were immediately interested in NCRI's information about the two secret sites. NCRI had only identified the site's location as near the town of Natanz. We were suspicious of NCRI's identification of the site as a fuel fabrication plant, since such a site does not warrant such elaborate secrecy. Using commercial, high resolution satellite imagery, we decided to hunt for the site ourselves.

ISIS was one of the first private organizations to incorporate commercial satellite imagery into its nuclear program analyses. It became available in the late 1990s with the launch of U.S. commercial satellites that could produce high resolution images that were once the exclusive domain of intelligence services. For several years, ISIS used this imagery to locate secret nuclear sites in Pakistan, Algeria, China, and South Africa. Our release of high resolution, annotated images of these sites often had a profound effect, shaping public debates about nuclear proliferation and attracting far more media attention than a written account. A picture is indeed worth more than a thousand words.

We ordered images from DigitalGlobe, the company with the highest resolution commercial satellite images at that time. Corey Hinderstein, then ISIS's imagery expert, did not know precisely where to look, so she started at the town of Natanz and expanded out in concentric circles until she found the most likely site. The close-up image showed the Natanz site as it looked on September 16, 2002. Three huge underground structures were largely covered over with dirt and concrete, but their outlines could still be seen. The two largest ones each had horizontal dimensions of about 190 meters by 170 meters, each roughly the area of six football fields, huge by any standard but not necessarily confirming the facility's purpose.

At first glance some of the above-ground buildings, which had prominent white roofs, looked similar to the centrifuge halls of URENCO centrifuge sites in Europe. Through a process of elimination and with help from trusted, knowledgeable sources, we became convinced it was a gas centrifuge plant.

We believed Iran would stall the IAEA indefinitely unless actual satellite images were released that corroborated NCRI's information. We decided to release the imagery publicly in an ISIS report in an attempt to prompt the Iranian regime to meet with IAEA head El Baradei.[12] Our assumption was that once the site was made public, any further delays with the IAEA would risk damaging its international credibility. In early December 2002, I approached David Ensor, a highly regarded national security and intelligence correspondent at CNN with our photos and analysis.

ISIS had teamed with CNN previously to pursue in-depth the nuclear weapons–related stories about al Qaeda after the Taliban fell. We respected Ensor and found him to be a careful and thorough correspondent. He quickly confirmed our assessment with U.S. intelligence and State Department officials.

CNN also contacted the IAEA's spokesperson's office, where officials were worried about the impact of our upcoming report. El Baradei's office asked me to delay our report, fearing that it would make the Iranians more defensive.[13] I respectfully disagreed, and CNN aired our images on December 12, 2002.

Iran's response was as we had anticipated—they agreed publicly to meet El Baradei in February. This demonstrates that Iran can be susceptible to public and international pressure. Soon afterward, we received an email from El Baradei's office thanking ISIS for its work to make the site public.

The reaction to our report from hardliners in the Bush administration was something we hadn't expected. A source in the office of the under secretary of state John Bolton alluded to regime change and war with Iran over its nuclear activities by telling CNN that when the United States got to Baghdad, it would "turn right" toward Tehran. Besides being a hopelessly overoptimistic and needlessly confrontational assessment (especially given what quickly transpired in Iraq following the invasion), this attitude revealed an administration that was unprepared to deal with an Iran that was beginning to open up about its secret nuclear program.

Iran started publicly disclosing key elements of its nuclear program on February 9, 2003, when President Mohammad Khatami admitted that Iran was building a huge enrichment facility near Natanz.[14] He said that the facility would be for the production of nuclear electricity and not for nuclear weapons, but after hiding so much information for so long, how could Khatami's statement be trusted? The essential proliferation dilemma of nuclear energy is that the same facilities and materials can serve either a civil or military purpose. Both can be redirected easily. Moreover, Khatami did not explain Iran's need for a vast underground gas centrifuge plant able to withstand a military attack or why a country with vast oil and natural gas reserves urgently needed nuclear power.

Khatami's announcement was soon followed by El Baradei's historic visit to the Natanz site on February 21, 2003.[15] He toured the facility and assessed that the above-ground pilot centrifuge was "sophisticated." The pilot enrichment plant, slated to hold 1,000 centrifuges, had about 160 spinning centrifuges and the components to make five times that number. The underground halls were slated to hold 50,000 centrifuges, a huge capacity for a country Iran's size and a project that would likely take well over a decade to complete.

Gholamreza Aghazadeh, the head of AEOI, had taken over the nuclear program in 1998. His professionalism is credited with much of the success at Natanz and the secret heavy water production facility at Arak. Heavy water would be an essential ingredient in a particular type of nuclear reactor that Iran was planning to build adjacent to the production plant. Despite the new openness and denials of any nuclear weapons program, suspicions remained high that these facilities were actually part of an effort to produce highly enriched uranium and plutonium. In one of his first interviews with a Western journalist about the Natanz and Arak sites, Aghazadeh said, "When I started activities on heavy water, I was not predicting I could be successful with enrichment." He added, "I was successful in heavy water and also uranium enrichment."[16] Although Aghazadeh denied any military intentions, his comments implied that he wanted to succeed in at least one of these projects in order to develop a capability to produce either weapon-grade plutonium in a heavy water reactor or weapon-grade uranium in a gas centrifuge plant.

Suspicions immediately arose that Iran had not declared all of its centrifuge facilities. And where did Iran learn to run centrifuges? No one builds a large, costly site like Natanz without first running small numbers of centrifuges and learning how to enrich uranium. Iran told the IAEA that it had learned to operate the centrifuges through computer simulations and had never enriched any uranium at Natanz or elsewhere.[17] Natanz's sheer size belied that statement. Few IAEA officials believed Iran's claims, suspecting there must have been another facility where the centrifuges and likely enriched uranium were developed.

They were right to be wary. On February 20, 2003, shortly before El Baradei visited Natanz, the NCRI announced that Kalaye Electric was a centrifuge research and development facility. This site was the most likely place at which Iran could have secretly enriched uranium, a step that would be a clear violation of the verification requirements of the Nuclear Non-Proliferation Treaty. The IAEA asked to visit the site soon after NCRI's revelations.

The United States and Britain were apparently aware of the centrifuge activity at Kalaye Electric before the NCRI February announcement. U.S. satellite imagery showed trucks coming and going from the site, suggesting that Iran was hauling away centrifuge equipment before allowing the IAEA access. When asked about the NCRI report, Iran told the IAEA that the facility was a watch factory, which also just happened to make a few centrifuge components.

Under international pressure, Iran allowed the IAEA limited access to Kalaye Electric in March 2003 and full access that May. However, Iran refused to permit the IAEA to take environmental sampling, a powerful detection tool that picks up minute amounts of enriched uranium. On their first visit, the inspectors became immediately suspicious when they saw a considerable amount of remodeling activity inside one of the buildings, which was newer than the others at the site. Walls had been freshly painted, or in some cases, moved, doors and door handles had been replaced, and a pit in the floor, which Iran would later reveal was where centrifuges were assembled, was filled in and the floor freshly retiled. One inspector joked about the grouting between the tiles being so fresh. The building also had a large hall that looked suitable for a centrifuge cascade. Adding to their suspicions, the IAEA was refused access to two of the rooms in the building.[18]

One of the inspectors, Trevor Edwards, was a British centrifuge expert with long experience at URENCO. He began working with the IAEA in Iraq in the 1990s, inspecting its former centrifuge program, and Heinonen had asked him for help on Iran. Edwards was not duped by Iran's attempts at concealment. On an early visit, he was exploring the remodeled building and found a box of gasket rings, made out of paper, which he recognized as spacers used for centrifuge magnets. This confirmed the earlier presence of centrifuges.

Iran continued to refuse the IAEA's request to conduct environmental sampling at Kalaye Electric until August 2003. By the time permission to sample was granted, inspectors had mentally reconstructed the layout of the earlier centrifuge building prior to the remodeling, allowing them to plan carefully where they would take the samples.

Not surprisingly, the samples showed the presence of enriched uranium, conclusively disproving Iran's declaration about the site. Iran was forced to admit that Kalaye Electric had been its primary centrifuge research and development site where it had first enriched uranium and gained the expertise to scale up its operations at Natanz. The IAEA had shown that Iran had violated its safeguards commitments under the Nuclear Non-Proliferation Treaty.[19]

The next time the IAEA inspected a new site, Iran was better prepared to thwart environmental sampling. In 2004, at a military-owned site called Lavisan, which had housed the Physics Research Center (PHRC), located in the northern suburbs of Tehran, Iran took extraordinary steps in an apparent attempt to thwart the IAEA's sampling for enriched uranium. Instead of remodeling a set of buildings, which the IAEA suspected of involvement in the gas centrifuge program based on the PHRC's earlier procurement activities, it leveled them, hauled away the rubble, and then scraped the dirt away before building a recreational facility on top of it. These actions made it all but impossible for the IAEA to find any traces of enriched uranium or other evidence of secret nuclear work.

The IAEA inspectors faced another question soon after they arrived at Natanz in February 2002: Whom did Iran obtain its centrifuge technology from? The centrifuges in the pilot facility at Natanz appeared to be copies of a type developed at URENCO in the early 1970s, a design Khan had stolen from URENCO and was suspected of selling to Iran.

The Pakistani Foreign Ministry spokesman categorically rejected any suggestion that Pakistan was involved in developing Iran's nuclear program.[20] A few months later, Pakistan would call such speculation "wild flights of fancy."[21] Iran also denied reports about foreign assistance. A spokesman for the Iranian Foreign Ministry said, "The nuclear activities of the Islamic Republic are indigenous and Iran uses its own know-how."[22]

Over the next six months, the IAEA gradually and systematically established evidence that its suspicions were warranted. It asked Pakistan in the early summer of 2003 about Iran's centrifuges, then pressed the United States to quietly ask Pakistan for more cooperation.[23] Iran was also warned that the IAEA governing board could refer the issue to the U.N. Security Council for consideration of sanctions and other punitive measures. Under this intense scrutiny, and in the wake of the recent U.S. invasion of Iraq, Iranian officials finally admitted in August 2003 that Iran had bought a set of centrifuge drawings in 1987 from "intermediaries," but they claimed they did not know where the intermediaries got them.[24]

Iran first showed IAEA officials centrifuge drawings in mid-August 2003. IAEA centrifuge experts could tell from looking at the measurements of the parts, their diameters, and their tolerances, that the drawings were based on a Dutch design from the early 1970s. Dutch centrifuge experts who had been asked to analyze these drawings agreed.[25] Khan had stolen this Dutch centrifuge design in the 1970s, renaming it the P1 centrifuge. Although the IAEA was not ready to name Pakistan publicly, its officials leaked their findings to the media, increasing pressure on Pakistan to cooperate. By the end of the summer, the IAEA had enough evidence to convince even skeptical nations that Pakistan supplied the centrifuge designs. The September 2003 resolution of the IAEA board of governors called on "all third parties" (which was code language referring to Pakistan) to provide information to the IAEA.

Around this time, Tahir and Khan started to realize their operations were threatened.[26] Khan was worried that Iran would reveal his enterprise to the IAEA, and he attempted to contact one of his Iranian associates by letter, a communiqué that was intercepted by a Pakistani intelligence agency.[27] In the letter, Khan said not to mention his name under any circumstances to the IAEA; instead, they should name dead people. He also suggested that the Iranians should blame the IAEA for any uranium contamination found in Iran and recommended that Iran withdraw from the Nuclear Non-Proliferation Treaty. Finally, Khan promised more assistance.

In the fall of 2003, Britain, France, and Germany, later known as the "EU-3," launched a major diplomatic effort to persuade Iran to stop building and installing centrifuges and to "suspend" its enrichment program. Throughout 2003, the principal Iranian reaction had been fear, for both their nuclear program and their regime because of the U.S. invasion of Iraq. In an attempt to calibrate its response between U.S. military actions in Iraq and the IAEA's demands, Iran's Supreme Leader Ayatollah Khamenei ordered the head of the National Security Council, Hassan Rowhani, to take over the nuclear portfolio from the AEOI. He was tasked with creating a new, more credible declaration to the IAEA. He also intensified negotiations with the EU-3, finally agreeing to suspend the Iranian enrichment program in October 2003.

The next month, Iran also agreed to adhere to the Additional Protocol. Rowhani did not agree that Iran would formally ratify it, reflecting the conditional nature of its commitment to intrusive inspections and foreshadowing more problems ahead in getting Iran to keep the suspension in place. Heinonen thought

that Iran may have come to the conclusion that it could end a
covert nuclear weapons program without admitting to what work
it had already accomplished. Four years later, the United States
would declare in an influential National Intelligence Estimate
(NIE) that it believed Iran had halted its secret work on nuclear
weapons in 2003.[28] Given the intense pressure on Iran in 2003
emanating from the Iraq war, IAEA inspections, and the EU-3,
this conclusion is not surprising.

One of the unexpected benefits of Iran's concessions was that
the IAEA learned a great deal about what has to be considered
the core of Iran's secret centrifuge manufacturing complex. As
part of its suspension, Iran agreed to stop making centrifuge
components and allowed the IAEA to monitor components and
manufacturing equipment to lessen the chance that Iran could
secretly make additional centrifuges during the suspension. The
IAEA lost no time taking full advantage of its new rights under
the suspension and the inspection access provided by the Additional Protocol, obtaining considerable information about Iran's
facilities that had been dedicated to making the many centrifuge
components that comprise the P1 centrifuge.

A crucial piece of information learned by the IAEA was
that, unlike the centralized centrifuge manufacturing facility at
Pakistan's KRL, the Iranian centrifuge program, owned by the
Kalaye Electric Company (not to be confused with the Kalaye
Electric facility), dispersed its centrifuge component manufacturing among a range of civilian and military facilities. Centrifuges
are expendable, but the equipment that makes them is not, particularly when it has to be illicitly purchased and smuggled into
the country. A dispersed manufacturing facility would render
them far less vulnerable to an Israeli or American military strike.

Kalaye Electric Company contracted with several of its own subsidiaries, small private companies, and at least three facilities that are part of, or associated with, the Defense Industries Organization (DIO).[29] This completely state-owned entity is under the umbrella of the Ministry of Defense and is responsible for manufacturing the equipment required by Iran's armed forces. The most important DIO contractor was located at a large industrial compound south of the historic city of Esfahan, often called 7th of Tir Industries. This large armaments and missile production facility is surrounded by perimeter fencing with guard checkpoints and several security gates. It has a number of manufacturing buildings and what appear to be underground facilities. Centrifuge components were manufactured in a relatively small, unidentified facility inside this large site. Under contract, 7th of Tir machinists made approximately twenty critical rotating components of the P1 centrifuge.

Although the IAEA used the suspension period to dig deeper into Iran's centrifuge program, the EU-3 negotiations with Iran quickly deadlocked. Iran insisted on resuming centrifuge operations. It was willing to negotiate only the pace of centrifuge deployment and the level of inspections. The EU-3 countered by offering Iran nuclear power plants and a wide range of other economic assistance, but these offers were not enough to convince Iran to sacrifice its gas centrifuge program. The EU-3 could not offer one concession Iran said it required—a U.S. commitment not to attack Iran or seek its overthrow. The Bush administration believed Iran was part of an "axis of evil" and would never negotiate in good faith. The United States declined to join formally the EU-3 process, though in June 2008, Secretary of State Condoleezza Rice added her name along with those of other foreign ministers to a sweeping diplomatic offer of incentives aimed at persuading Iran to relinquish its enrichment program.

With the United States bogged down in Iraq, its threats to attack Tehran grew hollow. Iran felt increasingly confident about defying the United States with little fear of military retaliation. Iran's suspension of its nuclear program ended in January 2006 and the building and installing of centrifuges at Natanz quickly resumed. Soon afterward, Iran stopped adhering to the IAEA's Additional Protocol. Iran was no longer obligated to allow IAEA monitoring of centrifuge components or the equipment and materials involved in the production of those components. Since then, U.S. and Israeli intelligence agencies have had difficulty learning where Iran produces and stores centrifuges. Does it happen at these original supplier facilities or in a whole new set of unknown companies with secret storage locations for manufactured components? The lack of fresh and reliable information also undercuts the efficacy of military strikes to set back Iran's nuclear weapons effort.

In a report issued in February 2006, the IAEA said that without greater cooperation from Iran, it "will not be able to provide assurances about the absence of undeclared nuclear material and activities in Iran or about the exclusively peaceful nature of that program."[30]

Iranian nuclear procurement efforts have accelerated, suggesting that Iran intends to expand its centrifuge program. A multitude of Iranian trading companies have sent enquiries to vacuum companies for thousands of valves, fittings, and pipes. Many companies did not fulfill these requests but Iran has often obtained essential goods in China.

In 2007, Iran sought large quantities of special oils that could withstand the corrosive effects of uranium hexafluoride inside centrifuges and in pumps that create the vacuum in centrifuge cascades.[31] Several of these orders arrived in Iran via Dubai trading companies. Iran succeeded in obtaining one order from a U.S. supplier by using an Iraqi trading company as a false end user. Iran also sought more vacuum equipment for its centrifuge plant and obtained 50,000 tiny steel balls for bottom bearings.[32]

Iran continued finding countries that it could use as "turntables," or points of diversion, to route its goods to Iran without the suppliers learning the real end user. Like Khan, Iran relied on trading companies in the UAE, exploiting the Dubai free trade zone to obtain a range of items for its military and nuclear programs. Of the more than 1,200 commercial firms registered in the free trade zone, a significant portion of them were Iranian front companies.[33] Smugglers have also used Singapore and Hong Kong as important turntables to route goods to Iran. However, tightened governmental scrutiny of these operations disrupted many of them. As a result of this greater scrutiny, Iran started routing goods through Malaysia which does not have export controls.

Iran has also needed a steady supply of spare parts for its aging manufacturing equipment. In 2006 or 2007, Iran sought to buy a used Leifeld flow-forming machine in Switzerland, but the government stopped the sale. This attempt almost slipped by unnoticed since Iran sought to buy a 1960s era machine and then contracted with another company to update it with modern computerized equipment and software. The Swiss government only learned of this scheme because sale of the software needed its approval.

While Iran was steadily increasing its centrifuge capabilities, the United States and its European allies were working to convince Iran to resume its suspension of its enrichment effort. Russia and China, two of the country's allies, joined in demands that Iran "re-suspend" its uranium enrichment program. As of spring 2009, the United Nations Security Council had imposed economic and political sanctions on Iran three times, in December 2006, March 2007, and February 2008.

Contrary to popular belief, U.N. sanctions have limited Iran's ability to obtain credit for large-scale capital projects and have spurred some dissent within the country. They have also likely exacerbated Iran's high unemployment and inflation rate. Its oil and gas industry continues to face shortages for spare parts and long-deferred investment in infrastructure. U.N. sanctions have undoubtedly increased Iran's difficulties in obtaining items for its nuclear program. They have also led to more prosecutions as companies are caught violating the sanctions. Despite these successes, there are simply too many unscrupulous suppliers and trading companies around the world. For every procurement attempt detected, many more are missed.

Iran has continued installing P1 centrifuges, reaching eight thousand by September 2009.[34] The centrifuges work satisfactorily, although not as well as those in European countries. Over time, Iranian operators at Natanz have managed to overcome a host of problems and have accumulated a growing amount of low enriched uranium. Iran plans to install many more P1 centrifuges underground before installing more advanced centrifuges based on the P2 centrifuge design supplied by Khan.

In early 2009, Natanz crossed a key technical milestone. It accumulated enough low enriched uranium to achieve a nuclear weapons breakout capability. This low enriched uranium would provide a significant head start on producing weapon-grade uranium, dramatically shortening by about two-thirds the time needed to produce enough of it to make a nuclear weapon. It would likely opt to build a secret facility to enrich the material because if it tries to further enrich the material at Natanz, it would risk a military strike by Israel, and perhaps the United States, that could destroy the underground centrifuges. If Iran's enrichment program continues growing in size and gaining experience, the number of ways it could produce weapon-grade uranium will also increase. Its nuclear weapon capabilities will multiply with time.

Indeed, on September 25, 2009, President Barack Obama, British Prime Minister Gordon Brown, and French President Nicolas Sarkozy announced that Iran was secretly building an illegal gas centrifuge enrichment facility deep in a mountain northeast of the city of Qom. Their intelligence agencies had reportedly tracked the site's construction for several years but obtained definitive evidence that the site was intended for enrichment only in early 2009. The construction of this covert nuclear site is exactly the reason why the IAEA and the United States have called on Iran to accept modern inspections.

Facing increased concerns about the misuse of its low enriched uranium to quickly make nuclear weapons, Iran agreed on October 1, 2009, to allow IAEA inspectors into the Qom facility and tentatively agreed to ship a majority of its existing LEU to Russia for further enrichment and ultimate return for use in a small civilian reactor in Tehran that produces medical isotopes. Although welcoming these confidence building measures, the United States and its western allies continued to insist that Iran must suspend its uranium enrichment program.

An ongoing mystery is whether Iran is actively working on developing the nuclear weapons technology itself, particularly on developing the capability to build a nuclear warhead for a ballistic missile. The 2007 National Intelligence Assessment judged with "moderate confidence Tehran had not restarted its nuclear weapons program as of mid 2007."[35] Yet there is evidence that indicates otherwise. Both British and German government officials regularly state to ISIS that Iran has resumed working on the nuclear weapon itself. An official from a European intelligence agency, speaking privately with ISIS in March 2009, stated that Iran has recently procured items linked to nuclear warhead development.

An internal IAEA working document written in late 2008 or early 2009 sheds light on just how much Iran already knows about making nuclear weapons deliverable by its ballistic missiles. According to the IAEA document, "Iran has sufficient information to be able to design and produce a workable implosion nuclear device."[36] The necessary information was "most likely obtained from external sources and probably modified by Iran." The report does not list any of these sources, although likely suspects are from Russia, Pakistan, or China. Overall the report concludes that Iran has not yet "achieved the means of integrating a nuclear payload into the Shahab 3 missile with any confidence that it would work; but with "further effort it is likely that Iran will overcome problems and confidence will be built up."

U.S. intelligence estimates of when Iran could be technically capable of producing its first nuclear weapon have been surprisingly broad, falling somewhere between 2010 and 2015. The wide range reflects uncertainties about how fast Iran could surmount technical problems in its centrifuge program and produce enough weapon-grade uranium for a weapon. If Iran wanted to build nuclear weapons, it is technically competent to start now. Moreover, 2010 is simply the year that it's assumed it will have the technology to build nuclear weapons. The Iranian regime would then need to make a political decision to build them, which does not appear to have happened yet, and then would need enough time to implement such a decision.

With a growing nuclear weapons capability, though, Iran could produce enough weapon-grade material for a bomb in short order if it chose to do so. Had the Khan network not been dismantled, there's no telling how much further along the path to nuclear weapons Iran would be.

TEN

Busting the Khan Network

In the early 1990s, CIA headquarters assigned a senior agent to be the station chief of one of its oldest stations in Europe. His small group of agents secretly put Khan's European members under surveillance, resulting in considerable knowledge about their operations. Normally, agents' responsibility was limited to collecting information for further assessment and action back in Washington. This station chief wanted to do more. He wanted to act against the Khan network and disrupt their procurement operations. Getting the go-ahead for such an action was controversial in the 1990s, before the 9/11 attack. Nonetheless, the CIA granted approval for its European operatives to move aggressively against Khan's network.

It took the CIA a decade of hard work and a bit of luck to develop the evidence about the Khan network's proliferation activities. While the operatives experienced false starts, setbacks, and a healthy dose of skepticism from Washington, their persistent work was handsomely rewarded. James Pavitt, then deputy director of operations, summarized this successful operation: "As the result of a patient, decade long operation involving million dollar recruitment pitches, covert entries, ballet-like sophistication and a level of patience we are often accused of not possessing, the clandestine service exposed the network of Pakistani scientist A.Q. Khan."[1]

It started in Switzerland, where Friedrich Tinner and Gotthard Lerch were known to be actively assisting Pakistan's nuclear program. CIA operatives planted eavesdropping bugs, broke into offices, and sometimes walked up to key sources on the street and asked for help. People began to contact them and volunteer information. They discreetly approached Swiss bank officials seeking information on financial transactions. The Swiss government formally warned each new CIA station chief not to violate any Swiss laws, but while some of the CIA activities were illegal, agents were able to ply their trade with little interference from authorities.

What operatives discovered in Switzerland convinced them of the fundamental importance of independent U.S. action. CIA operatives witnessed Swiss government officials helping suppliers send sensitive goods to Pakistan, making a mockery of the official Swiss policy to maintain strict export control laws. Moreover, the Swiss government demonstrated an unwillingness to take action to disrupt these activities or to work with the CIA.

At first, the CIA missed Khan's proliferation activities to Libya and Iran in the 1990s. The problem was that Khan's operations were surrounded by a "fog bank," in which procurements were detected but not tracked to their ultimate destinations in Libya or Iran. That started to change in 1996 when, according to a former intelligence official, the CIA got its first big break in information that Khan's proliferation efforts were increasing.[2]

By early 2000, the CIA and its frequent partner, Britain's MI-6, learned that Khan was at the center of an international nuclear proliferation network with one major customer in the Middle East, thought to be Libya.[3] By the fall of 2000, they knew the network was expanding to mass-produce centrifuge components for a large centrifuge plant.[4]

A major turning point in obtaining this information was finding sources inside the Khan network. The identity of these moles remains a mystery which the CIA has no interest in shedding light on. One is believed to be Urs Tinner, although the extent of his initial cooperation is difficult to determine. What is known is that the CIA pressured Tinner, who was living in the UAE at the time, to cooperate by threatening him with possible legal trouble in France for a crime he had allegedly committed earlier.[5] This threat was evidently enough to convince Urs to become a reluctant source. Urs has admitted to being approached by the CIA, although he has declined to state when it happened.[6] Another mole, likely recruited before Tinner was approached, might have been a friend of his in the UAE.[7]

With details trickling in about the network's operations in Dubai, the United States now had enough information to bust several members of the network, but it also knew that many of the network's activities remained unknown. A top secret meeting was convened in the Clinton White House in 2000 attended by a select group of officials responsible for stopping nuclear proliferation and senior members of the CIA's covert operations division. The CIA successfully argued for patience—their inside sources could reveal the whole picture if given time.[8]

By early 2002, it was learned that Khan had moved his export business to Dubai and was now controlling operations through his associates there. Also discovered was the depth of Khan's assistance to Iran, which might have given its centrifuge program even more of a head start than had previously been known.[9] To prevent further centrifuge assistance from happening, the CIA, or more likely Israel, targeted Gotthard Lerch, leaving him a letter at his house in eastern Switzerland.[10] "Herr Lerch" was warned not to sell the P2 design to Iran in cooperation with Urs and Marco Tinner, and was threatened with "grave consequences" if he proceeded. The letter was signed "your sincere friends." It concluded, "we will come to talk to you to work out a deal for both parties' interest." To disrupt Iran's centrifuge program further, the CIA bought dual-use equipment and secretly sabotaged it. Then, the CIA's operatives found their own middlemen in Europe and the Middle East to sell the equipment to Iran.

By late 2002, details about a deal to sell Libya a gas centrifuge plant were coming into focus, and they were alarming. Information had been collected on the Khan network's suppliers, financing, front companies, key scientists, agents, shipping companies, and manufacturing plants. Libya was close to having everything it needed to build a centrifuge plant. It was finally time to act.

At a summit meeting between President George W. Bush and Prime Minister Tony Blair in early 2003, most of which was devoted to planning the looming war in Iraq, the two leaders quickly agreed that Khan's network had to be stopped.[11] The problem was finding the best way to bust it. One former senior State Department official likened the Khan network to bamboo, which regrows rapidly unless completely removed.[12]

One approach would be to funnel the evidence to the authorities in the various countries Khan was operating in, who could then take action against the individuals and sites where the network was active. This was rejected as the CIA did not have confidence in other countries prosecuting the smugglers.

Some key countries, such as the UAE and Malaysia, did not even have export control laws, making prosecution impossible. Convincing Pakistan was another option, but the concern was that Khan's operations would only be temporarily suspended with no guarantees that Libya would be prevented from finishing its centrifuge plant.[13]

In mid-2003, the CIA "came up with a bold solution that involved a series of carefully orchestrated approaches to the network," according to George Tenet.[14] Planning for the operation was top secret, with information restricted to a few top officials. The key to their strategy was recruiting the Tinner family, the father Friedrich and sons Urs and Marco, as paid CIA agents. The details remain classified but it's assumed that by mid-2003 the three Tinners must have realized that cooperating with the CIA would keep them out of jail and perhaps earn them more cash.

The Tinners were like mafia informers, and their "Don" had a hard time accepting their betrayal. In 2008, Khan told the Italian journalist Stefania Maurizi that the "claims that Urs Tinner had become a CIA agent do not ring true." He added that the Tinners were a "proud, educated family and Urs would never have betrayed his father, brother, and other friends."

On June 21, 2003, six U.S. intelligence agents visited Marco at the Tinner home in Jenins, a Swiss mountain village in eastern Switzerland, with the intention of conducting a search.[15] Marco was apparently not expecting the visit but was persuaded to offer his full cooperation. This "persuasion" came in the form of a $1 million contract, signed that day at his family house by Marco and two CIA agents using the false names W. James Kinsman and Sean D. Mahaffey.[16] The contract was between Marco's company Traco Group International Inc. and Big Black River

Technologies, a likely CIA shadow company.[17] The million dollars may reflect payment for the information taken that day or the amount of money Marco could expect for future cooperation. In either event, what was found in Marco's house was a cornucopia of digitized blueprints for P1 and P2 centrifuges, procurement details, and nuclear weapon drawings—all the proof they'd need for busting the network.

Another part of the CIA's mission was to purchase centrifuge parts the Tinners had ordered in Switzerland but had not yet shipped to Libya. Total value of parts: 1,462,901.95 Swiss francs, or about $1.2 million, about half of the original contract.[18] Being shrewd businessmen, the Tinners billed the same amount of money to the CIA that it charged the Khan network for making the parts.

The Swiss television program *Temps Present*, citing the newspaper *Sonntagszeitung*, obtained another invoice from Traco Group International to Big Black River Technologies dated May 20, 2004: $2 million for a "license fee." The two invoices suggest that the Tinners, already the beneficiaries of millions of dollars from selling Libya gas centrifuge components, were paid over $3 million for working for the CIA in 2003 and 2004.

The CIA wanted more than what the Tinners could offer in Switzerland. One of the CIA's most important assignments went to Urs, who was in Malaysia at the SCOPE factory overseeing the manufacture of Libya's centrifuge parts. SCOPE had already made three shipments of centrifuge parts to Libya via Dubai. With Urs's help, the CIA could intercept the next shipment, the largest of the four. Seizing the shipment would get the items out of circulation and provide concrete evidence of Libya's secret nuclear weapons effort.

Urs had the nerve-wracking task of obtaining the shipping

information. Hating that his phones were tapped by the CIA and fearful Tahir would discover him, Urs lived in constant fear, going so far as checking into a hotel for several days because he feared that something bad could happen at his home.[19] Urs got the CIA the needed information without arousing Tahir's suspicion, allowing CIA operatives to watch the actual containers being loaded onto a ship, where it was tracked until it reached Dubai. There, the cargo was transferred to the *BBC China*, a ship which was owned by a German company. On the last leg of the trip in the Mediterranean Sea, an American naval vessel trailed the container ship in case it made a run for it.[20] It was an unnecessary precaution. An official of the German intelligence service phoned the *BBC China*'s owner, based in Germany; the message was relayed to the captain as his ship moved through the locks of the Suez Canal.[21]

The *BBC China* changed course and sailed about one hundred miles to the northwest to the southern Italian port of Taranto. Located near the arch of Italy's boot, Taranto is both a bustling commercial port and a naval base for the North Atlantic Treaty Organization (NATO). After the vessel entered the port on October 4, 2003, it was boarded by Italian authorities, accompanied by U.S. and British intelligence officials. Even with the container numbers, it took hours to find the five containers, each forty feet in length, and innocuously listed in the ship's manifest as "used machine parts."[22]

In October, Urs left SCOPE for the last time, after deleting his personal files from the company's records. He took with him a hard disk containing sensitive centrifuge design information.[23]

With the documentation and the seizure of the centrifuge parts bound for Libya, the United States and Britain now had

100 percent iron-clad evidence. The question now was: how to use it? They decided to use the seized cargo as a trump card in a series of negotiations that had been taking place with Libya since March. Colonel Qaddafi had contacted Britain and signaled his willingness to give up his weapons of mass destruction programs in exchange for ending sanctions. Britain immediately told the United States, which agreed to pursue the offer, but the subsequent, confidential negotiations were moving slowly, and by that October had stalled.

A senior British diplomat was sent to quietly notify Qaddafi about the seizure before it was made public. Libyans said that the shipment was organized long before negotiations to abandon the nuclear weapon program began, but Qaddafi viewed the "heads up" as proof that he could trust Britain and the United States.[24] He also realized that a great deal was already known about his nuclear weapons program. It was too late to turn back. According to Pavitt, "Working with British intelligence, we surprised Libya's leaders with the depth of our knowledge about its weapons programs. We pressed them on the right questions, exposed inconsistencies and convinced the Libyans that holding back was counterproductive."[25] As a result, the negotiations moved quickly and on December 19, 2003, Colonel Qaddafi announced that he was halting Libya's nuclear weapons program.

The *BBC China* seizure dealt the Khan network a near fatal blow, but getting Pakistan to arrest Khan would not be easy. About ten days before the seizure, Tenet had confronted President Musharraf in New York while he was attending the United Nations General Assembly. Tenet showed him centrifuge drawings and bomb designs the CIA and MI-6 collected from Khan's agents. He told Musharraf, "A.Q. Khan is betraying your country. He has stolen some of your nation's most sensitive secrets and sold them to the highest bidders."[26] Musharraf was outraged but also worried about how to protect his country from the inevitable fallout that Khan's arrest would cause.[27]

Musharraf started an intensive investigation in November 2003 but allowed Khan to remain free. Deputy Secretary Richard Armitage visited Islamabad and delivered a blunt message: unless Khan's days as a nuclear entrepreneur were ended, the United Nations might impose economic sanctions and the United States could halt a proposed $3 billion aid package. Secretary of State Colin Powell followed up with a phone call. "We're going to go public with it . . . and you need to deal with this before you have to deal with it publicly."[28] On January 31, 2004, Khan was finally arrested under the Pakistani Security Act for allegedly transferring nuclear technology to other countries.

On February 4, 2004, Khan read a prepared statement on television where he expressed the "deepest sense of sorrow, anguish, and regret," and said, "I take full responsibility for my actions and seek your pardon."[29] He added that while the government did not authorize his proliferation activities, he had acted "in good faith." To many of his supporters, this was akin to saying Musharraf coerced Khan into confessing. The next day, Musharraf gave Khan a full pardon and placed Khan under house arrest, where he lived in his lavish house until February 2009, when he was released as a "free citizen" though a security detail would control his movements. Khan became the second most highly decorated senior Pakistani nuclear official to be so sentenced. The first was Sultan Bashiruddin Mahmood, who was "arrested" for helping Osama bin Laden.

Khan defended his actions by implying that nuclear proliferation was official government policy. He told the Swiss journalist

Urs Gehriger in an email that "I did nothing wrong and whatever I did was done in good faith and in the national interest."[30] Musharraf and other senior government officials vehemently refuted Khan's statements, calling them nonsense. The widely respected Lt. General Khalid Kidwai (ret.), head of the Strategic Planning Division in the Pakistani government, said Pakistan had plenty of evidence to show that Khan betrayed his country.[31]

Nonetheless, no one has investigated the role of the Pakistani government in Khan's deals. President Musharraf, the Army, and his top aides maintain they did not have direct knowledge of Khan's proliferation activities, but a more commonly accepted view is that high level officials in many parts of the Pakistani government, intelligence community, and military probably turned a blind eye to Khan's actions because of his vital importance to Pakistan's nuclear weapons program.

Ultimately, sorting out the exact role of Pakistan's civil and military governments in proliferation remains exceedingly difficult. Khan's claim that senior government officials had approved his proliferation has some merit in certain cases, such as some of his centrifuge aid to North Korea and initial help to Iran. But such actual or assumed approval in a few cases does not answer for Khan's central role in so many known or attempted transfers of centrifuges and nuclear weapons technology that extended from the mid-1980s until 2004. While Pakistani military and political leaders came and went, Khan remained. He operated freely in a largely unregulated, sometimes corrupt, political and military environment. Top leaders might have sanctioned a few specific proliferation acts but in general they tolerated or did not know of, let alone have the ability or motivation to stop, his and his associates' many proliferation activities.

By the time the intelligence operation against Khan's network ended, CIA and MI-6 operatives had succeeded in getting into the network's computers, workshops, and homes.[32] One of the CIA officers told President George Bush, "With the information we've just gotten our hands on—soup to nuts—about uranium enrichment and nuclear weapons design, we could make the CIA its own nuclear state."[33]

That said, a senior former intelligence official involved in this successful operation commented that it was a fluke that the CIA succeeded in stopping Khan. Without the CIA/MI-6 operation, it is hard to see which combination of actions could have stopped Khan. The traditional approach of export controls, IAEA inspections, and diplomacy was no match for Khan and his transnational band offering one-stop shopping for nuclear weapons. Busting these rings is tough work, but it pales in comparison to what comes next: bringing them to justice.

———■———

AFTER KHAN'S ARREST in January 2004, the United States pushed for an international roundup of his network's key members. John Wolf, then assistant secretary of state for nonproliferation, traveled with a schematic of a P2 centrifuge that showed what parts were confiscated from the *BBC China*. His message to foreign governments whose citizens and companies were implicated in these sales was clear: prosecute network members and tighten your own anti-proliferation laws. Unlike the clandestine CIA operation against the Khan network, the U.S. government now wanted to be as transparent as possible to deter others from going down the same path.[34]

As part of Libya's remarkable turnaround, it allowed the United States, Britain, and the IAEA to thoroughly verify Libya's nuclear facilities, activities, and procurement of key equipment and materials. Warehouses filled with centrifuge equipment and components provided a virtual who's who list of suppliers and middlemen, all backed up with incriminating shipping documents and pro forma invoices.

Tipped off by the United States, the Malaysian police questioned Tahir in early 2004. He proved a cooperative witness, willing to reveal the inner secrets of the network. In May, Tahir was arrested under Malaysia's controversial Internal Security Act, which allows for detention without trial on the basis of committing actions against the country's interests. (In Turkey, Khan's contact Gunes Cire fared much worse—he died during a police interrogation.) Malaysia made Tahir available to investigators and prosecutors worldwide, and he became a key witness in many prosecutions.

Additionally, the IAEA distributed lists of people suspected of working with the Khan network, asking for information. Some nations were embarrassed into investigating these leads; others downplayed the information. More arrests followed throughout 2004. The UAE arrested Tahir's brother who ran the computer business. Peter Griffin, then living in southern France, was questioned and had his computer's hard drive duplicated. British prosecutors started an investigation (later dropped) of Griffin.

The South African government arrested Gerhard Wisser and Daniel Geiges in September 2004 and charged them with ten violations of export controls involving Libya and Pakistan. In exchange for clemency, Johan A.M. Meyer turned state's witness against them.

Germany asked Switzerland to arrest Gotthard Lerch and extradite him to stand trial for charges of committing treason and violating weapons and trade control laws. Because he remained a German citizen, he could be charged there even if he physically resided in another country. German federal prosecutors had developed their method of charging smugglers with treason against Karl Heinz Schaab, who pled guilty to assisting Iraq's secret gas centrifuge program in 1989 and 1990 and supplying classified advanced centrifuge drawings.[35] Treason carries a longer prison sentence than violations of export laws, but its application to proliferators is controversial. In Lerch's case, German prosecutors argued he had used his extensive secret nuclear knowledge and experience to help Libya acquire highly enriched uranium and in so doing accepted the possibility of a nuclear calamity. Yet under Swiss law, it is illegal to extradite suspects to other countries for a manifestly political crime.[36] The treason charge was dropped, foreshadowing the problems to come in the prosecutions.

Each country has its own rules governing evidence and witnesses, and this inhibits cooperation among different national prosecutions. The UAE did not have any export control laws and thus could not charge Griffin, Tahir's brother, or other members of the network with any crimes. Likewise, Malaysia did not have any anti-proliferation laws. While it held Tahir for four years before putting him under house arrest, it did not prosecute him or his alleged accomplices at SCOPE, Shamsul Bahrin bin Rukiban and Shah Hakim Shahnazim Zain.

Swiss authorities arrested Lerch on November 13, 2004, and he was transported to a jail in Mannheim, Germany, to await trial. There he was charged with violating weapons and trade laws in his dealings with Libya's nuclear weapons program. While in jail, according to the prison director, he was polite and decent, and endeared himself to other prisoners by fixing the remote controls for the prison's television.[37] Yet he told prosecutors almost nothing during his year in custody.

When his trial began in 2006, Lerch's experienced defense attorney Gottfried Riems raised frequent objections to the evidence and pushed for an early start to the trial, undermining the prosecutor's complicated case. Lerch's lawyer tried to make his client look like a victim of an elaborate CIA/MI-6 sting operation intended to topple Qaddafi.[38] The prosecution hinged on several foreign witnesses, two of whom were in jails in South Africa and Malaysia, and a complicated collection of information in the hands of German and foreign entities was turned over to the court in drips and drabs. Like many of the defendants, Lerch also had ample opportunity to destroy incriminating evidence at his home and office before the police arrived. He appears to have been tipped off about the impending bust of the network. On September 30, 2003, four days prior to the interdiction of the *BBC China*, Lerch met Wisser in Switzerland and instructed him to destroy the feed and withdrawal equipment they were manufacturing at Meyer's company Tradefin.[39] Wisser sent Meyer a text message: "The bird must be destroyed, feathers and all. They have fed us to the dogs."[40]

Frustrated by the pace of receiving critical evidence and worried that Lerch could not receive a fair trial, the judge suspended all proceedings on June 26, 2006. Lerch was released on bail and returned to his home in Switzerland, awaiting word of a new trial.

In the summer of 2007, Wisser and Geiges finally agreed to a plea agreement and pled guilty to most charges, largely due to incriminating documentation that had been found in a raid at Meyer's factory and Meyer's testimony. As part of the deal, they did not receive any additional jail time. Prosecutors opted for a plea deal because a court case would take three years and would not guarantee a harsher penalty. As a condition of their suspended sentences, Wisser and Geiges promised that they would fully disclose their activities to the authorities and testify in court proceedings, including overseas trials.

The sixty-five-year-old Lerch also decided to plead guilty in October 2008 to charges of supporting the development of nuclear weapons in Libya. Wisser's plea of guilty and his promise to cooperate fully with South African authorities likely was the decisive factor. Although German prosecutors encountered difficulties in getting South Africa to allow Wisser to testify in court against Lerch, they could question him through third parties and independently obtained key written evidence used in the case against Wisser and Geiges. In addition, Tahir testified about Lerch's participation in supplying Libya. Lerch was fined a token 3.5 million Euros (his wealth remained in the millions) and sentenced to five and a half years, reduced to the time he already served in jail in Switzerland and Germany.

Pakistan detained at least eight current or retired officials of the Khan Research Laboratories in late 2003 and early 2004 for questioning under the Security Act.[41] All but one were released by October 2004. Mohammed Farooq, a lead member of Khan's network and head of Khan Research Laboratories' Foreign Procurement Division, was held until April 2006 when, like Khan and Mahmood, he was sentenced to house arrest.[42]

President Musharraf refused all requests to interview Khan and his accomplices. The only means of communication permitted were questionnaires submitted via the Pakistani government; these were too often dismissed as a "fishing expedition," and ignored.

Although the Pakistani government promised to cooperate with other governments, several prosecutions suffered from not having access to key Pakistani witnesses. It's impossible to determine how much of Khan's operation remains intact or whether someone might emerge to take his place.

Khan remains a hero in Pakistan. Years of outlandish propaganda, much of which was actively propagated by the government, made any honest public discussion about him impossible. What's more, Pakistan has continued using Khan's techniques to acquire critical items for its aging nuclear program.[43] Since 2004, the PAEC is known to have sought chemicals for the mining and processing of uranium.[44] KRL has recently sought thick-walled aluminum tubes for use as outer casings of a centrifuge, along with ring magnets for centrifuges, specialized Fomblin oil, vacuum equipment, vacuum leak detectors, and spare parts for flow-forming machines.[45] Instead of Pakistan ending its dependence on illicit procurements, it redoubled its efforts.

Over five years after A.Q. Khan's arrest, the members of the Khan network have suffered only minimal penalties. This undoubtedly contributed to the U.S. State Department imposing sanctions on thirteen key members of the Khan network who are not permitted to have business dealings with either the U.S. government or private American firms. The sanctioned members include Gotthard Lerch, Peter Griffin and his son Paul, Selim Alguadis, Kursad Cire (the late Gunes Cire's son), Mohammed Farooq, Shamsul Bahrin bin Rukiban, Shah Hakim Shahnazim Zain, and A.Q. Khan.

Ironically, the network members for whom the United States extended the greatest leniency were the ones who received the harshest prosecutions elsewhere. On October 7, 2004, Urs Tinner was arrested as he crossed the German border from Switzerland.

Tahir had prominently fingered Tinner but his role with the CIA was a closely guarded secret. Urs promptly told the authorities he was a CIA agent, expecting a quick release; instead he would spend the next four years in solitary confinement in a high-security jail in Bern next to the Swiss attorney general's office, under investigation for violating Switzerland's anti-proliferation laws and money laundering. The alleged charges centered on the Tinners' manufacture of centrifuge components in Switzerland and Malaysia, but Swiss prosecutors also allege assistance to Libya by supplying parts of the gas piping systems for centrifuges, along with transferring centrifuge technology during training sessions and through the provision of centrifuge drawings. Marco Tinner spent over three years in an isolated jail cell in Zurich. Friedrich Tinner was also arrested but was released on bail after six months because of his advanced age and illness.

The CIA informed Swiss intelligence agencies in early March 2004 that the Tinners had worked with the United States in uncovering the Khan network. There were many reasons why the CIA wanted the Tinners to avoid prosecution. It wanted to stem disclosures exposing past and possibly ongoing operations, preventing a further "tuning of the horn," according to one senior CIA official. Aware that some of its activities were illegal, it wanted to inoculate its own agents and the Tinners for cooperating with the CIA. Because Switzerland is a neutral state, its laws expressly ban Swiss citizens from cooperating with foreign intelligence services and prohibit foreign intelligence services from working against another country in Switzerland. More broadly, if the Tinners were punished, it could have a negative impact on recruiting future foreign agents.

This notification did not stop the Swiss government from

launching its own investigation of the entire family. The Tinners refused to cooperate with the prosecutors, leading to the decision to keep them isolated so that they could not coordinate their cover stories. They also tried to hide their family's involvement in the initial Libyan deal, likely to avoid further implicating themselves. In early 2004, the Tinners approached the IAEA's chief investigator Olli Heinonen and agreed to cooperate, but they only revealed certain portions of their activities. On November 21, 2004, Marco wrote in private correspondence that he did not tell either Heinonen or his lawyer that "even back in the early 1990s, they already did business with Silver and Boss," their cover names for Tahir and Khan.[46]

At the end of 2004, the U.S. ambassador to Switzerland gave U.S. assurances about the Tinners to a sympathetic Christoph Blocher, the right-wing Swiss minister of justice and police who had earlier announced he would oppose prosecuting the Tinners.[47] More difficult to dissuade were Peter Lehmann and Alberto Fabbri, two tough-minded Swiss federal prosecutors who suspected that the Tinners as a family had a long history of crime stretching back into the 1970s. Lehmann and Fabbri viewed the Tinners' cooperation with the CIA as likely coerced and exaggerated in order to avoid jail, and insufficient to warrant immunity from prosecution for violating anti-proliferation laws.

Viewed as flight risks, the Tinners remained in jail. In 2005 and early 2006, Lehmann and Fabbri appealed to the U.S. government on multiple occasions for legal assistance in obtaining evidence key to their investigation. Each request was ignored. The CIA finally proposed using the IAEA as a way for the prosecutors to obtain their evidence while preserving the U.S. position not to provide the evidence directly.

It was a promising development but in March 2006, U.S. officials learned that the Swiss government had found a set of nuclear weapons drawings in computer files taken from the Tinners. The sensitive nuclear weapon information, which was composed of component drawings and "recipe" manuals, totaled about two hundred pages.[48] The United States immediately demanded the files as it did not want a nonnuclear weapon state to possess them. Swiss prosecutors opposed relinquishing or destroying critical evidence, at least until the judicial process was over.

Through the spring of 2006, U.S. officials pressed the Swiss government for the documents. As the conflict escalated, there remained the unanswered question of why these designs were still on the Tinners' computers. As paid CIA agents, they should have voluntarily surrendered all their printed and digital copies. At the very least, CIA agents should have removed the hard drives from the Tinners' computers. That they continued to possess these files, and might have hidden copies either in Switzerland or overseas, increases the likelihood that these detailed nuclear weapon designs are on the black market and available for purchase.

In the summer of 2006, Attorney General Alberto Gonzales appealed to the Swiss minister of justice for the files. Minister Blocher's concern was whether handing over the documents to the United States violated Switzerland's perceived sovereignty as a neutral state. Meanwhile, Swiss prosecutors asked their government for permission to investigate filing charges against the Tinners along with certain CIA agents for violating anti-espionage laws. Following an avalanche of protests from a host of senior U.S. officials, including Secretary of Homeland Security Michael Chertoff, Secretary of Defense Robert Gates, Secretary of State Condoleezza Rice, Federal Bureau of Investigation Director

Robert Mueller, and Director of National Intelligence Michael McConnell, the Swiss government decided not to allow the prosecutors to pursue charges against CIA agents.

Although this issue was settled, there was still the question of prosecuting the Tinners for violating anti-proliferation laws, and the matter of the disposition of the documents. Under Blocher's leadership, the Swiss government decided to destroy all the seized documents in an attempt to quash any hope of Lehmann and Fabbri successfully prosecuting the Tinners. U.S. officials went along with, and in some cases advocated, the destruction of almost all the evidence in the Tinner case.

Instead of abandoning the case, Lehmann and Fabbri sent the remaining decimated case file of evidence to a magistrate, Judge Andreas Müller, to review prosecutors' evidence and issue an opinion on the merits of filing charges. In the Swiss judicial system, the magistrate considers the evidence from both sides before making a recommendation on whether to charge the defendants. Perplexed by the missing files, Müller attempted to re-collect the destroyed evidence, which was possible because the key documents that had been introduced in court proceedings still existed. Many documents had been previously provided to other governments and experts in routine efforts to gather more evidence or seek overseas witnesses and assessments, assisting Müller's collection efforts.

Determined to prevent Müller from reassembling evidence, the Swiss government took the unusual step of refusing a direct magistrate's request for police assistance in reacquiring the destroyed records. Intense back and forth legal wrangling followed, during which the Swiss government declared the documents destroyed and was publicly rebuked by an independent Parliamentary oversight committee for its actions (only to discover copies of many documents a full year after they'd been declared destroyed). Sometime in late 2009 or 2010 Müller will recommend whether prosecutors should proceed with charges against the Tinners. Given how dogged Lehmann and Fabbri have been, it's safe to assume charges and a trial will be forthcoming. In the meantime, both Urs and Marco are free on bail.

The United States refusal to provide any assistance to Swiss prosecutors in investigating export violations put it in the awkward position of preferencing state secrets over anti-proliferation laws, a position it has accused so many other foreign governments of occupying. To set itself as an example, the CIA should have cooperated with the Swiss government in the same way we expect cooperation from other governments. The simple truth is that effective enforcement is crucial to stopping unlawful nuclear trade. As the Khan cases demonstrate, we cannot yet rely on the coordination of national prosecutions to serve the cause of justice.

ELEVEN

Suppliers: First Line of Defense

Ralf Wirtz, the trade control manager of Oerlikon and its important vacuum subsidiary Leybold, in Cologne, Germany, often compares purchase enquiries sent to him from his company's salesmen. He's looking for hints that a potential buyer, perhaps in Malaysia, Singapore, the UAE, or even just down the street, is seeking to supply a secret nuclear weapons program in Pakistan, Iran, or North Korea. Experience dating back to the early 1980s has taught Wirtz that "turntable" operations, in which items are secretly diverted to a nuclear program in another country, are difficult to detect and stop.

Sitting in his office, he looks for suspicious communications, typically emails (but also faxes and third party contacts) from a potential customer asking about prices for Leybold vacuum products. Enquiries provide an important early indication of current and potential nuclear smuggling. A military nuclear program may need to procure thousands of individual items, but will likely use relatively few front companies to attain them, making the front companies' identification critical to efforts to prevent or slow down proliferation. While such enquiries contain names of individuals and trading companies, the type and amount of items sought, they can also offer insight into the modus operandi of whichever nuclear program is placing the order.

Wirtz's team easily spotted October 2007 enquiries from a Pakistani trading company, which over a ten day period contacted two of Oerlikon Leybold's subsidiaries in Singapore and Ireland seeking vacuum pumps, Leybold's main product. The company claimed the pumps were needed for regenerating oil from industrial operations, a legitimate use of such equipment. After double checking with German authorities, Wirtz concluded this company was probably buying for Pakistan's nuclear weapons program. All such enquiries are maintained in his company's large database of trading companies and agents, which allows him to match similar enquiries from another trading company, perhaps with a less conspicuous address.

The global market in dual-use goods is enormous and the market in vacuum technology is an important subset of this international market. Almost all of this business in dual-use items is legitimate. Leybold estimates that procurement enquiries from smuggling networks make up less than a tenth of one percent of the total number of enquiries it receives. That small fraction makes detecting these enquiries challenging. To overcome this, Wirtz's export control office trains company personnel to spot suspicious procurement patterns and relays advice based on its analysis to its sales agents.

During the 1970s and 1980s, no supplier was more identified with the rise of the Khan network than Leybold-Heraeus, which included the Leybold division in Cologne and the division in Hanau, Germany. Leybold salesmen had greeted representatives of nuclear programs from Pakistan, South Africa, Iraq, Brazil, Libya, Taiwan, India, Iran, and North Korea. Leybold-Heraeus's former employees and agents, including Gotthard Lerch, Gerhard Wisser, and Daniel Geiges, bolstered their careers helping Khan.

Yet no supplier has undergone such a dramatic turnaround. Leybold is now part of Oerlikon, a Swiss high-tech corporation with 170 subsidiaries in thirty-five countries that employs about 20,000 people. Oerlikon Leybold is both an industry leader and a model for all responsible suppliers of sensitive equipment, consistently placing nonproliferation over its commercial interests. By its own reckoning this policy has cost Leybold $50–60 million in lost orders. If one believes it is possible to stop nuclear smuggling, Leybold's story offers hope.

Leybold's path to exemplary global citizen has not been an easy one. Several years before Oerlikon purchased it, Leybold AG's owners decided it was time to reform. The daunting task fell to Horst Heidsieck, a forty-three-year-old executive who had originally studied physics at the University of Bonn. In 1990, he was a senior executive at the German Degussa chemical corporation, which at the time owned Leybold AG. Heidsieck hoped for a promotion within Degussa where he had spent much of his career. Instead, in October 1990, Degussa's leaders made him Leybold AG's chairman of the board and chief executive officer.

Heidsieck was reluctant to take the job. Leybold AG had been suffering heavy financial losses and was laying off workers. Further undercutting revenue, the company was subjected to enormous criticism in Germany and the United States over its past sales. Leybold's board of directors was dealing with the ramifications of the company's past sales on what seemed an almost daily basis.[1] The company would need massive restructuring if Heidsieck was to make it profitable again.

Soon after he took the job, Heidsieck had to confront damaging revelations about Leybold's past proliferation sales to Iraq's nuclear weapons program. After the 1991 Persian Gulf War, IAEA inspectors discovered Leybold AG equipment in secret Iraqi nuclear weapon sites, the inspectors' reports incontrovertible proof of Leybold's wrongdoing despite its frequent earlier denials. Even today, Wirtz reminds his employees, "We don't want our stuff dug up from the desert."

In 1991, Leybold AG's reputation was in shambles. It faced further sales losses in Japan and the United States, two of its key markets, and was close to being put on a blacklist of organizations American companies were forbidden to do business with. For a company in which exports represented two thirds of its sales, disaster was looming.

Many of Leybold's questionable exports were known to German authorities, and in fact the government export regulators had either approved them or took no action to stop them. In the early 1990s, an embarrassed German government passed far stricter laws and regulations. In 1992, the government essentially blacklisted Iran, which had been an important recipient of German dual-use exports. Also it created special nuclear investigation teams, or "special nuclear commandos," that on several occasions raided Leybold, carrying away incriminating documents. Leybold officials were not prosecuted, because its sales in general did not violate the weak German export control laws, but the company was subject to large fines, not to mention further damage to its reputation.

Heidsieck decided that instead of simply complying with the new, tougher export laws, Leybold must become a leader in stopping the proliferation of equipment essential to building weapons of mass destruction. Industry and government "must cooperate in preventing the further proliferation of weapons of all types," he said. A corporation has the duty, he emphasized, to "check, on its own initiative, whether exports to certain countries can be responsibly justified or not."[2]

With a goal to thwart purchases from what had once been welcomed customers, Heidsieck's reforms were unpopular in many parts of the company. Several salesmen found the sales to sensitive countries lucrative and considered them legitimate. One Leybold official involved in many of the sales said they were like a "license to print money."[3] Customers from these countries would not just knock on your door, he added, but "pound" on it.

New German laws in 1991 required Leybold to establish an internal Corporate Export Controls Office (CECO) to ensure that the company was abiding by the new laws. Under revised German law, each company had to nominate a senior "export-responsible executive," who is held personally accountable for any illegal actions by the firm. Heidsieck made himself Leybold's responsible official. The stakes were high. If his mid-level managers violated the laws, he could face jail time.

In March 1992, Heidsieck instituted the Leybold Charter, a set of principles controlling the export of its products and services. These principles underscored Leybold's commitment to the non-proliferation of nuclear weapons and nuclear-capable delivery systems. The charter institutionalized the policy that the goal of nonproliferation of nuclear weapons is more important than commercial interests. Even if a particular export is legal, Leybold is committed to not selling the item if the company knows or has reason to believe the item will be used for the development or production of nuclear weapons in sensitive countries. Some of these countries, like India, Pakistan, and Israel, may not have signed the Nuclear Non-Proliferation Treaty. Other countries, such as Syria, Iran, Libya, and North Korea, are viewed as sensitive even if they have signed the treaty. Leybold's voluntary self-restraint was a marked difference from its previous policy of keeping one's head in the sand about the end user. It was also far beyond what most suppliers were doing at that time.

Many outside the company reacted skeptically to the charter, cynically interpreting it as part of a campaign to keep Leybold from being blacklisted by the United States. Heidsieck did in fact hire a well-known U.S. public relations firm, Burson-Marsteller, to work on improving Leybold's standing. He also did not hesitate to visit Washington, charter in hand, pleading for understanding. To back up his commitment, any shipments to a collection of sensitive countries, including Pakistan, North Korea, Iran, India, and Israel, were to be authorized by Heidsieck himself. He instructed his export manager, Bernhard Herkert, based in Hanau with Heidsieck, and Wirtz, then Herkert's assistant in Cologne, to send all enquiries from any of these countries to the German customs authorities. If they raised any suspicions about the end use of the item, Heidsieck would not permit the sale.

Herkert said in an interview in 1993 that in the past sensitive export matters rarely reached top management but that had "drastically changed."[4] By 1993, his office had dealt with about 3,500 export cases, and had turned down many orders that could not meet Leybold's strict policies. Company officials were required to know government export regulations and laws, and had to submit sensitive orders through a detailed company approval process that checked for possible misuse. His office required company personnel to obtain detailed information about the customer and final purpose of the equipment. If they did not follow these procedures, they risked being fired. In one case, Heidsieck fired a salesman who sold spare parts to an Iranian steel factory against company policy.[5]

Preventing future sales to sensitive countries was only part of the problem. Heidsieck also had to address problems within Leybold. To fully change the export culture, Heidsieck was forced to fire or push out several employees, including a top corporate official, who were linked to the most questionable past sales. Given Germany's strong laws protecting employees, this proved a challenging task. Because many of the controversial sales were approved by former leaders of the company or heads of the sales division, several employees could not be fired for these sales. This meant that at least a few bad apples needed to remain—but who were these people?

In 1992, Leybold received a warning from the United States that a German trading company was buying a large number of Leybold items, likely for export to Pakistan or other sensitive countries. Wirtz investigated and discovered that the address matched that of the trading company owned by the wife of a senior employee. This employee was in charge of sales to a range of sensitive countries including Syria, Iran, Iraq, Israel, Pakistan, South Africa, Taiwan, and North Korea. He was familiar with members of the Khan network and its associated fronts, including Arshad, Amjad, and Abid, or Triple A, the Pakistani trading company and Leybold agent that fronted for Khan's enrichment program in the late 1970s and early 1980s.[6]

Senior Leybold officials speculated that this saleman was worried about his loss of sales and commissions following the reforms and had decided to use this trading company to buy items directly from Leybold as a way to bypass the internal checks on end users. He would then route the items himself. In essence, a domestic company down the street from their headquarters was purchasing its own materials for a hidden Pakistani client.

This trading company had ordered from Leybold DM 750,000 worth of products. The employee was also suspected of selling Iran many items, some in quantities large enough to suggest their use in a centrifuge program. Wirtz took the information to Heidsieck, who wanted to fire this employee, but the offense of establishing a side business competing with Leybold was not serious enough to warrant dismissal under Germany's employment regulations. Cleverly, Leybold management offered this employee a lucrative termination package that led him to resign.

A few years later, in 1994, German authorities tipped off Leybold that its agent in Pakistan, the Industrial and Scientific Equipment Company (ISEC), could be selling to Pakistan's nuclear program. This information had come from the United States in the form of a non-paper, a diplomatic note stripped of official U.S. markings to hide its origin. According to the tip, ISEC was linked to Triple A, Leybold's original agent. An internal Leybold investigation discovered that Leybold-Heraeus middle managers had helped form ISEC secretly after Leybold's agent Triple A was exposed in the early 1980s as a key Khan buyer. The investigation uncovered that Leybold managers had formed ISEC, with Mohammed Azlam Sheikh as head, expressly to avoid the problems caused by Triple A's exposure.[7] The new Leybold management was unaware of ISEC's clandestine connections to Triple A and Pakistan's nuclear program. The old top management might have been likewise uninformed of ISEC's true role, since middle managers used to have considerable discretion to conduct their sales. Nonetheless, Heidsieck remained suspicious that some of these former officials knew about ISEC or had looked the other way to gain more black market business.

One of the items found during the investigation was a 1989 memorandum written by a middle manager establishing that ISEC was in the same group of companies as Pakistan Air Conditioning and Refrigeration Corporation (PARC). The German government considered PARC a purchaser for Pakistan's nuclear program. This information established a clear link and as a result, Leybold fired ISEC as its agent in November 1994, mere days after it had received the initial tip from authorities.

Leybold's new policy created a virtual embargo on business with sensitive countries but Herkert quickly learned that tough restrictions were not enough to dissuade persistent clients, especially those desperate for spare parts essential for aging Leybold equipment. The same requests now filtered in from trading companies. For example, Herkert received an enquiry from a trading company in Bangkok, and later from one in Russia, for a near identical order that had been denied to India. Since the orders matched so closely, Leybold's new export tracking system could detect these attempted purchases.

With Leybold's tighter regulations and the general strengthening of controls over exports in the early 1990s, more customers went underground, developing a number of strategies to fool suppliers about an item's true end user. Some trading companies, like ISEC and Krisch Engineering, knowingly engaged in fronting for the real customer to hide the true buyer from the supplier and any prying authorities. Most trading companies, however, are engaged in legitimate business, acting as middlemen for a wide range of companies. Legitimate trading companies, which can be located anywhere, pose difficult challenges to responsible suppliers. These companies mark up the price of the supplied goods and live off commissions from their clients. Out of fear of losing those commissions, trading companies usually hide the identity of their clients, complicating any attempt by the supplier to confirm the end user is not nefarious. Herkert, however, discovered that secret nuclear programs were using these legitimate trading companies to disguise themselves.

What if an enquiry came from a trading company, whether acting as a front company or an inadvertent middleman for a sensitive program, and Leybold had no information to challenge the sale? What could it do? In almost all cases, the company could legally export the item, even if it suspected that the item would then be illegally reexported to Pakistan or another sensitive country. To prohibit the sale, the company needed a governmental warning to not deal with a specific trading company or needed to obtain evidence that the export could be for a secret nuclear program. At the time, such warnings were infrequent and the ability of companies to develop evidence limited.

Heidsieck and his export control staff wanted to do more about the trading company loophole. Leybold instituted procedures that required trading companies, whether in Germany or in other countries, to provide evidence that the end user was not a sensitive nuclear program. If Leybold officials remained suspicious, it would not make the sale even if the export was technically legal. This unprecedented policy ran into fierce resistance from trading companies that insisted Leybold had no right under the law to ask for such information. After a careful explanation of its intent, Leybold won many converts, though not enough to plug this major loophole industry wide, which largely remains today.

Heidsieck's departure from Leybold in 1998, along with Leybold's sale to Oerlikon, raised concerns that its nonproliferation commitment would fade. Such was not the case. Wirtz continues to look for suspicious enquiries via his office's centralized data system where orders from sales agents around the world are checked against enquiries from other Leybold offices or sales agents.

As Oerlikon Leybold's export officials became more familiar with enquiries from sensitive countries, they noticed that increasingly the requested items were not on lists of nuclear dual-use items subject to the stricter licensing requirements of the newer laws. Instead of custom ordering vacuum pumps and valves manufactured specially for gas centrifuge plants and thus on the lists, sensitive programs ordered similar items from the Leybold catalog. The procurement specialists and scientists running these programs in Iran, Pakistan, or North Korea had learned that items on dual-use export control lists could be avoided by substituting another item from the catalog that was less capable than the listed item but still good enough for its intended purpose. Such items may need to be replaced more often, but the sacrifice is worth it if they're easier to obtain.

Starting in August 2002, right before Iran's Natanz site was revealed, Leybold received a series of enquiries from trading companies for large numbers of fast-acting valves suspected for use in P1 centrifuge cascades. These valves were not of the type found on lists of nuclear dual-use equipment that require a government-issued license to export.[8] Countries like Pakistan and Iran had learned that despite not being specifically designed to handle the highly corrosive uranium hexafluoride gas found in a gas centrifuge plant, these less-controlled valves worked adequately, although perhaps not as long. They also realized that such purchases would attract far less scrutiny from suppliers and authorities.

The first order was from a German trading company which said the valves were destined for a petrochemical factory in the UAE. Leybold officials linked this company to Iran and did not make the sale. This enquiry was followed by one in October from another German company, which cited Iranian universities as the end users. The trial order of 3,000 valves and a total order of 50,000 valves was an unusually large number for a university. Other requests followed. The largest order was from a South Korean company in May 2003 seeking an annual quantity of 50,000 to 100,000 valves. The end user of this request was an Iranian nuclear power plant, another unusual customer for such a high number of valves.

Wirtz was convinced the orders were for the Natanz enrichment plant, which would need at least 150,000 valves for all the P1 centrifuges Iran planned to deploy. In September 2003, he brought the enquiries to the German government agency responsible for exports. This agency, after doing its own internal technical evaluation, confirmed Wirtz's hunch that these valves were suitable for use in a centrifuge plant and should not be approved for export to Iran.

Many sensitive programs have approached Oerlikon Leybold for vacuum pumps, but as in the case of the valves, they do not order vacuum pumps specially manufactured for a centrifuge plant.[9] The purchaser again avoids ordering explicitly controlled items by buying less controlled items from a company catalog. Advancements in vacuum pumps make it easier for customers in Iran and Pakistan to then transform standard vacuum pumps into those able to handle uranium hexafluoride.

In 2006, Indian Rare Earths (IRE), the Indian governmental entity that procures items for the gas centrifuge plant near Mysore, advertised among European suppliers its desire to buy several vacuum pumps. The IRE advertisement sought vacuum pumps able to handle corrosive gases but that would likely be used for the corrosive gas uranium hexafluoride inside centrifuges. As this modification does not meet the condition of being specially prepared for a centrifuge plant, these modified pumps would not be on the usual suspect orders list. Leybold ignored the advertisement. Subsequently the German government learned of this Indian sales request and ruled that such an export would not be allowed by any German company. Although the government agreed that the pumps are not explicitly controlled by any export control list, the purchaser is a well-known procurement agent for India's gas centrifuge plant that makes enriched uranium for military purposes.

As is standard practice among members of the Nuclear Suppliers Group (NSG), the German government shared its decision to deny exports of the pumps with other NSG members. This practice reduces the chance that the Indian government could make the purchase in another country. This case is an example where catch-all export controls are useful. They can work when a supplier learns of a nuclear end user or determines that the end use is more likely than not nuclear. This stands in sharp contrast to Leybold's condition not to make a sale if it merely suspects that the end user is nuclear. In most cases, however, suppliers cannot concretely establish the former condition without government assistance.

Leybold has noticed that trading companies engaged in unlawful procurement are aware that their enquiries will often be met with skepticism and that many will be ignored and unfulfilled.

As a result, the trading companies might send out enquiries for the same items to as many manufacturers and their sales agents as possible. These trading companies also try to exploit any lack of communication among a single manufacturer's sales agents by sending a barrage of enquiries to many of its sales agents within a short period of time, or all at once. Without Leybold's centralized export control office, its individual sales offices would be unaware of the identical enquiries sent by the same trading company to other sales offices.

This system was tested in late 2006. Leybold's export control office noticed a suspicious pattern of enquiries from trading companies. On one day, Leybold offices in France, the Netherlands, and the main office in Cologne received identical enquiries for vacuum pumps from a trading company in Rawalpindi, Pakistan. A few days later, Leybold's daughter company in Singapore received a similar enquiry from a Dubai trading company. The export control office suspected that the items were for use in Pakistan's gas centrifuge uranium enrichment program and ignored the enquiries. The same Dubai and Pakistani trading companies continued to seek items from Leybold in 2007 and 2008 for what was suspected to be Pakistan's nuclear weapons programs.

Leybold's export control office has over the years become deeply experienced in receiving and analyzing suspicious enquiries from the manufacturer's many subsidiaries and sales agents. It is now an entrenched part of Oerlikon Leybold, functioning as a "detection hub" aimed at finding and stopping potential procurement attempts. This system, however, is by no means foolproof, depending increasingly on help from friendly governments to detect suspicious enquiries.

In 2006, a South Korean manufacturing company wanted to

buy vacuum pumps. For many applications, including use in centrifuge plants, two or more vacuum pumps work in tandem, each achieving a portion of the desired vacuum. This order was for fifteen such systems. A friendly European government notified Leybold that the end user could be Iran's centrifuge program, so it ignored the enquiry. Yet as with the earlier valve orders, South Korea was a place where smugglers successfully sought items from European suppliers. The country had passed stringent export control laws and had become member of the elite Nuclear Suppliers Group. But according to an experienced U.S. government official, the South Korean government's export laws were poorly implemented at that time. He said that South Korea was "part of the gap," a weak link in the international system to thwart smuggling. South Korea is not alone. The number of turntable countries, or "countries of transit concern," remains high. Secret nuclear procurement efforts have also used trading companies in Singapore, the UAE, Malaysia, and Poland to disguise their orders. In some cases, they also use companies in countries with highly developed national export control systems, such as the United States.

China poses special challenges for a company like Leybold. A rapidly industrializing country, it has struggled to implement effective export controls. Following tips from a European intelligence agency, Leybold discovered a new strategy used by Iran to circumvent export controls, in this case a clever scheme to obtain vacuum pump systems for its centrifuge program. The elaborate ruse involved a Chinese manufacturing company, an "original equipment manufacturer," or OEM, that had an established relationship with Leybold.

After reviewing enquiries and contracts, Wirtz soon found

that the OEM had ordered fifteen such pump systems, seven of which the OEM had already received via Leybold's Chinese subsidiary. The OEM had ordered the pumps as part of a larger order it had received to build oil purification equipment for electrical power plants. The supplier did not need its government's approval to supply the pumps because the sale did not require a license and was not overtly suspicious. The OEM had not previously been associated with unlawful activities but after the discovery, Leybold immediately contacted them and asked for the end user of the equipment. The head of this OEM said that the vacuum equipment, including the pump systems, had already been exported to an overseas customer that he refused to name. Leybold stopped any further shipments of pumps. The OEM, after demanding the rest of the pumps or all its money back, cancelled the order, perhaps to prevent admitting that its customer was Iran, which ended up receiving the pumps.

While these types of diversionary procurements are more common, by exercising vigilance and cooperating with friendly governments, Leybold is in a strong position to inform authorities early about suspicious enquiries. With its key position in the international vacuum market, Leybold is a valuable lookout. Few, if any, governments have the accumulated knowledge of these commercial companies. Their assistance can be invaluable in detecting and thwarting smugglers. In the end, according to a U.S. Department of Energy official, "Export controls are a net, not a brick wall." Increasingly, dual-use items sought by sensitive countries can be caught only by invoking catch-all laws or restrictive company policies. The former are difficult to make work, leaving the latter as the most practical strategy.

Oerlikon Leybold provides us with a valuable lesson. Working alone, government and industry are each weakened in stopping the spread of dangerous technologies. Private industries, no matter how adept their internal compliance systems, cannot on their own prevent smuggling networks from eventually obtaining targeted goods without cooperation from their respective governments. Government loses valuable information and assistance if industry is not actively involved. With just a small fraction of companies in a potentially sensitive industry acting responsibly, like Oerlikon Leybold, industry could become an effective first line of defense against nuclear proliferation.

———————

TWELVE

Illicit Nuclear Trade Today and the Way Forward

For most countries, the pathway to obtaining and improving nuclear weapons still centers on illicit nuclear trade. The countries and subnational groups in the table below buy, or would need to purchase, key equipment and materials unlawfully to produce nuclear weapons or improve their nuclear weapons technology.

Who's Who in Today's World of Illicit Nuclear Trade?[1]

I. Currently maintaining or improving nuclear arsenals via illicit trade	II. Nuclear wannabes dependent on illicit trade	III. To worry about
Pakistan	Iran	Egypt
India	Syria	Algeria
North Korea	Myanmar	Turkey
China (?)	Al Qaeda	Saudi Arabia
		South Korea
		Taiwan
		Other terrorist groups
		Failed states in Africa, elsewhere
		Transnational smuggling networks

Over the next several years, many states in dangerous regions of the world, along with terrorist organizations, are expected to pursue nuclear weapons. Governments' ability to detect and stop this perilous trade remains limited. Too often, major successes in thwarting nuclear proliferation have depended on the last line of defense—military attacks, intelligence operations, and cargo seizures. As important as these measures are, it is risky to depend on the last line of defense for our security. A former CIA official who was instrumental in busting the Khan network worries, "Can we count on intelligence when we need it again?" Finding new ways to thwart these efforts is critical.

Our security should rest on the first lines of defense, such as institutionalized approaches like the Nuclear Non-Proliferation Treaty, domestic and international trade controls, diplomacy, corporate vigilance, and international inspections. Yet these approaches all failed to detect, let alone stop, a nuclear reactor in Syria, the Khan network, and Pakistan's nuclear experts' assistance to al Qaeda. Five years after Khan's network was busted, these established arrangements are not performing much better at catching, prosecuting, or deterring smugglers.

States such as Iran, Pakistan, and North Korea continue to use their nuclear programs to create state-sponsored smuggling networks that seek the most effective ways to bypass export regulations, hide the end user, and avoid detection. For-profit, transnational smuggling networks can periodically arise and rival sophisticated suppliers in their ability to sell nuclear facilities and capabilities. All these networks have learned that suppliers in any country, including the United States, can be tricked into selling them sensitive goods. By using trading companies, intermediary shippers, and complex payment schemes, these networks can use any country as a transshipment point. They can successfully target any supplier, making their orders through a nearly endless stream of unwitting intermediaries. Once a trading company serves its purpose, it is jettisoned and a new company is found.

With the global spread of technology and rapid growth in international trade, smugglers find it easier to ply their dangerous trade. It's simpler now to obtain the materials, equipment, and know-how to produce nuclear weapons than it was ten years ago, and could be simpler still ten years from now. Many countries that are considered developing nations have sophisticated manufacturing and machine tool capabilities that can be exploited. These new suppliers are emerging in developing markets with few export controls and a culture of indifference to stopping the spread of nuclear weapons technology.

New technologies could also emerge that would simplify the task of making nuclear explosive materials or nuclear weapons. With experts in producing nuclear explosive materials and nuclear weapons spread throughout the world, we can expect more leakage of dangerous classified information along with a growing reservoir of expertise that networks can probe for assistance.

We face the risk of new "nuclear wannabes," whether they are states or terrorist groups. John M. McConnell, former Director of National Intelligence, in testimony before the Senate Armed Services Committee on February 27, 2007, said, "We are watching several states for signs of nuclear weapons aspirations, in part because of reporting of past contact with A.Q. Khan and his network when it was active. We also are concerned about rogue or criminal elements willing to supply materials and technology—alone or with a network—without their government's knowledge."[2]

If Iran's and North Korea's nuclear ambitions remain unchecked, in direct defiance of the major powers in the U.N. Security Council, the international community could face both a cascade of states seeking nuclear weapons and a severely weakened world order to stop proliferation. And what could happen in Pakistan if its government, along with its nuclear arsenal of sixty to one hundred weapons, falls into the hands of radical fundamentalists? Besides the obvious threat to the United States, a radical fundamentalist government may decide that spreading its nuclear capabilities to other nations is vital to its survival and its duty. Along with the additional danger of al Qaeda are hostile groups in failed states that might be able to import the equipment and materials to cobble together a crude atomic weapon. According to George Tenet, "In the current marketplace, if you have a hundred million dollars, you can be your own nuclear power."[3] With advances in technology and a wider diffusion of knowledge, that price might come down considerably.

We do not have to live in such a frightening world. Some pundits and cynics proclaim nuclear smuggling inevitable, a necessary price of global business, but fatalism is a deadly foe. We should not wait until a nuclear weapon goes off in a major city to act.

Three critical steps that must be taken are implementing universal laws and norms against nuclear smuggling, establishing more secure nuclear assets, and working toward earlier detection of illicit nuclear trade.

Making export laws universal and enforcing them is paramount. Export or trade controls are the foundation of efforts to stop the outfitting of nuclear weapons programs. These controls are deeply embedded in the Nuclear Non-Proliferation Treaty. They are also at the core of efforts of the widely respected Nuclear

Suppliers Group. While few industries look favorably on export control regimes, their intention is not to stop progress or interfere in the pursuit of business. Preventing the misuse of civilian goods in nuclear weapons programs should be a global moral imperative.

Rigorous prosecution of major export violations is more of a goal than a reality in most parts of the world. Too many transnational nuclear smugglers evade punishment because rules of evidence vary among countries, international cooperation is uneven or nonexistent, and judicial attitudes vary widely. Under the Nuclear Suppliers Group or NPT, major suppliers must agree to implement universal guidelines for prosecuting transnational nuclear smugglers that include commitments to aid other countries' prosecutions. As a backup to national prosecutions, the United Nations Security Council should sanction major transnational nuclear smugglers. To further deter such smuggling, it should also make the most extreme cases of such smuggling activity a crime against humanity and an offense punishable under international law and tribunal. The transfer of the capability to develop, produce, or trade nuclear weapons deserves international censure, because acquisition of nuclear weapons severely threatens international security and the detonation of a single nuclear weapon can kill tens or even hundreds of thousands of innocent people.

Another problem is that not all countries have export controls. The United Nations Security Council has already mandated in Resolution 1540 that all countries should establish and implement export controls. President Barack Obama has made this goal central to his efforts to stop nuclear proliferation. However, many countries have refused to create laws to enforce this resolution, or if they have them, have not effectively enforced them. Certain states' lack of cooperation should be deemed unacceptable. It is outrageous that Malaysia, an important base of operation for the Khan network and a favorite global smuggling hub for Pakistan and Iran, has refused to create and implement export controls. China has also done far too little and remains a shopper's paradise for nuclear smugglers.

The UAE is a special case because of Dubai's long history of acting as a smugglers' safe haven. In recent years, it has taken steps to bust up smuggling operations, including creating export controls, but Dubai still resists needed changes. If the UAE (and for that matter, Malaysia) wants to continue importing U.S. goods either for use domestically or for transshipment elsewhere, it must show that these goods are not diverted to Iran's or Pakistan's nuclear weapons efforts. Other key transit points, such as Singapore and Hong Kong, have changed dramatically for the better. The UAE has much more to do.

America must press countries—both friends and foes alike—to do more to clamp down on smuggling. In the case of a partner such as Pakistan, we need to stop acting as if we are powerless to prevent it from "picking our pocket" to obtain goods illegally. Under U.S. pressure in the 1980s and early 1990s, Israel, which formerly rivaled Pakistan in the extent of its nuclear smuggling, decided to stop its illicit procurement for its nuclear weapons program. We should expect no less from Pakistan or India.

For countries such as Iran and North Korea, negotiated agreements to limit their nuclear programs must include commitments to stop proliferating nuclear technology and engaging in illegal smuggling. Negotiators have shied away from demanding verifiable commitments for far too long.

In April 2009, President Obama spoke in Prague of a world free of nuclear weapons. Achieving that goal will take a long time.

The methods developed today to prevent the misuse of dangerous technologies are an important building block in creating the world Obama wants. They help provide critical assurances that countries are not pursuing nuclear weapons and an early warning system if a country or subnational group seeks to build them.

In his Prague speech President Obama also called for securing all vulnerable nuclear material within four years. He committed the United States to work with Russia and other partners to lock down these sensitive materials. Protecting nuclear assets against theft is vital, but we must do more. Developing uniform international standards on what technology and information is sensitive is long overdue.

Pakistan's long history of inadequate controls over its sensitive nuclear information has created an unprecedented risk that requires special steps to undo. Among Khan's most dangerous innovations were ingeniously marketing designs and manufacturing instruction booklets for centrifuges and nuclear weapons, developing packages containing key equipment and, often times, digitized documentation. Although the danger that such detailed designs would emerge on the Internet has not been realized, these digitized nuclear weapon designs, and others like them that we know nothing about, may now be in the hands of smugglers.

It is imperative that responsible governments seek to recover these materials and other sensitive information. Past efforts to find and recover sets of stolen classified centrifuge information have succeeded. After the fall of Baghdad in April 2003, one of ISIS's goals was to find the classified centrifuge drawings and manufacturing instructions sold by German experts to Iraq in the late 1980s. Despite the Iraqis' dubious claims that they had destroyed all such documents (dubious because its engineers knew that they had little chance of obtaining another set), we figured that Mahdi Obeidi, the former head of Iraq's gas centrifuge program, would know the whereabouts of these documents. Obeidi telephoned me from Baghdad admitting he had hidden the entire set of centrifuge information, along with key centrifuge components, in a plastic drum which he buried in a garden behind his house. He sought my help in approaching the U.S. government to negotiate a deal for asylum in return for the documents.[4] The negotiations were not easy, but Obeidi traded the entire set for asylum for him and his immediate family in the United States, where they now live today. Fortunately, Obeidi had not digitized this collection, making recovery far easier once we established no other copies existed.

Although digitized information is far easier to copy and hide than paper copies, it too is recoverable. Smugglers place digitized information on CDs or secretly on Internet servers. Governments and the IAEA should remove classified information from circulation whenever they get the opportunity. Although such a practice might not eliminate all copies, it can reduce the chance that this information will spread.

The single most significant shortcoming we face today is the lack of systematic, universal methods to detect illicit nuclear trade. Early detection is vital. In this effort, an unutilized tool is the IAEA Additional Protocol to the Nuclear Non-Proliferation Treaty and IAEA investigatory capabilities.

One of the IAEA's central inspection tools is the Additional Protocol, developed in the mid-1990s to expand the IAEA's inspection rights and make it much easier to detect when a country has a secret nuclear facility. The protocol makes a country's nuclear program far more transparent than what was provided for with inspections in years past. Under the protocol, the inspectors can investigate questionable imports and exports to determine whether a state is in compliance with its treaty obligations. If the IAEA learns of suspicious purchases, it can press the country for more information.

Not surprisingly, this detection tool remains largely unimplemented among countries most prone to proliferate. Syria, Iran, and North Korea have refused to implement the Additional Protocol. The IAEA and its key member states have, up to this point, not made accepting the Additional Protocol a requirement among countries that have signed the Nuclear Non-Proliferation Treaty. This should change immediately. Any country that refuses the Additional Protocol should not receive any further nuclear assistance from the IAEA or elsewhere.

The IAEA's experienced and technically sophisticated inspectorate is unique in its ability to collect and analyze nuclear information. Even intelligence agencies rarely have the technical depth of the IAEA or a sustained commitment to maintaining that level of expertise. Because of its experiences uncovering the nuclear smuggling activities of Iran, Libya, and the Khan network, the IAEA established a special program solely dedicated to tracking smuggling networks. On a limited basis, it tracks transnational nuclear networks and nonstate actors to increase its chances of detecting and responding to nuclear proliferation risks. To that end, it collects and analyzes nuclear trade information, seeking to better understand existing networks and reveal unknown ones.

Yet its potential often lies dormant. A key part of this initiative is collecting suspicious enquiry data from high-technology manufacturers that volunteer to help. The IAEA contacts an individual company only after obtaining the support of the company's home country. While there are now outreach programs in many countries, the Bush administration did not give the IAEA the green light for its effort to collect information from U.S. companies. The Obama administration should do so.

Currently, the U.S. intelligence community, in cooperation with its foreign partners, works to identify, penetrate, and disrupt nuclear smuggling and proliferation networks. These operations are often successful, but they miss most transactions. Innovative approaches to detection can be built upon both multilateral governmental cooperation and responsible company citizenship efforts. Companies like Oerlikon Leybold demonstrate how new methods can complement intelligence and enforcement efforts and significantly improve chances of catching suspicious enquiries.

U.S. enforcement agencies tend to focus on prosecutions for illegal exports, even in accidental cases where goods ended up in a proliferant state despite a company's best efforts to verify an end user's identity. This emphasis on prosecution inhibits companies from taking part in the type of broad, sustained cooperation that Oerlikon Leybold practices in Europe. When companies cooperate with law enforcement in the United States, they typically do not know if they themselves are under investigation. Moreover, U.S. companies that make voluntary disclosures of potential violations of export requirements—disclosures that can identify hitherto unknown foreign parties—risk criminal prosecution and substantial administrative fines based on disclosures. Companies are rightly concerned about their exposure to penalties when making disclosures and are left to determine on their own to what extent they need to protect themselves from voluntarily disclosing accidental violations.

There is a better way to expand cooperation. In Britain and Germany, companies regularly provide information to authorities, while their governments tip off companies about illicit procurement networks targeting their products in order to prevent an inadvertent sale. In Britain, authorities maintain contact with about 2,500 British companies, trade associations, and academic institutions through phone calls, emails and personal visits. Common to these systems is the notion that industry and government can work together to better identify illicit procurement attempts before an enquiry becomes a sale.

As a result of this cooperation, the British and German governments receive an unprecedented amount of operational intelligence. In a large number of cases, follow-up actions result in disruptions of shipments or improved compliance. Just as important, the government receives a significant amount of strategic intelligence about secret nuclear programs, providing new insights and key corroboration of intelligence assumptions and estimates.

A new approach is needed in the United States. This effort should place an emphasis on facilitating an equitable flow of information between the U.S. government and industry. Finding an institutional home for this cooperative effort may be difficult, but one possible candidate is the Commerce Department. It has experience with the intricacies of export control laws and its staff is trained to effectively communicate with companies. This would allow it to glean information on suspicious enquiries as well as provide useful tips on illicit procurement attempts.

Albert Einstein said, "The unleashed power of the atom has changed everything save our modes of thinking and we thus drift toward unparalleled catastrophe." Underlying these reforms must be a shift in the way we think about nuclear proliferation. We must have a greater awareness about the risks to our security and our future if this trade is to stop.

Notes

INTRODUCTION

1. Mark Mazzetti and Helene Cooper, "U.S. Confirms Israeli Strikes Hit Syrian Target Last Week," *The New York Times*, September 12, 2007.
2. Barbara Opall-Rome and Vago Muradian, "Bush Privately Lauds Israeli Attack on Syria," *Defense News*, January 14, 2008.
3. As of September 2009, Israeli government officials still had not provided any details about the attack.
4. BBC, "Analysis: Syria-Israel Tensions," October 3, 2007.
5. Glenn Kessler, "Syria-N. Korea Reports Won't Stop Talks," *The Washington Post*, September 15, 2007.
6. KCNA, September 18, 2007.
7. George Friedman, "Israel, Syria and the Glaring Secret," Stratfor, Strategic Forecasting, September 25, 2007.
8. David Albright and Paul Brannan, "Suspect Reactor Construction Site in Eastern Syria: The Site of the September 6 Israeli Raid?" *ISIS*, October 23, 2007, www.isis-online.org; and Robin Wright and Joby Warrick, "Photographs Said to Show Israeli Target Inside Syria," *The Washington Post*, October 24, 2007.
9. Interview with senior Israeli official, October 2007.
10. Many of the countries that have sought nuclear weapons are described on the ISIS website, www.isis-online.org.
11. George Jahn, "Syria Contacted by Nuclear Black Market," Associated Press, December 19, 2007.

ONE: OUT OF THE COLD

1. "Coming out of the cold" refers to a spy returning from a dangerous mission; interview with Munir Khan by Shahid-Ur-Rehman, quoted in Rehman, *Long Road to Chagai* (Islamabad: Printwise Publication, 1999), p. 51.
2. *Investigative Group Report on the Activities of Dr. A.Q. Khan*, Dutch government

report, 1979 (in Dutch), also referred to in this and the next chapter as secret 1979 Dutch report.

3. Ibid.

4. Ibid.

5. R. B. Kehoe, *The Enriching Troika—A History of URENCO to the Year 2000* (Buckinghamshire UK: URENCO Limited, 2002), p. 228; and interview with Marcel van Silfhout, Zembla, October 6, 2005.

6. *Investigative Group Report*, op. cit.

7. Ibid.

8. *The Enriching Troika*, p. 228.

9. Zahid Malik, *Dr. Abdul Qadeer Khan and the Islamic Bomb, Part 2* (Islamabad: Hurmat Publications, 1998), chapter 9.

10. *Long Road to Chagai*, p. 48.

11. Interview with S.A. Butt by Shahid-Ur-Rehman, quoted in *Long Road to Chagai*, p. 48.

12. S. Shabbir Hussain and Mujahid Kamran (eds.), *Dr. A.Q. Khan on Science and Education* (Lahore: Sang-E-Meel Publications, 1997), p. 12.

13. *Dr. Abdul Qadeer Khan and the Islamic Bomb, Part 2*, chapter 9.

14. Years later, discoveries about Iran's and Libya's gas centrifuge programs—see Chapter 6—would demonstrate exactly how much information Khan stole from URENCO. Khan's and Pakistan's denials are an attempt to fend off any potential legal action and prevent any international efforts to stop Pakistan's nuclear program. Khan's story has also been drummed into the minds of Pakistanis, elevating Khan to a larger-than-life figure.

15. *Investigative Group Report*, op. cit.

16. *Long Road to Chagai*, p. 50.

17. "Twenty Years of Excellence and National Service: Dr. A.Q. Khan Research Laboratories 1976–1996," undated, p. 4.

18. Ibid.

19. "Worrying Times?" *The Guardian*, November 8, 2001, and Qazi Kashif Niaz and Irshad Ahmed Arshad, "Pakistani Scientist Says Al-Qaida's Nuclear Briefcase is a Fiction," *Jamaatud Daawa Pakistan*, April 7, 2006, in Urdu. Mahmood would later become a Taliban supporter and be placed under house arrest for suspicion of helping Osama bin Laden build nuclear weapons in Afghanistan. See Chapter 8, "Al Qaeda's Bomb."

20. Steven Weissman and Herbert Krosney, *The Islamic Bomb* (New York: Times Books, 1981), p. 182; *Long Road to Chagai*, p. 48.

21. *Long Road to Chagai*, p. 51.

22. Ibid.

23. *Investigative Group Report*, op. cit.

24. Interview with Marcel van Silfhout, Zembla, October 6, 2005; and Panorama, BBC-1, June 16, 1980, written transcript.

25. *Long Road to Chagai*, p. 50.

26. *Investigative Group Report*, op. cit.

27. Ibid.

28. Ruud Lubbers, "The Threat of Nuclear Proliferation in the Era of Globaliza-

tion," Muller Lecture 2005, Netherlands Society for International Affairs, December 13, 2005.

29. Ibid.
30. *Investigative Group Report*, op. cit.
31. The part was a maraging steel tube 500 millimeters long, with an outer diameter of 101 millimeters and wall thickness of one millimeter. The bellows is about 60–100 mm in length, implying that each tube could result in 5–8 bellows.
32. *Investigative Group Report*, op. cit.
33. "The Threat of Nuclear Proliferation in the Era of Globalization," op. cit.
34. *Investigative Group Report*, op. cit.
35. Ibid.
36. Ruud Lubbers, "Moving Beyond the Stalemate: Addressing the Nuclear Challenge by Supranational Means," Chingendael International Energy Programme, Briefing Papers, August 2005.
37. NHK Japan Broadcasting, "AQ Khan Network," Interview with Ruud Lubbers, undated, p. 2 of written transcript.
38. Interview with former senior CIA official, October 2005.
39. Ibid.
40. *Investigative Group Report*, op. cit.

TWO: PAKISTAN GETS THE BOMB

1. *Dr. Abdul Qadeer Khan and the Islamic Bomb, Part 2*, op. cit., chapter 9.
2. *Long Road to Chagai*, pp. 51–53; and *Dr. Abdul Qadeer Khan and the Islamic Bomb, Part 2*, chapter 9.
3. *Long Road to Chagai*, op. cit., p. 51–52.
4. Egmont Koch, "Wanted . . . Bomb Business: Nuclear Aid for Pakistan and India," West German Broadcasting (WDR), 1986, written transcript, translated from German.
5. *Investigative Group Report*, op. cit.
6. Ibid.
7. Ibid.
8. Ibid.
9. Ibid.
10. Ibid.
11. Ibid.
12. Ibid.
13. Ibid.
14. Ibid.
15. *Islamic Bomb*, op. cit., p. 184.
16. *Investigative Group Report*, op. cit.
17. Ibid.
18. "Twenty Years of Excellence and National Service," op. cit., p. 9.
19. Ibid.
20. Zembla, "The Netherlands' Atomic Bomb," Hilversum Nederland-3 Television Network in Dutch, November 5, 2005 (translated from Dutch).

21. *Investigative Group Report,* op. cit.
22. Abdus Salam shares a name with the Pakistani physicist who won the Nobel Prize in 1979. They are not the same person.
23. *Investigative Group Report,* op. cit.
24. Ibid.
25. Sreedhar, *Pakistan's Bomb: A Documentary Study* (New Delhi: ABC Publishing House, 1986), chapter 4, "Letters of A.Q. Khan."
26. *Islamic Bomb,* p. 186: Steve Coll, "The Atomic Emporium," *The New Yorker,* August 7 & 14, 2006, p. 5; and Adrian Levy and Catherine Scott-Clark, *Deception* (New York: Walker, 2007), p. 38.
27. *Investigative Group Report,* op. cit.
28. "Wanted . . . Bomb Business: Nuclear Aid for Pakistan and India," op. cit.; and *Investigative Group Report,* op. cit.
29. *Investigative Group Report,* op. cit.
30. Ibid.; each tube was 100 millimeters long and 100 millimeters in diameter.
31. Zembla, "The Netherlands' Atomic Bomb," Hilversum Nederland-3 Television Network, in Dutch, November 5, 2005.
32. *Investigative Group Report,* op. cit.
33. Ibid.
34. Ibid.
35. Jaco Alberts and Karel Knip, "About an Engineer from Alkmaar and the Pakistani Bomb—Dutch Government Monitored Activities of Trader in Nuclear Know-How for More that 30 Years," NRC Handelsblad (Internet version). Cire was a trusted Khan confidant until he was arrested by Turkish authorities in 2004. He died in prison before he could be brought to trial. Slebos was convicted on minor export violations on December 16, 2005. He served four months in prison and paid a modest fine.
36. *Islamic Bomb,* op. cit. p. 186.
37. Mark Hibbs, "Convicted German Preform Exporter Had Kahuta Contacts for 20 Years," *Nuclear Fuel,* September 7, 1998.
38. Stefania Maurizi, "Interview with A.Q. Khan," June 2008.
39. Interview with former U.S. official, May 11, 2006.
40. Interview with former U.S. official by Joel Wit, New York City, April 18, 2007.
41. Interview with former U.S. official, May 11, 2006. This information was far less sensitive than what Khan stole.
42. Interview with former URENCO official, 2007.
43. Interview with former U.S. official, May 11, 2006.
44. Norman Lamont, Undersecretary of State for Energy, Hansard, official record of debate in the British House of Commons, "Joint Centrifuge Project, Almelo," December 18, 1979, p. 567.
45. "Memorandum for the President," Department of State, SECRET, May 7, 1980, Approved for Release 2005/01/31:NIC-7-23-3-1-5; Leonard Downie, Jr., "U.S., Swiss At Impasse on A-Policy," *The Washington Post,* September 22, 980, p. A1; Leonard Downie, Jr., "Swiss, U.S. Prepared to Resume Nuclear Cooperation," *The Washington Post,* December 31, 1980.

46. "International Agreement on Tighter Export Controls on Gas Centrifuge," *Nucleonics Week*, (Vol. 24, No. 34) August 25, 1983, p. 3; "The 21 Members of the So-Called Zangger Committee Exchanged Notes," *Nucleonics Week*, (Vol. 25, No. 5), February 2, 1984, p. 3.

47. Gary Milhollin and Kelly Motz, "Nukes 'R' Us," *The New York Times*, March 4, 2004.

48. George Tenet, *At the Center of the Storm* (New York: HarperCollins, 2007), p. 284.

49. Interview with former U.S. official by Joel Wit, 2006.

50. General Advisory Committee on Arms Control and Disarmament, Department of State, Friday Morning Session, September 14, 1979, Washington D.C., SECRET, Declassified 2004, p. 319.

51. Z.A. Bhutto, *If I Am Assassinated* (Delhi: Vikas, 1979), p. 203, as cited in Ashok Kapur, *Pakistan's Nuclear Development* (London: Croom Helm, 1987), p. 244.

52. Interview with former U.S. official by Joel Wit, 2006.

53. Interview with former U.S. official by Wit, March 23, 2006.

54. Interviews with former U.S. government officials by Wit and Albright, 2006; and Thomas Reed, "A Tabulation of Chinese Nuclear Device Tests," *Physics Today*, September 2008, http://ptonline.aip.org/journals/doc.PHTOAD-ft/vol_61/iss_9/47_1s.shtml. Supplemental material for "The Chinese Nuclear Tests, 1964–1996," by Reed in the same edition. Several U.S. officials stated that China also provided enough highly enriched uranium for two nuclear weapons.

55. "Pakistan's Procurement for Its Nuclear Programs—Examples of Materials and Equipment," U.S. Non-Paper, undated, delivered to the Dutch government in 1984.

56. Jaco Alberts and Karel Knip, "About an Engineer from Alkmaar and the Pakistani Bomb," op. cit.

57. Egmont Koch and Simon Henderson, "Taking the Low Road to Atomic Power," *Der Stern*, April 30, 1986, pp. 152–156.

58. Holger Koppe and Egmont Koch, *Bomben-Geschäfte* (Knesebeck & Munich: Schuler, 1990), pp. 67–72.

59. Interview with a former U.S. government official, July 11, 2005; and "Taking the Low Road to Atomic Power," op. cit.

60. "Pakistan's Procurement," op. cit.

61. Central Intelligence Agency, "Soviet Short-Term Options in South Asia," Special National Intelligence Estimate, TOP SECRET, January 5, 1982, Declassified 1994, p. 2.

62. Interview with former senior U.S. official, July 2005.

63. Interviews with anonymous U.S. government officials. PAEC might have received the Chinese bomb assistance, and A.Q. Khan obtained the design from the PAEC with the approval of senior Pakistani officials. Other information, however, suggests that KRL personnel were also recipients of the bomb information in China.

64. Interview with a former U.S. government official by Joel Wit and Albright, July 11, 2005.

65. A.Q. Khan in a Khan Research Laboratories promotional video, undated.

THREE: IT'S JUST BUSINESS

1. *Note,* Meeting in Vienna, Austria, on June 17, 2004, between German Federal prosecutors and senior IAEA officials with regard to "Preliminary proceedings against unknown on suspicion of treason by delivering gas ultracentrifuge technology to Libya," Date of Note, July 2, 2004.

2. Witness Hearing of Mario Staggl, April 28, 2005, Vaduz, Liechtenstein, conducted by German Public Prosecutor, Federal Court of Justice, Karlsruhe.

3. Interview with ex-employee of Leybold-Heraeus, April 16, 2007.

4. Summary of court proceedings, Lerch Trial, Mannheim, Germany, day nine of the trial, May 23, 2006.

5. *Long Road to Chagai,* op. cit., p. 61.

6. Interview with ex-employee of Leybold, April 16, 2007.

7. "UF6 Feeding System," *Preliminary Process Description,* V3A Vacuum Plant, Job no. 17–324, August 8, 1977, sheet 1 of 20; "Requisition Sheet: Heating Tank," V3A Vacuum Plant, job no. 17–324, August 12, 1977, sheet 1 of 2; and interview with knowledgeable German source.

8. Interview with Lerch's former colleague in the High Court of South Africa, *Indictment: The State versus Daniel Geiges and Gerhard Wisser and Summary of Substantial Facts,* case number CC332/2005, served on the accused April 26, 2006, p. 26.

9. *Verdict,* Cologne Local Court, in the criminal matter Gotthard Lerch and Otto Herman Anton Heillingbrunner, July 1, 1992 (in German). As discussed later, neither was convicted in this matter.

10. Ibid.

11. Holger Koppe and Egmont Koch, *Bomben-Geschäfte* (Munich: Knesebeck & Schuler, 1990), pp. 84–87.

12. *Long Road to Chagai,* op cit. p. 60.

13. *The Islamic Bomb,* op. cit.

14. *Quotation for Planning of Assembly for V 3A Vacuum Plant, Including Purification System,* Customer: Special Works Organization; Supplier Leybold-Heraeus, August 16, 1978. Ref. no. 057–18–253.

15. *Islamic Bomb,* op. cit., p. 297. Khan told the Swiss television journalist Hansjürg Zumstein that Cora exported two additional small feed and withdrawal systems with the assistance of Tinner, e-mail from Khan to Zumstein, December 16, 2008, in supplementary materials to the Swiss national television program SF DOK, "Wie ein Schweizer Mechaniker die Welt Veränderte," January 22, 2009.

16. *Islamic Bomb,* op. cit., p. 296.

17. *Bomben-Geschäfte,* op. cit., pp. 67–72.

18. Ibid.

19. Email from Khan to Zumstein, December 16, 2008, op. cit.

20. Internal Leybold-Heraeus memorandum from Otto Heilingbrunner about a recent media request from ZDF, July 23, 1981 (in German).

21. Interview with Leybold official, August 16, 2007.

22. Egmont Koch and Simon Henderson, "Let Us Just Call Him Kotari," *Stern,* April 27, 1989 (translated from German); and Interrogation Testimony, by

German Customs officials, of Anton Benedikt Schoeb, March 26, 1987 (translated from German).

23. Interrogation Testimony, Schoeb, "Chronology of Events," op. cit. (translated from German).

24. Transcript of the Hearing on February 27, 1984, at Uranit GmbH, Stetternicher Staatsforst, D-5170 Juelich, Germany, File number: 31 Js 3/84 StA Aachen, statement of Hagen Fink (translated from German).

25. Interrogation Testimony of Margrith Lippuner, by the German Customs Office, Cologne, March 26, 1987 (translated from German).

26. Ibid.

27. Interview by author of Heilingbrunner and unnamed Leybold employee.

28. Letter to Albright from Heilingbrunner, August 14, 2007.

29. Interview by author at Leybold, August 11, 2006.

30. "Let Us Just Call Him Kotari," op. cit.

31. Memorandum by Public Prosecutor Vielhaber, Public Prosecutor's Office, Cologne, March 16, 1989 (translated from German).

32. Interrogation Testimony, Spass Dagarov, by German Customs officials, March 26, 1987 (translated from German).

33. Interrogation Testimony, Robert Karl Ostheimer, by German Customs officials, April 27, 1987 (translated from German).

34. *Verdict*, op. cit.

FOUR: KHAN'S FIRST CUSTOMERS— IRAN AND IRAQ

1. IAEA internal working document, "Possible Military Dimensions of Iran's Nuclear Program," undated. For more information about this document see, ISIS, "Excerpts from Internal IAEA document on Alleged Iranian Nuclear Weaponization," October 2, 2009. See also Frances Harrison, "Iran Mulled Nuclear Bomb in 1988," *BBC News*, Tehran, updated September 29, 2006.

2. Interview with Naraghi by author, September 7, 2004.

3. ISIS, "Iraq's Acquisition of Gas Centrifuge Technology," www.exportcontrols. org. Started in 1987, the Iraqi centrifuge group was under the authority of Saddam Hussein's brutal son-in-law Hussein Kamel, who also controlled the chemical weapons and ballistic missile programs that had devastated Iran. The program was led by engineer Mahdi Obeidi, who would buy classified URENCO centrifuge know-how from four German centrifuge experts who had no known connection to A.Q. Khan. Per interviews with a senior Iraqi centrifuge official, June 1996, in addition to telling Iraqi engineers about its sale to Iran in 1985, Leifeld salesmen showed them a video containing sensitive information about producing maraging steel rotors for a URENCO-type gas centrifuge. One wonders if Leifeld told the Iraqis about Iran's budding interest in an attempt to increase sales.

4. *Implementation of the NPT Safeguards Agreement and Relevant Portions of Security Council Resolutions 1737 (2006) and 1747 (2007) in the Islamic Republic of Iran*, GOV/2007/58, November 15, 2007, p. 3.

5. Ibid.

6. NHK interview with Naraghi, 2007.

7. To increase sales in Iran, Heilingbrunner hired a Leybold-Heraeus agent in Tehran after a year-long search. M. Khorsandian, CEO of a company called Messo, would play an important role in selling items to Iran's nuclear programs.

8. Interview with Heilingbrunner, August 11, 2007.

9. According to the German television journalist Egmont Koch, Naraghi visited the offices of the Cologne branch in 1985 seeking help with the technology of enriching uranium. Koch's report is partially corroborated by the official Iranian declaration to IAEA inspectors made after Iran was caught hiding its centrifuge program in late 2002 and early 2003. Iranian officials told the inspectors that a project leader got in touch with Europeans who could help him with the technology for uranium enrichment. The IAEA did not reveal the name of the project leader.

10. NHK interview, 2007.

11. Now called Oerlikon-Leybold, the company is a world leader in stopping nuclear proliferation.

12. Egmont Koch, interview by author, August 2006. This type of pump is a turbomolecular pump that is also driven by a frequency converter.

13. Interview with Heilingbrunner by author, August 11, 2007.

14. NHK interview, 2007.

15. Interview with Naraghi by author, September 7, 2004.

16. Egmont Koch, "The Physicist of the Mullahs," *FR-Online*, www.fr-online.de/in_und_ausland/dokumentation/?em_cnt+1053209, in German; see also documentary of same name by Koch, shown on ARD and WDR in Germany in January 2007.

17. NHK interview, 2007.

18. *Implementation of the NPT Safeguards Agreement and Relevant Portions of Security Council Resolutions*, GOV/2008/4, November 15, 2007, op. cit., p. 3. Mousavi was the last Iranian Prime Minister, serving until 1989 when Iran's constitution was changed and the position abolished. He ran for President in 2009 as a reformist candidate but lost in a disputed election.

19. NHK interview, 2007.

20. Interview with a senior official close to the IAEA, August 2006. At the time of the interview, Allahdad was still an administrator of the centrifuge program. He had been interviewed by the IAEA, but he had not been that helpful. The IAEA wanted to talk to him again, but Iran had refused to allow the meeting to take place.

21. NHK interview, 2007.

22. NHK interview, 2007.

23. NHK interview, 2007.

24. *Note*, Meeting in Vienna, Austria, on June 17, 2004, between German Federal prosecutors and senior IAEA officials with regard to "Preliminary proceedings against unknown on suspicion of treason by delivering gas ultracentrifuge technology to Libya," July 2, 2004 (translated from German).

25. In 1996, Khan gave Iran a full set of general P2 drawings. In 2008, a modi-

fied version of the P2 centrifuge began testing at the pilot plant in Natanz. *Implementation of the NPT Safeguards Agreement and Relevant Portions of Security Council Resolutions* November 15, 2007, op. cit., p. 4.

26. Ibid., p. 3.
27. Koch, interview by author, 2006.
28. "The Physicist of the Mullahs," op. cit.
29. John Lancaster and Kamran Khan, "Pakistanis Say Nuclear Scientists Aided Iran; Iran Nuclear Effort Said Aided in Secret '80s Deal," *The Washington Post*, January 24, 2004.
30. Ibid.
31. John Lancaster and Kamran Khan, "Musharraf Named in Nuclear Probe," *The Washington Post*, February 3, 2004.
32. Interview with a senior official close to the IAEA, November 26, 2005.
33. *Implementation of the NPT Safeguards Agreement and Relevant Portions of Security Council Resolutions*, November 15, 2007 op. cit.; and Director General, *Implementation of the NPT Safeguards Agreement and Relevant Portions of Security Council Resolutions 1737 (2006) and 1747 (2007) in the Islamic Republic of Iran*, *GOV/2008/4*, February 22, 2008.
34. Director General, *Implementation of the NPT Safeguards Agreement and Relevant Portions of Security Council Resolutions 1737 (2006) and 1747 (2007) in the Islamic Republic of Iran*, GOV/2008/14, May 26, 2008; and a senior official close to the IAEA.
35. NHK interview, 2007.
36. *Implementation of the NPT Safeguards Agreement and Relevant Portions of Security Council Resolutions*, GOV/2007/58, November 15, 2007, op. cit., p. 3.
37. *Implementation of the NPT Safeguards Agreement and Relevant Portions of Security Council Resolutions 1737 (2006) and 1747 (2007) in the Islamic Republic of Iran*, GOV/2008/14, May 26, 2008, op. cit.
38. Interviews with senior Leybold official, 2006 and 2007.
39. Interview with former senior official close to the IAEA, January 5, 2007.
40. German BND report on Pakistan overseas procurement for its nuclear programs, February 1981 (in German).
41. The original has the word "pursued" in point 5, but IAEA analysts took the word to mean "persuaded."
42. Letter from Mr. Aala al-din Hussein al Samaraae to Mr. Dhafer Rashid Selbi, Head of PC-3 Group 3, dated October 6, 1990, stamped top secret and personal. The typed Project A.B. offer was attached (translated from Arabic).
43. Mahdi Obeidi and Kurt Pitzer, *The Bomb in My Garden* (New Jersey: John Wiley & Sons, 2004); and "Case Studies," www.exportcontrols.org. The three known centrifuge experts were Bruno Stemmler, Walter Busse, and Karl Heinz Schaap, all of whom had or had held important positions at MAN New Technologies in Munich Germany. A fourth expert, who also was working at MAN, was never identified.
44. John Barry, "Pakistan's Bomb Builder," *Newsweek International*, June 8, 1998. A shorter piece appeared earlier in the U.S. edition. The following description of

the interactions among Barry, the IAEA, and Pakistan is based on interviews with persons directly involved and on my access to the documents referenced here. The set includes the fax to Barry from the Pakistani embassy and a summary of a meeting between IAEA and Pakistani officials in Vienna.

45. Zahid Malik, *Dr. Abdul Qadeer Khan and the Islamic Bomb, Part 2* (Islamabad: Hurmat Publications, 1998), chapter 22, "Conspiracy to Malign Dr. Abdul Qadeer Khan."

46. Ibid.

47. BBC, "Nawaz Sharif Calls for US Shift," April 16, 2008.

48. IAEA inspectors found much of this equipment listed in this paragraph at Natanz and other centrifuge facilities during their visits in 2003. The inspectors developed long lists of this equipment which included suppliers, serial numbers, and locations for these parts in the centrifuge facilities. Iran also provided the inspectors with names of foreign nationals who assisted Iran. The IAEA supplied these lists to trusted member states such as Germany and Britain, which queried suspect companies and personnel for more specific information. This was, in turn, provided to the IAEA for further investigation and verification. Such collaboration on illicit trade started during inspections in Iraq following the 1991 Persian Gulf War and proved an effective way to uncover secret nuclear activities.

49. *Implementation of the NPT Safeguards Agreement and Relevant Portions of Security Council Resolutions*, GOV/2007/58, November 15, 2007, op. cit., p. 4.

50. KRL promotional video found by the IAEA in Libya and South Africa.

51. NHK interview, 2007.

52. Ibid.

53. Ibid.

54. Ibid.

55. Director General, *Implementation of the NPT Safeguards Agreement in the Islamic Republic of Iran*, GOV/2005/67, September 2, 2005, p. 5.

56. Egmont Koch, interview, August 2006.

57. Interview with a senior official close to the IAEA, December 14, 2004.

58. Interview with a senior official close to the IAEA, August 20, 2006.

59. Interviews with senior officials close to the IAEA, June 29, 2004, and August 2006.

60. Interview with senior U.S. intelligence official, February 28, 1995.

61. David Albright, "The Russian-Iranian Reactor Deal," *The Nonproliferation Review*, Spring-Summer 1995.

62. Interview with former Clinton administration official, January 2008.

63. Interview with Einhorn, February 21, 2006.

FIVE: FINDING A NEW HIDEOUT—
SOUTH AFRICA

1. Interview with Heilingbrunner, August 11, 2007.

2. Wisser, statement for South African police, application for firearm license, October 22, 1984.

3. High Court of South Africa, *Summary of Substantial Facts*, The State vs. Daniel

Geiges, Gerhard Wisser, and Geiges and Wisser, Directors of Krisch Engineering Co., undated.

4. In the High Court of South Africa, *Indictment: The State versus Daniel Geiges and Gerhard Wisser and Summary of Substantial Facts*, case number CC332/2005, served on the accused April 26, 2006, p. 18.

5. Witness Hearing, Mario Staggl, April 28, 2005, Prosecutor General at the Federal Court of Justice, Karlsruhe, April 28, 2005 (translated from German).

6. Steve Coll, "The Atomic Emporium," *The New Yorker*, Augut 7 & 14, 2006, p. 58; and *Summary of Substantial Facts*, op. cit.

7. *Summary of Substantial Facts*, op. cit., p. 24.

8. Roxound web site, archived at http://web.archive.org/web/20011203135744/roxound.com/projects.htm.

9. *Summary of Substantial Facts*, op. cit., p. 26.

10. "The Atomic Emporium," op. cit., p. 58.

11. www.web.archive.org/web/20011203135744/roxound.com/projects.htm

12. *Summary of Substantial Facts*, op. cit., p. 27.

13. Testimony of Peter Griffin, trial of Gotthard Lerch, Mannheim, Germany, May 16, 2006.

14. *Summary of Substantial Facts*, op. cit., pp. 26. The country of origin of the client is not mentioned in this court document. However, a confidential source provided the country.

15. Daniel M. Kemp, Pieter J. Bredell, A. Albert Ponelis, and Einar Ronander, "Uranium Enrichment Technologies in South Africa," Atomic Energy Corporation of South Africa, Ltd., paper presented at the International Symposium on Isotope Separation and Chemical Exchange Uranium Enrichment, October 29-November 1, 1990, Tokyo, Japan.

16. Interview with South African official by author, July 2, 1992.

17. David Albright and Susan Basu, "India's Gas Centrifuge Enrichment Program: Growing Capacity for Military Purposes," *ISIS*, January 18, 2007.

18. *Summary of Substantial Facts*, op. cit., p. 30.

19. Ibid., pp. 31–33.

20. See also "The Queen v. Abu Bakr Siddiqui," in the Crown Court at Southwark, Pleas and Directions Hearing, January 3, 2001.

21. *Summary of Substantial Facts*, op. cit.

22. Written Statement by Wisser to the Magistrate, September 1, 2004, p. 5.

23. "Terms of Agreement," *Annexure to the Plea and Sentence Agreement*, September 2007, p. 8.

24. Confidential memorandum to the Department of Energy from an attorney representing Peoples' Steel Mill seeking support for its effort to gain German government approval for a controversial export to this mill, December 1994.

25. Witness Hearing, Fridolin Zahner, April 27, 2005, Prosecutor General at the Federal Court of Justice, Karlsruhe, April 28, 2005 (translated from German).

26. Telefax to Leybold, Cologne from British Leybold London, May 30. 1995.

27. Interview with Wirtz, August 20, 2004.

28. High Court of South Africa, *Summary of Substantial Facts, The State vs. Daniel*

Geiges, Gerhard Wisser, and Geiges and Wisser, Directors of Krisch Engineering Co., undated.

29. "Extract from the Statement of Sayed Abu Tahir Bin Bukhary, Managing Director of SMB Group of Companies, Kuala Lumpur," Malaysia, June 7, 2006.

30. Telefax, from G. Wisser., Krisch Engineering to G. Lerch, AVE, June 9, 1995, typed notation on telefax to Mr. Wisser from CH, an employee of Krisch Engineering.

31. *Affidavit* of Jeffrey Bedell, paragraph 7, August 17, 2007.

SIX: LIBYA: A MAJOR SALE AT LAST

1. Director General, *Implementation of the NPT Safeguards Agreement of the Socialist People's Libyan Arab Jamahiriya*, GOV/2008/39, September 12, 2008, Annex, p. 3.

2. Ibid., and interview with a senior official close to the IAEA, September 12, 2008.

3. Interview with a senior official close to the IAEA, January 6, 2004.

4. Interview with senior IAEA official, January 6, 2004. The name is from a confidential source, September 4, 2006.

5. Director General, *Implementation of the NPT Safeguards Agreement of the Socialist People's Libyan Arab Jamahiriya*, GOV/2004/12, February 20, 2004, par. 21.

6. Director General, *Implementation of the NPT Safeguards Agreement of the Socialist People's Libyan Arab Jamahiriya*, GOV/2008/39, September 12, 2008.

7. Ibid., Annex, p. 3.

8. Interview with a senior official close to the IAEA, December 11, 2007.

9. KRL promotional video found in Libya and South Africa. Script by Huma Fawad and Shamoon Hashmi, and made by Pakistan National Television.

10. Interview with former URENCO expert, August 20, 2006.

11. Interview with a senior official close to the IAEA, December 11, 2007. Each test module contained a vacuum pump, control and measuring equipment, a small feed autoclave, two withdrawal stations, or "cold traps," filled with liquid nitrogen.

12. *Nuclear Proliferation Network, Technology and Equipment Procurement*, undated chart produced by the IAEA. Other sources list the names of Cire's and Alguadis' companies somewhat differently.

13. U.N. Security Council Resolution 748.

14. Interview with a senior official close to the IAEA, December 11, 2007.

15. Director General, *Implementation of the NPT Safeguards Agreement and Relevant Portions of Security Council Resolutions*, GOV/2007/58, November 15, 2007, p. 4.

16. Interview with knowledgeable source, October 21, 2004. The assistance to Egypt was offered prior to 1992.

17. Director General, *Implementation of the NPT Safeguards Agreement of the Socialist People's Libyan Arab Jamahiriya*, GOV/2004/12, February 20, 2004, par. 22.

18. "Extract from Statement of Sayed Abu Tahir Bin Bukhary" (Tahir statement), Managing Director of SMB Group of Companies, Kuala Lumpur, Malaysia, June 7, 2006. Annexure L in *Plea and Sentence Agreement, State vs. Geiges,*

Wisser, and Krisch Engineering, September 2007. See also "Press Release by Inspector General of Police in Relation to Investigation of the Alleged Production of Components for Libya's Uranium Enrichment Program," February 20, 2004, accessed at http://www.rmp.gov.my/rmp03/040220scomi_eng.ht

19. Tahir statement, op. cit.
20. *Implementation of the NPT Safeguards Agreement of the Socialist People's Libyan Arab Jamahiriya,* GOV/2004/12, February 20, 2004, op. cit., par. 6.
21. Tahir was born April 17, 1959.
22. Interviews with senior IAEA officials, 2006 and 2007. As part of the IAEA's investigations into Khan, Heinonen visited Farooq unannounced a few years earlier at his home. He was unwilling to cooperate with Heinonen, providing the IAEA inspector with only limited information about the network.
23. Email interview with Khan by Urs Gehriger, *Weltwoche,* published January 2009, http://www.weltwoche.ch/ausgaben/2009-04/artikel-2009-04-interview -khan-english-version.html.
24. *Implementation of Safeguards Agreement of Libya,* February 20, 2004, op cit.
25. Interview with a senior official close to the IAEA, April 1, 2005.
26. Interview with a senior official close to the IAEA, January 6, 2004.
27. George Tenet, *At the Center of the Storm* (New York: HarperCollins Publishers, 2007), p. 296.
28. Douglas Jehl, "CIA Says Pakistanis Gave Iran Nuclear Aid," *The New York Times,* November 24, 2004.
29. *Plea and Sentence Agreement,* op. cit.
30. The bulk of the enrichment effort goes into making the 3.5 percent enriched uranium, requiring 67 percent of the centrifuges.
31. *Affidavit of William Tobey,* U.S. Department of Energy, who represented the views of the U.S. enrichment expert, *Plea and Sentence Agreement, State vs. Geiges, Wisser, Krisch Engineering, Pretoria, South Africa,* Case No. CC332/ 2005.
32. Confidential source that has seen the document; interview with source in August 2006.
33. The larger amount of weapon-grade uranium in the Chinese design appears to reflect a decision to make the warhead smaller by increasing the amount of weapon-grade uranium and decreasing the amount of high explosives compressing the nuclear core.
34. The division of responsibilities for supplying the Libyan order is from Tahir's statement, op. cit., and interviews with senior IAEA officials.
35. Interview with a senior official close to the IAEA, December 14, 2004.
36. Interview with a senior official close to the IAEA, February 8, 2005.
37. Interview with a senior official close to the IAEA, December 14, 2004.
38. Interview with a senior official close to the IAEA, May 13, 2004.
39. Ilhan Tasci, "Nuclear Services to the Islamic World," *Cumhuriyet,* July 6, 2004 (translated from Turkish).
40. The White House, "Memorandum of Conversation, Meeting with President Evren of Turkey," June 27, 1988.
41. See for example, Leon Fuerth, "Turkey, Nuclear Choices Amongst Danger-

ous Neighbors," *The Nuclear Tipping Point,* edited by Kurt Campbell, Robert Einhorn, and Mitchell Reiss (Washington, DC: Brookings Institution Press, 2004).

42. Tahir statement, p. 7.
43. Interview with a senior official close to the IAEA, February 1, 2004.
44. Interview with a senior official close to the IAEA, June 26, 2004.
45. Interview with a senior official close to the IAEA, November 3, 2004.
46. *Nuclear Proliferation Network, Technology and Equipment Procurement,* undated chart produced by the IAEA.
47. Ibid.
48. Interview with a senior official close to the IAEA, June 26, 2004.
49. Interview with a senior official close to the IAEA, May 13, 2004.
50. Tahir Statement, op. cit.
51. *Plea and Sentence Agreement,* op. cit., p. 16.
52. Interview with a senior official close to the IAEA, February 28, 2004.
53. Abdul Mabood Siddiqui, *Timbuktu, City in the Middle of Nowhere* (Islamabad: Hurmat Publications, undated), p. vi.
54. Statement of John M. McConnell, director, National Intelligence, Committee on Senate Armed Services, February 27, 2007.
55. Interview with a senior official close to the IAEA, January 20, 2006.
56. Interview with a senior official close to the IAEA, February 20, 2004 and August 21, 2008.
57. Interview with a senior official close to the IAEA, August 21, 2008.
58. Alan Sipress, "Key Player in Nuclear Trade Ring Found Hospitable Base in Malaysia," *The Washington Post,* February 24, 2004.
59. Abdul Mabood Siddiqui, *Timbuktu, City in the Middle of Nowhere* (Islamabad: Hurmat Publications, undated), p. 16 and pp. 48–50.
60. Isa Ismail, "28 April 03: Brokers' Digest," *The Edge Daily,* website, accessed at www.theedgedaily.com.
61. Raymond Bonner and Wayne Arnold, "Business as Usual at Plant That Tenet Says was Shut," *The New York Times,* February 7, 2004.
62. *Summary of Testimony of Thorsten Heise,* Lerch Trial, summary of testimony, 11th day, Mannheim, Germany, June 20, 2006.
63. Ibid.
64. German Prosecutor, *Preliminary Proceedings Against Anonymous on Suspicion of Treason by Delivering Gas Ultracentrifuge Technology to Libya,* Interview of Olli Heinonen, Trevor Edwards, and Mrs. Yonemara, Karlsruhe, July 2, 2004.
65. "Malaysian Firm Denies Nuclear Black Market Role," *TodayOnline,* September 15, 2006; and Kyodo News Service, "Mitutoyo Exported 10,000 Devices Since 1995, Most of them Illegally," August 31, 2006.
66. David Crawford, "How a Nuclear Ring Skirted Export Laws," *The Wall Street Journal,* March 22, 2004.
67. Susan Basu, "Transactions of Bikar Metal Asia and Scomi Precision Engineering, 2001–2002," ISIS memorandum, undated, based on internal Bikar Metal documents.

68. Ibid. ASMP is a marketing representative for a Russian group of companies.

69. Bikar Metal Asia Pte Ldt, Transaction for Al tubes, Al 6061, 168 mm inner diameter, data table prepared by ISIS from internal Bikar Metal Asia documents, undated.

70. *Summary of testimony of Heise*. Lerch Trial, 11th day, op. cit.

71. Interview with a senior official close to the IAEA, December 11, 2007.

72. Polis Diraja Malaysia, "Press Release by Inspector General of Police in Relation to Investigation on the Alleged Production of Components for Libya's Uranium Enrichment Programme," February 20, 2004, http://www.rmp.gov.my/rmp03/040220scomi_eng.htm.

73. Interview with a senior official close to the IAEA, January 9, 2004.

74. Interview with a senior official close to the IAEA, January 6, 2004.

75. Table prepared by ISIS from Bikar Metal Asia documents listing all quotations, invoices, and deliveries of the motor housing preform (210 mm outer diameter, height 105 mm).

76. Memorandum from Bikar Metalle GmbH to Bikar Metal Asia, September 9, 2001; and Martin Stoll, "On the Radar of the CIA," *FACTS*, March 10, 2005 (translated from German).

77. Confidential source, August 14, 2007.

78. *Plea and Sentence Agreement*, op. cit., p. 11; and Summary of oral judgment by Judge Juergen Niemeyer against Gotthard Lerch at Oberlandesgericht, Stuttgart, October 16, 2008, prepared and translated by Ralf Denninger. (German courts do not prepare written transcripts or allow recordings.)

79. *Plea and Sentence Agreement*, op. cit., pp. 11 and 13.

80. Ibid., op. cit., p. 15; senior official close to the IAEA.

81. In the High Court of South Africa, "Summary of Substantial Facts," *Indictment, The State vs. Geiges and Wisser*, undated.

82. Interview with a senior official close to the IAEA, August 22, 2006.

83. Interview with a senior official close to the IAEA, August 22, 2006.

84. Director General, *Implementation of the NPT Safeguards Agreement of the Socialist People's Libyan Arab Jamahiriya*, GOV/2004/12, February 20, 2004.

85. Director General, *Implementation of the NPT Safeguards Agreement of the Socialist People's Libyan Arab Jamahiriya*, GOV/2004/33, June 1, 2004; and *Implementation of Safeguards Agreement of Libya*, February 20, 2008, op. cit.

86. *Implementation of Safeguards Agreement of Libya*, February 20, 2008, op. cit.

87. German Prosecutor, *Preliminary Proceedings Against Anonymous on Suspicion of Treason by Delivering Gas Ultracentrifuge Technology to Libya*, Interview of Olli Heinonen, Trevor Edwards, and Mrs. Yonemara, Karlsruhe, July 2, 2004 (translated from German), and interview with a senior official close to the IAEA, April 30, 2005.

88. Ibid.

89. Michael Adler, "Iran May Have Received Advanced Centrifuges: Diplomats," Agence France-Presse, January 20, 2006.

90. Stefania Maurizi, "Interview with A.Q. Khan," June 2008.

91. Interview with Khan by Urs Gehriger, via email address of his wife, *Weltwoche*, December 2008; and www.draqkhan.com.pk. It is unclear who wrote

the website, although its email contact is Dr. Ahmad Nazeer, who was a former chief engineer in the metallurgy department at KRL and was arrested in January 2004 for questioning by Pakistani authorities. An examination of the page properties reveals that the domain name was created on June 6, 2001.

92. Videotaped interview with A.Q. Khan by Egmont Koch, August 17, 1998, time stamp: 6:16.

93. Farah Stockman, "Pakistan Had Case Against Scientist," *The Boston Globe*, February 13, 2004, quoting a 120-page dossier by the Pakistani government's National Accountability Bureau. This dossier was discussed in more detail in Douglas Frantz and Catherine Collins, *The Nuclear Jihadist* (New York: Twelve Hachette Book Group, 2007), chapter 23.

94. Videotaped interview with A.Q. Khan by Egmont Koch, August 17, 1998, time stamp: 6:27.

95. "Dr. Khan's Transfer of Centrifuge Designs Did Not Help N. Korea Become N Power: Musharraf," *Online International News Network*, August 25, 2005.

96. *Timbuktu, City in the Middle of Nowhere,*

97. Interview with a senior official close to the IAEA, December 14, 2005; interview with European intelligence official, August 16, 2006.

98. "Pakistan Had Case Against Scientist," op. cit.

99. In the Crown Court at Southwark, The Queen v. Abu Bakr Siddiqui, Case Summary, T2000 1338, January 3, 2001.

100. "UK Court Sentences Man Over Helping Pakistan Nuclear Project," Associated Press, October 8, 2001.

101. Omar Hassan would eventually direct a campaign of murder, rape, and pillage against civilians in Darfur, leading the International Court of Justice to issue a warrant for his arrest in 2009.

102. Interview with former U.S. intelligence expert, August 16, 2005; and *Sudan*, German Early Warning Letter published by German government No. 18/02, May 15, 2002 (translated from German).

103. *Sudan*, German Early Warning Letter, No. 18/02, op. cit.

104. Videotaped interview with A.Q. Khan by Egmont Koch, August 17, 1998, time stamp: 6:08.

105. Ibid., timestamp: 6:03.

106. *Zembla*, "The Netherlands' Atomic Bomb," Nederland-3 Television Network (translated from Dutch), op. cit.

107. Albright, "Team GmbH and Ernest Piffl: The Case of the Illegal Centrifuge Preforms Exports to Pakistan," www.exportcontrols.org.

108. Videotaped interview with A.Q. Khan by Egmont Koch, August 17, 1998, time stamp: 6:03–04.

109. Interview with a senior official close to the IAEA, February 26, 2004.

110. Interview with a senior official close to the IAEA, February 28 and March 24, 2004.

111. Joby Warrick and Peter Slevin, "Libyan Arms Designs Traced Back to China," *The Washington Post*, February 15, 2004.

112. Heinonen, in interview with Swiss national television program Hansjürg Zum-

stein, "Wie ein Schweizer Mechaniker die Welt Veränderte," SF DOK, January 22, 2009 (in German).

113. Urs Gehriger, interview with Khan, in "Eine Ehrliche, Aufrechte Familie," *Weltwoche,* January 21, 2009, http://www.weltwoche.ch/ausgaben/2009–04/ artikel-2009–04-interview-khan-english-version.html. See also "Libyan Arms Designs Traced Back to China," op. cit.

114. William J. Broad and David E. Sanger, "Warhead Blueprints Link Libya Project to Pakistan Figure," *The New York Times,* February 4, 2004, p. 1.

115. In the South African case against Wisser and Geiges, "Extract from the Statement of Sayed Abu Tahir Bin Bukhary, Managing Director of SMB Group of Companies, Kuala Lumpur," Malaysia, June 7, 2006; and "Libyan Arms Designs Traced Back to China," op. cit.

116. Interview with confidential source with access to official documents that included a discussion of Pakistani nuclear weapons, February 2007.

SEVEN: NORTH KOREA

1. Robin Wright and Joby Warrick, "Purchases Linked N. Korean to Syria," *The Washington Post,* May 11, 2008. The name of the company varies. For example, a German Early Warning Letter of 2005 calls it Nam Chongang High-Tech Engineering Corporation. It is common for such trading companies to modify their names. The address is from an invoice dated September 18, 2002, to NCG from a German company. The full address was Senkujia Dong 11–2 Mangyong District, Pyongyang, DPRK.

2. German Early Warning Letter, *Nordkorea,* July 1, 2005.

3. Ibid.

4. Albright and Kevin O'Neill, *Solving the North Korean Puzzle* (Washington, DC: ISIS Press, 2000).

5. R. Jeffrey Smith, "N. Korea and the Bomb: High-Tech Hide-and-Seek; U.S. Intelligence Key in Detecting Deception," *The Washington Post,* April 27, 1993.

6. Quoted in "Atom Smuggling: The North Korea Connection," by Georg Mascolo, *Der Spiegel,* 39/2003, September 22, 2003 (translated from German).

7. *German customs investigation of Hans Werner Truppel,* July 18, 2003 (translated from German).

8. "Atom Smuggling: The North Korea Connection," op. cit.

9. Joby Warrick, "N. Korea Shops Stealthily for Nuclear Arms Gear," *The Washington Post,* August 15, 2003.

10. *German customs investigation of Hans Werner Truppel,* op. cit.; and "Chaoyang District," *Beijing This Month,* March 2002. This publication is sponsored by the Information Office of the Beijing Municipal Government.

11. Interview with senior Chinese official, November 5, 2005.

12. Michael Hayden, "Director's Remarks at the Los Angeles World Affairs Council," September 16, 2008.

13. Shyam Bhatia, *Goodbye Shahzadi: A Political Biography of Benazir Bhutto* (New Delhi: The Lotus, Rolli Books, 2008); "Benazir Reveals Plot to Kidnap A.Q. Khan and ISI Links to Nuclear Black Market," *South Asia Tribune,* No. 83, March 14–20, 2004.

14. "Benazir Reveals Plot to Kidnap A.Q. Khan and ISI Links to Nuclear Black Market," op. cit.
15. Pervez Musharraf, *In the Line of Fire* (New York: Free Press, 2006), p. 296.
16. Associated Press, July 4, 2008; Haq Nawaz, "Kidwai Comes Out with Guns Blazing," *The Nation*, July 5, 2008.
17. A shorter version of this fact sheet is on the website of the Federation of American Scientists: November 2002 National Intelligence Estimate on North Korea, www.fas.org/nuke/guide/dprk/cia111902.html.
18. Author conversations with North Korean Foreign Ministry officials, 2005 and 2007.
19. Albright, "North Korea's Alleged Large-Scale Enrichment Plant: Yet Another Questionable Extrapolation Based on Aluminum Tubes," ISIS, February 23, 2007, http://www.isis-online.org/publications/dprk/DPRKenrichment22 Feb.pdf.
20. Director General, *Implementation of the NPT Safeguards Agreement of the Socialist People's Libyan Arab Jamahiriya*, GOV/2004/59, August 30, 2004, par. 16; a confidential source who provided the name of the company, 2007.
21. *Nuclear Proliferation Network, Technology and Equipment Procurement*, undated chart produced by the IAEA.
22. Interview with a senior official close to the IAEA, June 11, 2004.
23. Director General, *Implementation of the NPT Safeguards Agreement of the Socialist People's Libyan Arab Jamahiriya*, GOV/2004/33, May 28, 2004, par. 20.
24. Interview with a senior official close to the IAEA, May 24, 2004.
25. Interview with a senior official close to the IAEA, June 12, 2005.
26. Pervez Musharraf, *In the Line of Fire* (New York: Free Press, 2006), p. 291.
27. Interview with a senior official close to the IAEA, April 15, 2005.
28. Interview with a senior official close to the IAEA, April 1, 2005.
29. Ibid., April 1, 2005.
30. Interview with a senior official close to the IAEA, February 19, 2009; and Director General, *Implementation of the NPT Safeguards Agreement in the Syrian Arab Republic*, GOV/2009/9, February 19, 2009.
31. Albright and Paul Brannan, *The Al Kibar Reactor: Extraordinary Camouflage, Troubling Implications*, ISIS report, May 5, 2008.

EIGHT: AL QAEDA'S BOMB

1. George Tenet, *At the Center of the Storm* (New York: HarperCollins Publishers, 2007), p. 264.
2. ISIS, *Osama bin Laden's Quest for Nuclear Weapons Based on Open Source Information*, October 10, 2002. This compilation contains several references to statements by bin Laden, including: (1) On or about May 29, 1998, Osama bin Laden issued a statement, translated by the U.S. State Department, entitled: "The Nuclear Bomb of Islam," under the banner of the "International Islamic Front for Fighting the Jews and the Crusaders," in which he stated that "it is the duty of the Muslims to prepare as much force as possible to terrorize the enemies of God." [United States District Court Southern District of New York, Indictment 2(9) 90 Cr. 1023 (LBS), United States of America v. Usama Bin

Laden, 1998, p. 32.], and (2) The German television station, ARD, published an interview with Osama bin Laden that included the full text to a 1998 statement made by bin Laden. It said: "We just want to be freed from the repression of the Americans. Self-defense is, after all, the right of every human being. Israel has hundreds of nuclear warheads and the Western crusaders have nuclear bombs. Thus, we also have a right to that. Only a crazy person can accuse a soldier of wearing a good armor. We as Muslims have the duty to possess such weapons and God has given them to us as a gift." [ARD, "Angst vor dem Atom—Besitzen Bin Ladens Terroristen Nuklearmaterial?" October 15, 2001]

3. *At the Center of the Storm,* op. cit., p. 261.
4. Interview with former senior intelligence official, March 2009.
5. *At the Center of the Storm,* op. cit., p. 263.
6. Asmir Latif, Islam Online, "Two Pakistani Atomic Scientists Arrested," October 24, 2001. Accessed at www.islam-online.net/English/News/2001-10/25/article3.shtml.
7. Quoted in "Pakistan May Ease Restrictions on Renegade Scientist," by Saeed Shah, *Globe and Mail,* April 11, 2008.
8. Rory McCarthy, "Worrying Times," *The Guardian,* November 8, 2001.
9. See for example, Farhatullah Babar, "Recalling a Patriot," *The News International* May 2, 2002.
10. In an article he co-authored with Muhammad Nasim and published in January 2000 in the Pakistani newspaper *The Nation* and on *Pakistan Link,* Mahmood identified himself as the chief designer and director of the Khushab reactor.
11. Ibid.
12. For a short critique of Mahmood's methodology, see http://lists.isb.sknpk.org/pipermail/earth-sky-old/1999-July/000008.html.
13. "Worrying Times," op. cit.
14. Peter Baker, "Pakistani Scientist Who Met Bin Laden Failed Polygraphs, Renewing Suspicions," *The Washington Post,* March 3, 2002.
15. www.tanzeem.org, December 29, 2000, press release.
16. www.tanzeem.org, January 28, 2000, and October 15, 1999, press releases.
17. "Pakistan Atom Experts Held," op. cit.
18. Molly Moore and Kamran Khan, "Pakistan Moves Nuclear Weapons," *The Washington Post,* November 11, 2001. The date when Mahmood resigned varies in press reports. Dates of 1998, 1999, and 2000 are all given; 1999 is taken as the most accurate date: see Anwar Iqbal and Khawar Mehdi, "Nuclear Scientist Opposes Pakistan Accepting CTBT, *The News,* Internet version, April 10, 1999; Susan B. Glasser and Kamran Khan, "Pakistan Continues Probe of Nuclear Scientists," *The Washington Post,* November 24, 2001, or Haider K. Nizamani, "Imperatives of the CTBT Debate," *Dawn,* February 28, 2000. For a date of January 1, 2000, see Arshad Sharif, "Assets of Nuclear Scientist Frozen," *Dawn,* January 31, 2002. See also Munir Ahmad, "Attacks-Scientist," Associated Press, October 24, 2001; and "Pakistan Atom Experts Held," op. cit.
19. *At the Center of the Storm,* op. cit., p. 262.
20. Robert Windrem, *NBC News,* November 1, 2001.

21. *At the Center of the Storm*, op. cit., pp. 266–67.
22. For more detailed information about these drawings, see Chris Stephen, "Kabul House of Anthrax Secrets," *The Evening Standard*, November 22, 2001; Douglas Frantz and David Rohde, "2 Pakistanis Linked to Papers on Anthrax Weapons," *The New York Times*, November 28, 2001; and David Rohde, "Germ Weapon Plans Found at a Scientist's House in Kabul," *The New York Times*, December 1, 2001.
23. "Pakistani Scientist Says No Anthrax Plant in Afghanistan, Discusses Prevention: U.S. Provides Chemical Weapons to Northern Alliance-Dr. Sultan," *Islamabad Khabrain*, October 6, 2001, in Urdu (available in English from FBIS, document number FBIS-NES-2001–1006).
24. *At the Center of the Storm*, op. cit., p. 272.
25. Ibid., p. 275.
26. Interview with a knowledgeable former senior U.S. intelligence official, March 2009.
27. Ibid.
28. *Report to the President of the United States*, Commission on the Intelligence Capabilities of the United States Regarding Weapons of Mass Destruction, March 31, 2005, p. 273.
29. Ibid., p. 274.
30. Documents found by CNN in Kabul at the offices of Baracat Islami Investment General Trading and Contracting Co. in the Hotel Intercontinental.
31. "Pro-Taliban Nuclear Scientist Planned Large-Scale Investment in Afghanistan," Nawa-i-Waqt, October 31, 2001, in Urdu (English version in FBIS, document number FBIS-NES-2001–1031).
32. Shujaat Ali Khan, "Nuclear Scientists' Case Hearing Adjourned," *Dawn*, November 28, 2001.
33. Peter Baker and Kamran Khan, "Pakistan to Forgo Charges Against 2 Nuclear Scientists," *The Washington Post*, January 30, 2002.
34. Fact sheet distributed by the White House when President George W. Bush announced the addition of UTN, Mahmood, and Majeed to the list of organizations and individuals supporting terrorists on December 20, 2001. See also Kamran Khan and Molly Moore, "2 Nuclear Experts Briefed Bin Laden, Pakistanis Say," *The Washington Post*, December 12, 2001; and Kamran Khan, "Pakistan Releases Nuclear Scientists for Ramadan's End," *The Washington Post*, December 16, 2001.
35. "2 Nuclear Experts Briefed," op. cit.
36. Julian West, "Al Qaeda Sought Nuclear Scientists," *The Washington Times*, April 11, 2002.
37. *At the Center of the Storm*, op. cit., p. 268.
38. Bin Laden Almost Had Uranium Bomb," *London Sunday Times*, March 3, 2002.
39. "2 Nuclear Experts Briefed," op. cit.
40. Carla Anne Robbins and Jeanne Cummings, "How Bush Decided that Hussein Must be Ousted from Atop Iraq," *The Wall Street Journal*, June 14, 2002.
41. These and other controls are discussed in Kenneth Luongo and Brig. Gen.

(Ret.) Naeem Salik, "Building Confidence in Pakistan's Nuclear Security," *Arms Control Today*, December 2007.

42. Peter Baker and Kamran Khan, "Pakistan to Forgo Charges Against 2 Nuclear Scientists," *The Washington Post*, January 30, 2002.

43. Statement of Rolf Mowatt-Larssen, Department of Energy, before the Homeland Security and Governmental Affairs Committee, U.S. Senate, April 2, 2008.

44. Quoted in "Statement for the Record of Charles E. Allen, Undersecretary for Intelligence and Analysis, U.S. Department of Homeland Security" before the Homeland Security and Governmental Affairs Committee, U.S. Senate, April 2, 2008.

45. Speech by El Baradei, Carnegie Endowment for International Peace, Conference, June 2004.

46. Michael May, "Nuclear Forensics," *APS News*, April 2008; and Nuclear Forensics Working Group of the American Physical Society's Panel on Public Affairs and the American Association for the Advancement of Science, chaired by May, *Nuclear Forensics: Role, State of the Art, Program Needs*, released on February 16, 2008, available at http://cstsp.aaas.org/content.html?contentid=1546.

47. Statement of Allen, op. cit.

48. The quantities in this paragraph are from the ISIS website, www.isis-online .org.

49. www.isis-online.org. See pages on stocks of fissile materials.

50. Statement of Mowatt-Larssen, op. cit.

51. Ibid.

NINE: UNCOVERING IRAN'S ILLICIT GAS CENTRIFUGE PROGRAM

1. Interview with a senior official close to the IAEA, May 13, 2004.

2. Interview with an Iranian American who traveled to Iran frequently during this period and learned this information from a colleague in the construction industry, November 10, 2004.

3. "Alireza Jafarzadeh Holds News Conference on Iran's Attempts to Acquire Nuclear Weapons," National Council of Resistance of Iran, Washington, DC, August 14, 2002, FDCH Political Transcripts. The NCRI has never revealed its sources. Based on analyzing the information, the sources may have been Iranians associated with the construction of nuclear facilities who may have known about the facilities but were unaware of their end purpose. Suspicions also remain that U.S. or Israeli government officials provided information to the NCRI.

4. Mark Hibbs, "U.S. Briefed Suppliers Group in October on Suspected Iranian Enrichment Plant," *Nuclear Fuel*, December 23, 2002, p. 1.

5. Interview with a senior official close to the IAEA, March 13, 2003; and a senior State Department official confirmed that the IAEA asked the United States about this site after August 2002, and the United States provided the IAEA some intelligence information, interview by CNN correspondent, December 2002.

6. Interview with a senior official close to the IAEA, March 13, 2003. A senior

Iranian official once told me in the late 1990s, after being confronted multiple times with evidence of a centrifuge program, that Iran is pursuing "all parts of the fuel cycle," implying that enrichment was also being developed.

7. Director General, *Implementation of the NPT Safeguards Agreement in the Islamic Republic of Iran*, June 2003.

8. Steve Coll, "Nuclear Inspectors Check Sites in Iran," *The Washington Post*, November 20, 1993.

9. Interview with Bruno Pellaud, January 27, 1995.

10. *Implementation of NPT Safeguards Agreement*, June 2003, op. cit.

11. Interview, IAEA official, December 9, 2002.

12. Albright and Corey Hinderstein, "Iran Building Nuclear Fuel Cycle Facilities: International Transparency Needed," December 12, 2002, at www.isis-online .org; for a more detailed description of ISIS's release of the images, see Steven Livingston, "NGOs as Intelligence Agencies: The Empowerment of Transnational Advocacy Networks and the Media by Commercial Remote Sensing," prepared for presentation at the meetings of the Association of American Geographers, San Francisco, April 17–21, 2007.

13. Senior IAEA official, December 10, 2002.

14. Mohammad Khatami, Speech by Iranian President Khatami at a meeting with University Chancellors in Tehran, Tehran Vision of the Islamic Republic of Iran Network 1, February 9, 2003 (in Persian, translated by U.S. government).

15. Ali Akbar Dareini, "U.N. Inspects Iranian Nuclear Facility," Associated Press, February 21, 2003.

16. Text in email to David Albright from Elizabeth Neuffer of *The Boston Globe*, February 26, 2003.

17. *Implementation of the NPT Safeguards Agreement*, June 2003, op. cit.

18. Interview with senior State Department official, March 25, 2003.

19. Jacqueline Shire and David Albright, "Iran's NPT Violations—Numerous and Possibly On-Going?" September 29, 2006, available at www.isis-online.org.

20. Islamic Republic News Agency, "Pakistan Rejects Reports of Nuclear Cooperation with Iran," February 24, 2003.

21. Agence France-Presse, "Pak Says Alleged Links to Iranian Nuke Program 'Flights of Fancy,' " August 6, 2003.

22. Reuters, "Iran Denies Claim Buying Western Nuclear Technology," March 27, 2003.

23. Interviews with a senior official close to the IAEA, August 19, 2003, and February 7, 2004.

24. Interview with a senior official close to the IAEA, 2003.

25. Interview with a senior official close to the IAEA, September 25, 2003.

26. Interview with a senior official close to the IAEA, February 8, 2005.

27. Musharraf, *In the Line of Fire*, op. cit., p. 296.

28. National Intelligence Council, *Iran: Nuclear Intentions and Capabilities*, National Intelligence Estimate, November 2007.

29. Albright, Paul Brannan, and Jacqueline Shire, *Can Military Strikes Destroy Iran's Gas Centrifuge Program? Probably Not*, ISIS report, August 7, 2008. Available at www.isis-online.org.

30. *Implementation of the NPT Safeguards Agreement in the Islamic Republic of Iran,* GOV/2006/15, February 27, 2006.
31. Interview with a European intelligence agency official, March 27, 2007.
32. Interview with a knowledgeable senior government official, July 8, 2008.
33. German early warning letter, "Dubai: The Role of Dubai (UAE) in the Procurement of Technology by Proliferation Countries," July 1, 2005, No. 02/05 (translated from German).
34. *Implementation of the NPT Safeguards Agreement and Relevant Provisions of Security Council Resolutions 1737 (2006), 1747 (2007), 1803 (2008) and 1835 (2008) in the Islamic Republic of Iran,* GOV/2009/55, August 28, 2009.
35. National Intelligence Council, *Iran: Nuclear Intentions and Capabilities,* National Intelligence Estimate, November 2007.
36. IAEA, "Possible Military Dimensions of Iran's Nuclear Program," op. cit.

TEN: BUSTING THE KHAN NETWORK

1. Remarks by James Pavitt, Deputy Director of Operations at the Foreign Policy Association, June 21, 2004, https://www.cia.gov/news-information/speeches -testimony/2004/ddo_speech_06242004.html.
2. Interview with a confidential source, 2009.
3. Lord Butler, Review of Intelligence on Weapons of Mass Destruction, Report of a Committee of Privy Counsellors, July 14, 2004, referred to as the "Butler Report."
4. Butler Report, op. cit.
5. Douglas Frantz and Catherine Collins, *The Nuclear Jihadist* (New York: Twelve Hachette Book Group, 2007).
6. Hansjürg Zumstein, "Wie ein Schweizer Mechaniker die Welt Veränderte," SF DOK, Swiss national television, January 22, 2009.
7. Interview in 2008 with knowledgeable U.S. government official who was receiving information about the Tinners at that time.
8. Interview by Joel Wit of a former senior U.S. official, November 16, 2007.
9. Ibid.
10. Letter dated about February 2002 obtained by European officials and seen by the author.
11. Interview by Joel Wit of former U.S. official, Washington D.C., April 5, 2005.
12. Interview with former senior State Department official, April 3, 2006.
13. *At the Center of the Storm,* op, cit., p. 284.
14. Ibid.
15. *Fall Tinner: Rechtmässigkeit der Beschlüsse des Bundesrats und Zweckmässigkeit seiner Führung,* Geschäftsprüfungsdelegation der Eidgenössischen Räte, January 19, 2009.
16. Martin Stoll, "Millionen für Atom-Kundschafter," *FACTS,* April 4, 2007: http://classic.facts.ch/dyn/magazin/schweiz/737789.html (see also video: Swiss television *Temps Present,* January 22, 2009 citing *Sonntagszeitung*).
17. Martin Stoll, "Very Close to the Spider," op. cit. (for a view of a portion of the contract see video: *Temps Present,* January 22, 2009, citing *Sonntagszeitung*). In his article, Stoll called the company Little White River Technologies to protect

his sources. The actual name was provided by a knowledgeable Swiss official, August 2006.

18. Pro forma invoice, dated January 19, 2004, from Marco's company, Traco Schweiz AG, to Deramo Systems Design, where the address is given as a Chicago post office box.

19. SF DOK, January 22, 2009, op. cit.

20. William Broad, David E. Sanger, and Raymond Bonner, "A Tale of Nuclear Proliferation: How Pakistani Built His Network," *The New York Times*, February 12, 2004, p. 1; William J. Broad, David E. Sanger, and Raymond Bonner, "How Pakistan's network offered the whole kit; Nuclear proliferators/ Scientist and black marketer," *The New York Times*, February 13, 2004, p. 2; "German Ship With WMD Components Bound for Libya Stopped, Seized in October," *Munich Süddeutsche Zeitung*, January 2, 2004; "Nuke Components Headed to Libya Seized," *The Mercury* (Australia), January 2, 2004, p. 18.

21. William Hawkins, "Interdict WMD Smugglers at Sea," U.S. Naval Institute Proceedings, December 2004, http://www.military.com.

22. "The Sixth Container," *Ohmy News*, May 31, 2006, http://english.ohmynews. com/articleview/article.

23. Polis Diraja Malaysia, "Press Release by Inspector General of Police in Relation to Investigation on the Alleged Production of Components for Libya's Uranium Enrichment Programme," February 20, 2004, http://www.rmp.gov.my/ rmp03/040220scomi_eng.htm.

24. Interviews with a former senior CIA official, February and May 2006.

25. Remarks by James Pavitt, Deputy Director of Operations at the Foreign Policy Association, June 21, 2004, https://www.cia.gov/news-information/speeches -testimony/2004/ddo_speech_06242004.html.

26. *At the Center of the Storm*, op. cit., p. 285.

27. Pervez Musharraf, *In the Line of Fire* (New York: Free Press, 2007), p. 292–3.

28. Christian Science Monitor Newsmaker press briefing, Washington D.C., December 21, 2004.

29. "Abdul Qadeer Khan Apology," Pakistan television, February 4, 2004. The full text is at "In the News," *Disarmament Diplomacy*, No. 75, January/February 2004.

30. Urs Gehriger, interview with Khan, in "Eine Ehrliche, Aufrechte Familie," *Weltwoche*, January 21, 2009, http://www.weltwoche.ch/ausgaben/2009–04/ artikel-2009–04-interview-khan-english-version.html.

31. See for example, Iftikhar A. Khan, "Offer to Share 'Proof with Neutrals': Govt's Riposte to A.Q. Khan's Tirade," *Dawn*, July 6, 2008.

32. Interview with former senior State Department official, April 3, 2006.

33. *At the Center of the Storm*, op. cit. p. 284.

34. Interview with former senior State Department official, April 3, 2006.

35. ISIS case studies. www.exportcontrols.org.

36. Swiss Federal High Court, Judgement from 23 June 2005 (translated from German). The name of the defendant is deleted in this document, but the person is obviously Lerch.

37. Juergen Dahlkamp, Georg Mascolo, and Hoger Stark, "Network of Death on Trial," *Der Spiegel*, March 13, 2006 (in English), www.spiegel.de/international/ spiegel/0,1518,405847,00.html.
38. Summary of oral judgment by Judge Juergen Niemeyer against Gotthard Lerch at Oberlandesgericht, Stuttgart, October 16, 2008, prepared and translated by Ralf Denninger.
39. *Plea and Sentence Agreement*, op. cit., p. 18.
40. High Court of South Africa, "Summary of Substantial Facts," *Indictment, The State vs. Daniel Geiges and Gerhard Wisser*, undated.
41. Rafaqat Ali, "Court Bars KRL Men Shifting," *Dawn*, January 24, 2004. Seven of those still detained in late January 2004 were Mohammed Farooq, then director general of KRL; Maj. (retd) Islamul Haq, then principal staff officer of A.Q. Khan; Sajawal Khan, retired as director general of Maintenance and General Services Division at KRL; Naseemuddin, then head of Missile Manufacturing at KRL; Mansoor Ahmad, former director general of Health and Physics Department, KRL; Brig. (retd) Mohammad Iqbal Tajwar, former director general of security, KRL; and Nazeer Ahmad, then chief engineer of Metallurgy Department, KRL.
42. Shahzad Raza, "Dr. Farooq of KRL Released," *Daily Times*, April 29, 2006.
43. German Early Warning Letter, *Pakistan: Procurement Activities for the Nuclear Program*, No. 11/05, July 1, 2005 (translated from German).
44. "Procurement Activities for the Pakistani Nuclear Programme Since Beginning 2004," undated handout, but produced in 2006 for a Nuclear Suppliers Group meeting.
45. *Pakistan: Procurement Activities*, op cit.; and "Procurement Activities for the Pakistani Nuclear Programme," op. cit.
46. Swiss Federal Court (Supreme Court), *Judgment*, Lausanne, October 9, 2007, translated from German; interview with knowledgeable official, August 2007.
47. *Fall Tinner*, op. cit.
48. Ibid.

ELEVEN: SUPPLIERS: FIRST LINE OF DEFENSE

1. "Winning Back Confidence Through a New Export Policy, An Interview with Heidsieck," *Blickpunkte*, March 1992 (internal Leybold publication).
2. Ibid.
3. Interview at Leybold, Cologne, August 11, 2006.
4. Albright, "Lessons of Leybold," in *ISIS Report: Building a Corporate Nonproliferation Ethic*, June 1993.
5. Interview with former Leybold AG employee in 2007.
6. Interview at Leybold, Cologne, August 11, 2006.
7. Senior Leybold official, based on an interview of a company employee knowledgeable about the formation of ISEC.
8. These valves were made of stainless steel, while the valves on the lists were made from aluminum, aluminum alloys, or other materials resistant to uranium hexafluoride. U.S. exports to North Korea are an exception, where all items on

a special list that includes valves and vacuum pumps require U.S. government permission to export to them to North Korea.

9. Vacuum pumps in general are not listed on control lists. Vacuum pumps for a calutron enrichment plant are an exception as a result of the scandal caused by Iraq's construction of secret electromagnetic isotope separation (EMIS) facilities prior to the 1991 Persian Gulf War.

TWELVE: ILLICIT NUCLEAR TRADE TODAY AND THE WAY FORWARD

1. This table is a current snapshot. The first column comprises states which have nuclear weapons and use illicit trade to support their weapons programs; the second column includes states and terrorist groups who could seek nuclear weapons and would depend on illicit trade to succeed; the third column includes states and subnational groups that might seek nuclear weapons and would need to use illicit nuclear trade or launch smuggling networks to succeed in acquiring them. The nuclear weapon states Britain, France, and the United States do not engage in illicit trade to maintain their nuclear arsenals. Israel has committed not to do so, at least unilaterally. Countries like Japan would likely not need foreign suppliers to build nuclear weapons if they decided to do so.

2. Statement of John M. McConnell, Director, National Intelligence Committee on Senate Armed Services, February 27, 2007.

3. George Tenet, *At the Center of the Storm* (New York: HarperCollins, 2007), p. 287.

4. Mahdi Obeidi and Kurt Pitzer, *The Bomb in My Garden* (New York: John Wiley & Sons, 2004).

Acknowledgments

Peddling Peril is the result of work undertaken over many years at the Institute for Science and International Security in Washington, D.C. This book has been made possible by generous grants from the Smith Richardson Foundation, Inc., and the MacArthur Foundation. The Ploughshares Fund and the Ford Foundation supported the collection of information and its assessment.

I am grateful to the staff at ISIS, both current and past, who worked tirelessly on this multi-year project. Several staff members deserve special thanks. While at ISIS, Corey Hinderstein helped launch ISIS's project on the A.Q. Khan network and contributed significantly to this effort. Until she left ISIS, Susan Basu pored over complicated invoices and shipping documents to draw valuable insights, and Jacob Blackford provided key research. Jacqueline Shire provided useful inputs and consistently improved the manuscript. Paul Brannan's contributions were too numerous to mention, serving as a close collaborator through the process of writing this book. Andrea Scheel deserves special thanks for devoting long hours when I needed assistance most, during the arduous period as work on the book drew to a close.

I would like to give special thanks to Joel Wit whose contribution made this book possible. He first conceived the idea of this book and put much energy into convincing first me and then foundations and Free Press of its value. He also made important contributions to the book itself.

This book draws upon information from a wide variety of sources, who generously shared their time and expertise. Over many years, current and former staff at the International Atomic Energy Agency (IAEA) devoted considerable time to discussing with me this complicated subject. Many thanks go to especially Jacques Baute, Phil Caulfield, Garry Dillon, Trevor Edwards, Mellissa Fleming, Olli Heinonen, Robert Kelley, and Mauritzio Zifferero.

This book has built on the work of many journalists who were always generous with their time to discuss key findings and questions. In particular, I wish to thank Glenn Kessler, Joby Warrick, and Robin Wright (formerly) at *The Washington Post*, John Barry and Mark Hosenball at *Newsweek*, William Broad and David Sanger of the *The New York Times*, Steve Coll, Douglas Frantz, Mike Nichoson at NHK, Johannes von Dohnanyi of *SonntagsBlick*, Marcel van Silfhout of the Dutch television show *Zembla*, Georg Mascolo at *Der Spiegel*, Julian Borger and Ian Traynor at *The Guardian*, Stephen Fidler, formerly at the *Financial Times*, Michael Adler, formerly at *Agence Press-France*, Louis Charbonneau and Mark Heinrich at *Reuters*, George Jahn at *Associated Press*, Mark Hibbs at *Nuclear Fuel*, Urs Gehriger at *Weltwoche*, and the Italian journalist Stefania Mauriti.

The German journalist and filmmaker Egmont Koch shared generously his insights, his videotaped interview of Khan, and many court documents dating from the 1980s. His multi-decade, groundbreaking work into A.Q. Khan and his associates has received far too little exposure and credit in the English-speaking world.

ISIS benefited from considerable documentation and information from investigations and prosecutions of members of the Khan network in the United States, Europe and South Africa. I would also like to thank several prosecutors in Germany and Switzerland who took the time to explain difficult legal and evidentiary issues that they face in bringing transnational smugglers to justice in this globalized world.

I would like to thank ISIS board member and lawyer Michael Rietz for his key help in navigating legal issues with German prosecutors over my possible appearance as a witness in the trial of Gotthard Lerch. I am also grateful to Ralf Denninger for his willingness to attend the Lerch trial and report on the court's verdict.

I am particularly grateful to the German company Leybold for sharing information. Their experience is an inspiration for all companies. In addition, several former Leybold staff, who wish to remain anonymous, provided important historical insights.

Gernot Zippe deserves special credit. For over fifteen years, he patiently guided me into the highly specialized world of gas centrifuges and the people who developed them. He helped open my eyes to how gas centrifuges have spread through the world and the personalities behind this spread.

Many former government officials generously provided critical knowledge about the Khan network, U.S. policy, nuclear terrorism, and illicit nuclear trade. In particular, I would like to thank Richard Barlow, Joseph DeThomas, Robert Einhorn, Mark Fitzpatrick, Robert Galluci, Thomas Graham, Marc Grossman,

Khalid Hassan, Fred McGoldrick, Rolf Mowatt-Larssen, Joseph Nye, Gary Samore, Howard Shaffer, and John Wolf.

There is a longer list of government officials in the United States and abroad who greatly assisted this endeavor but prefer to remain anonymous.

I want to especially thank Bruce Nichols and Emily Loose at Free Press for their vote of confidence in acquiring this book and their dedicated editing and guiding hands despite the difficulty of the subject. I was extremely fortunate to work with Brando Skyhorse who patiently and skillfully took the original manuscript and fashioned a readable book.

I am deeply indebted to my agent Alice Martell, who fought and advocated for this book at every turn. Without her professionalism, dedication, and support, this book would not have happened.

I would also like to thank Ulrike and Anna Lea, for their love and support through all the trials of writing a book.

Index

About the Author

DAVID ALBRIGHT IS the president of the Institute for Science and International Security (ISIS) and was its founder. He has been quoted over 150 times in the *The New York Times* and *The Washington Post* and has appeared over 200 times on network television news shows, including Wolf Blitzer, Anderson Cooper, *Nightline*, *NBC Nightly News*, *60 Minutes*, and *The Lehrer Report*. He is one of the world's most respected and sought-out specialists on nuclear proliferation. He lives in Alexandria, Virginia.